PRAISE FOR *Generation MySpace*

"As an educator who has seen firsthand how the Internet has changed teen culture and the viciousness in which teens are attacking each other online, I believe *Generation MySpace* is an absolute must-read. Seriously, please read this book. It gives you insights into technology's power over young people and concrete strategies so you can teach [kids] to use technology safely and responsibly. You can't understand young people today without reading this book."

—Rosalind Wiseman, *New York Times* best-selling author of
*Queen Bees and Wannabes: Helping Your Daughter Survive
Cliques, Gossip, Boyfriends, and Other Realities of Adolescence*

"A must-read for any parent. Kelsey soars beyond our knee-jerk fear of MySpace predators and offers a detailed, practical guide to understanding—and protecting—the modern 'screenager.'"

—Wendy Shalit, author of *Girls Gone Mild:
Young Women Reclaim Self-Respect and Find it's Not Bad to be Good*

"This book—an essential guide to the world of MySpace.com specifically written for the parents of the millions of teens who use it and other social networks—can't be cataloged quickly enough. Kelsey, a teacher, counselor, and parent, believes that parents must find out how overpowering and influential social sites have become . . . Eye-opening."

—*Library Journal*, starred review

"Kelsey takes a no-nonsense and no-sensationalism approach to the online world of kids. Even better, her strategies are holistic—raising a healthy, savvy child in a marketing-saturated world. That's what makes this book so valuable for parents in the real world."

—Joe Kelly, President, Dads and Daughters
(www.DadsandDaughters.org) and See Jane (www.SeeJane.org); author of
Dads and Daughters: How to Inspire, Understand, and Support Your Daughter

"*Generation MySpace* levels the virtual playing field. Every parent and teacher should have a copy to understand the unique temptations that call out through alluring computer screens to every child out there. A well-researched, easy-to-read resource."

—Jeffrey Bernstein, PhD, author of
10 Days to a Less Defiant Child

"A desperately-needed, soup-to-nuts guide to the electronically-based youth social landscape that is driving new forms of personal, aggressive, and sexual expression to disturbing levels. A wake-up call to parents that we can no longer rely on standard notions of at-risk and not-at-risk kids."

—Dr. Janet Sasson Edgette, adolescent psychologist and author of
*Stop Negotiating with Your Teen: Strategies for Parenting Your
Angry, Moody, Manipulative, or Depressed Adolescent*

"However sophisticated and savvy they consider themselves, many parents are blissfully unaware that their early adolescent children are corrupting and even endangering their lives on their bedroom laptop computers. But after Candice Kelsey's findings offered in this book, we have no excuse for ignorance or inaction."

—D. Bruce Lockerbie, author and educator,
Chairman, PAIDEIA, Inc.

"Whether or not your kids check their MySpace 73 times a day, they have access to a complicated world you've probably long ignored. Let Candice Kelsey show you how to remedy that—because children's online activities are all of our business."

—Linda Perlstein, author of
Not Much, Just Chillin': The Hidden Lives of Middle Schoolers

"An alarming but intensely informative and helpful guide to the rapidly escalating hazards of our teens' online world. Read it: It may save not only your parent-child relationship, but also your child!"

—Jane M. Healy, PhD, educational psychologist and author of
Failure to Connect: How Computers Affect Our Children's Minds

Generation
MySpace

*Helping Your Teen Survive
Online Adolescence*

Candice M. Kelsey

Marlowe & Company
New York

To Georgia Rae and Mike

• • •

GENERATION MYSPACE: *Helping Your Teen Survive Online Adolescence*

Copyright © 2007 by Candice M. Kelsey

Published by
Marlowe & Company
An Imprint of Avalon Publishing Group, Incorporated
245 West 17th Street • 11th Floor

AVALON
publishing group incorporated

New York, NY 10011-5300

Lyrics to "The MySpace Song" copyright © by Brian "B-Roc" Jenkins and Benjamin "Benofficial" Kemp, DaCav.5. www.dacav.com and www.myspace.com/dacav5. Used with permission.

Special thanks to www.TheAntiDrug.com, The National Youth Anti-Drug Campaign, and to Lindsey Kirn, Sean, Cherie, Cheyenne, and their families.

Library of Congress Cataloging-in-Publication Data

Kelsey, Candice M.
  Generation MySpace : helping your teen survive online adolescence / Candice M. Kelsey.
       p. cm.
  ISBN: 978-1-60094-011-8
  1. Internet and teenagers. 2. Online social networks. 3. MySpace.com. 4. Parenting. 5. Internet--Safety measures. I. Title.
  HQ799.2.I5K45 2007
  305.235028567--dc22

                                                                                    2007005262

ISBN-10: 1-60094-011-0
9 8 7 6 5 4

Designed by Bettina Wilhelm
Printed in the United States of America

To Georgia Rae and Mike

Contents

Introduction

"My daughter is obsessed with YouTube; I don't even know what it really is. Is it something like TiVo?"

—Marlene, parent

"I'm so fed up with adults worrying about MySpace. They need to stick to their own world and stay out of ours!"

—Gus, 16

"I refuse to let my son have a laptop because I know he'll just chat with his friends till all hours of the night, but he swears it will help him do better in school. I'm not sure what to do."

—MiKailie, parent

"If I miss one night of checking my MySpace, I feel so left out! I wish I could have it by my side all day."

—Jeannie, 15

———

Adults Are the Only Ones Who Say
"Online Social Network"

MySpace, Facebook, YouTube, Xanga, Flickr, Bebo, LiveJournal, Imbee, Hi5, Orkut, CyWorld, vMix, WhyVille, Tagged, CherryTap, Friendster, b-linked, eSPIN, Piczo, and Sconex. If you're like me, most of these words seem strange, perhaps akin to lost characters or places from *Gulliver's Travels.* But to most teens, at least a handful of these names mean something, something very important. With a combined forty-five million users under age eighteen, these are all the most popular and/or up-and-coming websites that are classified by us over-thirty crowd as "online social networks." What does that mean? Well, it means different things on different sites, but for the most part, an online social network is a website that encourages its users to interact with, or network with, other users. That is, they're websites where your teen logs on to hang out and socialize with other people—some they may know "in person," others they may not.

This social interaction can take the form of:

E-mailing: sending electronic messages to another's inbox.

Blog (web log) posting: the hottest new trend of keeping a journal (open to commentary) online.

Comment posting: quick responses to and about a friend's pictures, page layout, or video music selection.

Instant messaging: a real-time dialogue between two parties contacting each other's screen names (multiple conversations with friends can be pursued at once).

Picture, video, and music sharing: the uploading and sending via e-mail of songs, video clips, and images.

Gaming: meeting other players online and competing in virtual competitions.

Survey and quiz taking: filling out personal information that creates a desired persona or answering teen magazine-style questions to find out things like what type of coffee drink you are.

Bulletin posting: mass-delivered messages not unlike a memorandum in an office.

Personalized content: including web page "wallpaper" (background graphics), animated graphics, photos, and the like.

Got all that? Think of it this way: essentially, a "social-networking site" is a souped-up e-mail jalopy sporting new rims, whitewall tires, chrome runners, a V-8 engine, and Dolby Surround Sound: it's a multimedia experience that encourages the linking together, however superficial or fertile, of as many people as possible. Oh, and only adults call them "social-networking sites"—your teen just refers to them by name.

"My dad is so weird. He insists on asking me about my 'online networking.' Half the time I don't know what the heck he's talking about."

—Anton, 12

"These things frighten me. As if I'm not having a hard enough time connecting to my teenager as it is, now I have to learn a whole other new thing."

—Javier, parent

Many people (and especially my students) ask, what's the big deal about hanging out on the Internet? On the opposite end of the spectrum are those who, if given a Rorschach test involving an image of the word *MySpace*, would blurt out "predators" without hesitation. That you've picked up this book is an indication that you may be curious about what your kids are doing online—or have a sneaking suspicion that your son is replacing his homework time with MySpace time, or wonder what kind of language your daughter is using in her instant messages (and how she can carry on four conversations at once!), or why your son seemed so upset after his last computer session, or fear your daughter could be sharing information with Internet predators, or all of the above. Are these websites natural, even helpful ways for teens to express themselves? Are they "harmless fun"? Are they dangerous? These sites, whatever they are, are integral to the social landscape of your teenager. They are where she spends her free time, hangs out with her friends, and defines who she is. This book will supply you with every bit of information you will need to come to your own conclusion—and to successfully talk with your children about their activities online.

The Scene

I n an effort to be as comprehensive as possible, I have dissected the online scene as best I can for you. The hottest sites are listed here under their respective categories.

Social Networks

- b–linked
- Bebo
- Bolt2
- College Tonight
- CyWorld
- eSPIN
- Facebook
- Flickster
- Hi5
- Imbee
- MySpace
- MyStack
- MyYearbook
- Piczo
- Sconex
- Tagged
- Vox

Teen Blogging Sites

- Blogger
- Red Blogs

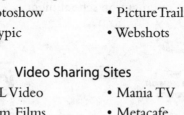

- Bolt2Journals
- The Diary Projec
- LiveJournal
- TypePad
- Xanga

Photo Sharing Sites

- Filmloop
- Imager Dump
- Photoshow
- Tinypic
- Flickr
- Photobucket
- PictureTrail
- Webshots

Video Sharing Sites

- AOL Video
- Atom Films
- Break
- Grouper
- Google Video
- iFilm
- Mania TV
- Metacafe
- MySpace Video
- Yahoo Video
- YouTube

What Are the Popular Networking Sites?

According to the Harrison Group's 2006 Teen Trends Study, 68 percent of American teens have an online profile. Let's take a brief look at some of the more popular sites in an effort to understand the climate in which our kids are growing up.

MySpace

MySpace.com is a cultural phenomenon of the digital age. Founded in 2003 by University of California graduates Tom Anderson and Chris DeWolfe, and acquired by News Corp for $580 million in July 2005, MySpace is essentially an online social-networking community in which teens are encouraged to meet, communicate, and share personal information and pictures. It now has over 140 million members and is growing at a rate of 150,000 new members worldwide each day, with plans to significantly expand outside the United States. According to Nielsen/NetRatings, MySpace has spent time as the number one most-viewed site on the Internet, outranking both Google and eBay. In addition, an estimated 25 percent of MySpace members are between the ages of thirteen and seventeen. Many teens spend four or five hours a day on MySpace (including after midnight on school nights).

It's been compared to the speakeasies of the '30s, the soda shops of the '50s, and even the scandalous impact of Elvis Presley. However, the truth is MySpace.com is none of these things . . . and all of these things. As the most popular—and notorious—website on the Internet, I've focused my attention on it here in this book.

Facebook

Originally founded as "thefacebook.com" by Mark Zuckerberg, a student at Harvard, this social network took the Ivy League by storm in early 2004. After a surge of popularity, it did what most starlets do: it changed its name and headed west (albeit to Palo Alto, California) later that year. Facebook is a social-networking site similar to MySpace but a distant second in popularity. With nearly four million users as of June 2006, it attracts mostly college students because of the college e-mail address requirement for membership; however, recently the site expanded to include high schools and companies. Because of the academic connection to Facebook, users tend to use their real names and supply less fabricated or fantastical information. Facebook has made the scene with this T-shirt:

YouTube

YouTube is a wildly popular and free video-sharing website founded in San Mateo, California, in 2005. The site made news in September 2006 when it was acquired by Google in a megadeal for $1.65 billion. YouTube uses Adobe Flash technology to display movie, television, music video clips, and video blogs. Visit YouTube and you can view, download, or upload a clip of almost anything—from the previous night's television shows to obscure music videos, from amateur cartoons to embarrassing moments captured via the digital video camera of a cell phone. With the slogan "Broadcast Yourself," YouTube is responsible for the growing trend of video blogging (better known as "vlogging," or a blog that includes embedded video or a link to video), which in turn is responsible for some newfound celebrity and is widely utilized by MySpacers. You can also post a YouTube video to a page of another site, like MySpace.

Bebo

Bebo.com, with close to two million users and growing, is one of the most popular social-networking sites in the United Kingdom; while it requires users to be thirteen to register, it used to allow one to enter "my age is secret" instead of an actual birthdate. British Internet security expert Rachel O'Connell has changed this feature in an effort to "make Bebo one of the most hostile environments for users with ill intent. "The typical profile includes a "White Board," where other Bebo users can draw pictures for everyone else to see using a simple program called ffArt (free form art). An interesting fact about Bebo is that it won the People's Choice Award in Social Networking for the 2006 Webby Awards (international awards presented to the best websites.)

Xanga

Xanga.com, officially launched as a full-fledged social networking site in New York in April 2006, dates back to 1999 as a rudimentary site for sharing book and music reviews. With almost seven million subscribers as of June 2006, it is known for its blogging features. Chief Executive John Hiler is not interested in adding instant messaging or chat features until he can have "safety features built into them."

LiveJournal

LiveJournal (LJ), a site where users can post their own diaries, was perhaps the first site to start the blogging craze. Started by Brad Fitzpatrick in 1999 as a way of keeping up with his friends, this San Francisco company was soon bought out. Its popularity among teens is waning, however, because it doesn't offer the multimedia experience that a site like MySpace does, while many other sites now offer blogging features. What LiveJournal does offer is a chance to journal in a more sober online environment.

A Place for Predators?

Lately, as you've no doubt heard, many of these sites are getting a bad rap. According to a recent report by CBS News, MySpace.com is "a sexual predator's dream come true." A front-page article in the *New York Times* declared, "Parents, educators and law enforcement officials are reacting with alarm to MySpace.com, the Internet hangout for teenagers and young adults, the content of which is shocking parents and, according to the police, attracting sexual predators." And the attorney general of New York has called MySpace "a threat to child safety." There is now even a special website, www.mycrimespace.com, dedicated solely to crimes linked to MySpace. In the last six months CNN, *The Today Show*, Fox News, the *New York Times*, the *Los Angeles Times, USA Today*, CBS News, ABC News, *Nightline, Newsweek*, the *New Yorker*, and *Good Morning America* have all reported on the dangers of teens using MySpace.com.

Seventeen-year-old Monica Sharp met fifty-seven-year-old Jeffrey Nichols through MySpace.com. Monica was missing for an entire month before returning home in October 2005. A thirteen-year-old girl in Brevard County, Florida, met a teenage boy in a chat room on MySpace.com. When she agreed to meet him in person, the boy turned out to be an adult. He is now under arrest and charged with rape. Currently in Hartford, Connecticut, police are investigating whether as many as seven teenage girls have been sexually assaulted by men they met on MySpace.com.

The site is also problematic at schools across the country. Threats against teachers, discrimination against other students, intimidation, and conspiracy to commit acts of school violence are commonplace. Jim Boyce, the dean of student affairs at White River High School in Buckley, Washington, says, "MySpace has hit schools with a vengeance." Below is a small sample of recent news headlines involving school-based problems related to MySpace.com:

- "Teenager Is Accused of Menacing Hispanic Students" (*New York Times*)
- "Teenagers Accused in Plot" (*New York Times*)
- "Teen Charged with Threatening Official on MySpace Blog" (CNN)
- "School Shooting Foiled after MySpace Messages Intercepted" (Fox)
- "The School Bully Is Moving into CyberSpace" (*L.A. Times*)
- "Boys' MySpace Prank Results in Sex Offense Arrest" (MSNBC)

These true stories are just a few examples of the countless incidents of abduction, sexual battery, statutory rape, secretive plans, illegal behaviors, teen runaways, bullying, racial intimidation, threats, conspiracies to commit violence at school, and missing children that authorities attribute to MySpace.com. Parents do need to be alert to the potential dangers of this enormous influence on their children.

But how major—or minor—is the predator problem? Some MySpacers joke that the site is no longer safe for predators—their point being that the excessive media hype has successfully discouraged any weirdos with pedophilic desires, forcing them to look elsewhere. A recent study done at the University of New Hampshire confirms this fact. Apparently, unsolicited communication is on the decline for teens on MySpace. The question remains, is it a real worry worthy of your concern? Of course, especially if your teen is posting personal information, including photos; I talk in more detail about this in chapter 10. However, most teens I know are sufficiently prepared in how to recognize a creepy instant message and how to delete it.

According to journalist Julia Angwin, who spent a week surfing the social-networking scene, "Young kids (say, under thirteen) probably shouldn't be on any of these sites." Later on in this book, I'll encourage you to log on, create a profile, and surf these sites; check them out for yourself in an effort to become more familiar with the social landscape of today's youth.

However, this book does not focus on the Internet sexual predator controversy associated with MySpace in the media recently. While the seemingly increasing occurrence of young girls being lured into dangerous face-to-face encounters with older men who have less than honorable intentions is clearly one concern, it is one aspect of a much larger problem. As I talked to teens and their parents, researched the Internet behavior of adolescents, interviewed countless experts in teen psychology, and experienced social-networking sites for myself, I *am* able to conclude that MySpace is as much solely about predators as elections are about ideals. That is to say: there are many additional reasons to take an interest in what your child is up to online.

How I Became Interested in MySpace

I've taught middle school and high school for the past eight years. Each year since 2000, I have asked my ninth-grade students to turn off their televisions, Internet, computer games, and other media for an entire week, in an effort to participate in National TV-Turnoff Week—to me, an important sociological experiment. The goal of this week is to disengage from the screen time that dominates our day and reengage with our families and friends, as well as to remember what it's like to experience life without electronic devices. And in 2000, my students begrudgingly signed their oaths, unplugged their televisions, logged off their computers, handed their PlayStations to their younger brothers, and wept.

Talk about making a name for yourself as a teacher! Pretty soon subsequent classes were dreading that fateful week in April when I would rob them of their God-given right to entertainment and advertisements. On the whole, however, the project is always successful; most students are honest, disciplined, and surprisingly positive about the experience.

- "I've been able to play the piano . . . I haven't played in so long, and I forgot how relaxing it is."
- "I've been a lot happier these past few days, and I have to admit it feels awesome!"
- "It was weird because I had no idea how much our family revolved around the TV and the computer."
- "I can't believe I'm saying this, but I'm kind of glad I don't have the TV, computer, or cell phone to distract me."
- "I would normally eat dinner in front of the TV, but instead I ate dinner with my mom and dad; it was nice."

However, I noticed a marked change in the reaction to "no screen time" week from the 2004 through 2006 school years. While it's always a black day when I hand out the TV-Turnoff guidelines to an angry mob of adolescents, recently the outcries have evolved from the former need for television shows ("I just *have* to watch *The O.C.!*") to the more recent need for the Internet—specifically, for social networking. Exclamations of outrage ("She has no right to sabotage my social life like this!") and expressions of terror ("But how will I keep in touch with my friends from Beverly Hills High?" "My grade better be A+++ for enduring this inhumane form of torture!!!") echoed from the walls of my humble classroom and down the halls toward the gym. In fact, during last year's TV-Turnoff Week, many students flaunted "cheating"; word travels fast when students trust their teacher, and many came to me in private to rat another student out. What surprised me is that these students weren't watching the NBA championship or the *American Idol* finalists. They were circulating the latest gossip on the new screen of choice, MySpace.com. While I had been well aware of the site, it wasn't until this breach in the "no screen time" clause of TV-Turnoff Week that I began to fully realize the consuming nature of this cyber-village. And I took notice.

I also took notice because fewer and fewer days would go by that didn't end with a distraught student sitting on the floor of my office in search of advice about how to respond to various MySpace-related dilemmas. Whether it was someone "talking trash" about her, a boy removing her from his Top 8 Friends List, or her mother's forbidding her to log on during school nights, the nature of my students' problems was changing. And it was obvious that the problems revolved around MySpace.

As a teacher and a parent, whenever I see a child hold on to something with an irrationally tight grip, whether it's a bag of hot Cheetos, a spray bottle of Axe, or a hot pink Razr V3 phone, I see a red flag. After all, adolescence is a time of complete chaos, inse-curity, and rash behavior. Or, as my husband, also a high school teacher, explains the teen specimen, "They're not human." (Tongue in cheek, of course.) So, I asked myself, *why* are these young people so hooked on this MySpace site?

A perpetual slave to my curiosity, one sleepless night I decided to invade that space. I'd visit some of the MySpace pages my students were constantly referring to. Cardinal sin, right? At least most teenagers would think so. And I admit, I felt some hesitation about logging on. But it is a public domain, I am an adult, and my intentions are always to help my students, even when they believe otherwise.

What I proceeded to experience that night was a disconcerting cyber-journey. And at the time it really shocked me. Let me tell the story of a fourteen-year-old student whom I'll call Jennifer.

Jennifer is a quiet, demure, intelligent young woman who dresses conservatively and speaks softly. She is one of the most polite students I have ever encountered. She sings in the school choir, attends a local church, and has a close relationship with her parents. However, her MySpace profile contradicted this image 180 degrees. Jennifer's photo showed an angry young woman in full gang attire, hand signals and all. Her headline, an important signifier for teen MySpacers, was "Suck it slo, Ho!" In her brief bio, she warned "all you bitches" not to mess with her because she's friends with "a lot of big ass nigg-uhs, ya'll!" Her background image, or "wallpaper," was a huge spread of musical artist and sex kitten extraordinaire Beyoncé, sporting just the right amount of sequins to showcase her bulging breasts. I scrolled down to see that she listed a fictional business that takes in over $250,000 per year called "Pimps 'R Us." When I finally got back into bed, I couldn't help but wonder if I had been on the wrong MySpace page. I mean, there was no possible way that this avatar represented the Jennifer I knew each day in class. Deep inside, I knew it was true. But I was left with the nagging question: *Who are these kids really?*

This and many other MySpace moments have affected me in a very real way. Each day I devote myself to honest and open dialogue with my students. Nothing is more important to me professionally than fostering sincere relationships with my students. I value their thoughts, opinions, hopes, and dreams as well as their creativity, and I bank on understanding these things. After all, that is the only true way of reaching them intellectually, let alone influencing them personally. Jennifer's portrayal of herself left me feeling confused, even bamboozled.

Millions of teens spend hours and hours on a daily basis ensconced in this culture of MySpace. I asked one of my more savvy sophomore girls which teenage identity is real, the one I see at school or the one displayed so brazenly on the Internet. She promised me that for most kids, the MySpace profile is the most honest. I have to admit I still have a hard time believing that.

So began my journey into the online jungles.

Parenting in the Age of MySpace

Peel that bored exterior off your teen and you'll find a complex being who seeks your love and approval; peel off that media-generated image of predator-saturated MySpace and you'll find a window into today's teen culture.

As a parent, I am sure you are well aware of the ubiquitous role media and technology play in kids' lives today—and how different it is from just a decade or two ago. It cannot be exaggerated to what extent teens are bombarded with media information and images and encouraged to incorporate each techno-gadget into their daily lives. It is this new adolescent world that we as parents must be committed to understanding. Anyone who undertakes a super-media-saturated way of life is at risk of becoming a disconnected and lonely individual, but a preteen or teen whose delicate coming-of-age process is set to a 24-7 backdrop of reality television, iPod videos, and MySpace messages is at risk of more lasting and less trivial effects. As one cultural critic wisely claimed, "The medium is the message." And if the medium for our teens is permanently rooted in an electronic screen, what ultimately is the message our kids are hearing?

1. I Must Be Entertained All the Time.

The first message teens have heard loud and all too clear is that entertainment comes above all else. The true products of our leisure society enraptured by celebrity, today's teens have been raised in the multi-television home and nursed on a steady diet of advertisements. One might imagine that teens today would be too cynical about media to take it seriously, but they are so lost in the middle of the forest that they don't even know there's a path in to town. Now we are more alienated and disconnected from them than ever before. They'll even tolerate overt marketing schemes as long as they're funny or entertaining in some manner. So video games and MP3s and sites like MySpace.com have swooped in and stolen the interest of our kids. Why? Simply because they provide endless entertainment, and this total access to all things entertaining reinforces a culture of consumption, inactivity, and the self-righteous expectation to never be bored.

2. If You've Got It, Flaunt It.

The second message teens are embracing is that modesty is uncool—a thing of the past, stifling, disempowering—and that privacy is lame. The emergence of what I term the "screenager," the product of teens who spend excessive amounts of time online, marks the emergence of a new breed of kid, one who values the public much more than the private. When the majority of an adolescent's time is spent evaluating images and messages emanating from a screen, a shift occurs in the being's self. Because screen culture is one that is rooted in a peekaboo mentality anchored in images, today's teens are expert exhibitionists, vigilant voyeurs, and novice narcissists. In the words of cultural critic Jerry Mander, "When environments change, creatures change to match the environment." Teens raised on tabloid television that boasts the latest celebrity gossip as national news quickly learn to value the scandalous. It's no wonder that a gossip trap like MySpace thrives among the under-eighteen crowd.

3. Happiness Is a Glamorous Adult.

A third message being absorbed by our youth is that happiness is found in becoming an adult, or at least what they think is an adult. And they're not defining adulthood as parenthood, mind you. No, what they have accepted as the coveted form of adulthood is the salacious world of *Desperate Housewives* and *The Man Show*. These shows would have you believe that the more pathetically in search of sex, humiliation, and self-degradation a person is, the more mature he or she truly is. Once again, the pursuit is for excitement, not substance. References to drunken shirt-lifting on a Cancún hotel balcony, oral sexual favors, and belittling and mocking of peers dominate the evolving teen MySpace culture.

4. Success Means Being a Consumer.

The MySpace marketing machine harvests private data from unsuspecting teens, ranging from e-mail addresses and personal information to likes and dislikes and hopes and dreams, and uses it to target this vulnerable demographic with products that you, as a parent, may not want them to buy. For example, one of the most marketed products targeted to fourteen- and fifteen-year-old girls is body spray. According to an article in *BusinessWeek*, "The advertising on MySpace can be so subtle that kids don't even know that it's advertising." On MySpace, you can be "friends" with a product. A recent article in the *San Diego Business Journal* touted that "MySpace's . . . members, nearly all in their teens . . . represent the sasquatch of the advertising world— elusive and hunted." According to the Harrison Group's 2006 Teen Trends study, teenagers spend about $195 billion annually on clothes, eating out, cars, movies and cell phones, and this figure does not include technology expenditures. Because teens spend money, and they spend time on MySpace, the reality is that MySpace is a marketer's dream. It is no coincidence that since Rupert Murdoch's News Corp purchased MySpace recently, advertisements for Fox television shows have proliferated on the pages. In fact, according to *BusinessWeek*, the whole marketing industry is "changing because of MySpace."

Clarification

In no way am I claiming that social-networking sites are solely responsible for the normal problems of adolescence, or the sometimes deviant or dangerous behaviors of teens today. Adolescent insecurities abound today just as they did thirty years ago, but the advent of MySpace has changed the way teenagers cope. Although MySpace is only a medium, a platform, I do believe that integral to the popularity of this website are many elements that encourage, provoke, justify, and condone the behaviors mentioned above. This book will help you understand your teen's struggles in navigating the social landscape, her attempt at finding her identity, and the hurdles of establishing healthy boundaries between private and public realities. In short, yes, MySpace is at the front lines of redefining today's teenager.

What You'll Find in This Book

I encourage parents of children as young as nine years old to read this book. While your young child, hopefully, is not actively participating with a live profile and daily blogs, he or she is quickly entering into a social reality embedded with strands of networking culture. To be an effective parent of a preteen today, I cannot stress strongly enough that one must be knowledgeable about and actively involved in the morphing teenscape. Plus, your nine-year-old is only T minus three years away from full blastoff into social-networking sites. What if social networking becomes obsolete by that time, you ask? Don't worry, it won't.

For those of you with full-fledged teenagers: although the angst of adolescence has not changed, your teenager lives in a world very different from the one you once knew. MTV is so yesterday, and e-mail is clip-clopping its way into the sunset; even texting is losing its shine. If you want to know your teenager's world, you have got to know MySpace. This book will not only peel the onion for you, it will offer you sound resources, helpful tools, wise advice, and practical strategies for dealing with your Generation MySpace teenager.

I researched this book over the course of about eighteen months. I began by collecting any and all print media on the topic—from academic texts on contemporary teen culture and technology to six months of every relevant newspaper and magazine article on MySpace and teens. (The headlines have so proliferated that I actually had to invest in an industrial-size super-binder.) In short, the behemoth that has become my research file forms the skeleton of my book. Much of what you are about to read is grounded in professional studies like the Pew Internet and American Life Surveys, live interviews with licensed psychotherapists and sociologists, conference travel, including the National Youth Anti-Drug Media Campaign's "Teens, Technology, and Drugs" roundtable, heartfelt vignettes from experienced parents, and candid discussions with brave and willing teens who wanted to share their online experiences. The latter are the most important. This book is the result of many years of getting to know teens, being real in their lives, and devoting my professional life to them.

As you read each chapter, you will find some common landmarks. First, you'll hear my thoughts and observations from my work with teens. Second, you will read interviews, vignettes, blogs, and quips from teen experts, other parents, and teens themselves. Please be aware that teen names and identifying details have been changed to protect teenagers as they are minors, and while some stories are composites of several teens, all of the anecdotes are real and their relevant details are true.

You will learn when to talk to your teen and how to broach some difficult subjects, and you will be exposed to copious testimonials dealing with drugs, sex, bullying, gossip, and even suicide. Most of all, however, you will be ushered into a lively debate about your child's privacy and your role in his or her cyber-life. In addition, this book will cover the following topics:

Real-Life Issues Affecting Your Teen

- The skyrocketing craze of teen exhibitionism and voyeurism
- The emerging culture of narcissism as encouraged by the medium
- The redefining of friendship and popularity for this generation
- The pressure teens face to invent an identity online
- The sexual, bullying, and drug-friendly culture of MySpace
- The widening disconnect from reality as experienced by teens

Practical Safety Issues Facing Your Teen

- Whether you should find and assess your child's personal web page
- How to assess your child's involvement level and risk
- A glossary of popular IM and online slang terms, acronyms, and other online language
- How to talk successfully to your child about online social networking
- Practical steps for navigating MySpace.com
- Guidelines for blocking, monitoring, or limiting MySpace usage
- Innovative ways to protect children from Internet predators

All Is Not Bleak

Teens are resilient creatures; they (we) somehow make it through adolescence, and most of us become functioning, productive adults.

And teens will survive this MySpace craze. Countless parents of teen and preteen children have expressed to me a strong desire to read a book such as this. Obviously, there is nothing more important to parents than the welfare of their children. However, a widening chasm between adolescence as experienced by the adult generation and adolescence as experienced by teenagers today is crippling multitudes of family relationships. We can be at a disadvantage when it comes to all things wireless, and often we tend to shut out or ignore that which we don't understand, especially when the culture misleads us. This book intends to provide a prescriptive strategy to bridge the gap between you and your tech-savvy children.

I hope this book will help you not only to protect your children, but to truly know them, and to fully understand the reality in which they are coming of age.

Addicted to MySpace

Why Kids Are Bewitched

"I am so tired of trying to peel my daughter away from the computer on a sunny Saturday afternoon; this whole MySpace craze is out of control!"

—*Bill, parent*

"My parents spend hours reading the newspaper and their stupid magazines, so what's the big deal if I spend hours reading messages from my friends? The hypocrisy really gets to me."

—*Ellen, 13*

"During the 2006 power outage in L.A., MySpace was down for about twelve hours. It was a dark, dark time in more ways than one. However, the outage has helped me to identify my addiction to MySpace. While it was out, I kept checking to try and log in until finally I got in there, and I breathed a sigh of relief. I read my boring e-mails and felt at ease."

—*Jassa, 17*

"Can anyone help me understand why my son and his friends really only ever talk about what transpires on MySpace.com; I mean what is the appeal?"

—*Sarah, parent*

———

Think back to when you were fifteen or sixteen years old. Try to remember the things your parents and other adults said to you. "Be home by 11:00." "Where is your report card?" "Who are you going out with tonight?" "What kind of party is it?" "You're wearing that?!" "You're grounded!"

No doubt about it, the teen years are a constant balancing act between earning parental approval and fearing parental disapproval. And as I recall from my own childhood, sometimes adolescence feels like a balancing act on a tightrope with no safety net. Perhaps most annoying of all is the feeling that parents are watching and waiting for just one little wobble or misstep.

Now imagine, in the midst of this world dominated by adult supervision, that every teen was a member of a private club. In the clubhouse they can do as they please. They can socialize with their friends, discuss their innermost feelings, gossip, rant, flirt, curse, trade pictures, share music, and express themselves openly because there are no parents anywhere. What's even better, in this parent-free zone every teen can pretend to be anything or anyone they want. Whenever they like, they can re-create their own persona—real or imagined—and everyone will believe they are as cool as they appear to be.

Herein lies the appeal of MySpace.com. Except MySpace is a real club. It's open twenty-four hours a day. And there are 500 million doors to the clubhouse across the United States alone (Europe and the Far East are unlocking their doors as I write)—every home computer, laptop, PDA, middle or high school computer lab, and now some cell phones. The highly entertaining nature of

MySpace—24-7 access to constant stimulation, global communication, and anonymity—makes for quite a combustible compound in a teen's volatile world.

It Begins in Middle School

According to the Pew Internet and American Life's "Teens and Technology" study, going to middle school seems to be the point of entry for many teens who were not previously online to get connected. Findings show that "while about 60 percent of sixth graders reported using the Internet, by seventh grade, it jumps to 82 percent." Most MySpace users cross the online social-network threshold by the seventh grade.

The Siren Call

Ancient Greek sailors feared the enticing song of the Sirens because it would steal their desire for home. For the modern teenager, MySpace has a similar allure—it's utterly transfixing, it commandeers their time, and it can lead them far from home. I've witnessed many a student become so enthralled with checking his MySpace messages or revamping his profile that he is no longer able to concentrate in class or socialize at lunch (which becomes the time when he holes up in the computer lab).

Fifteen-year-old Nadia began to fall asleep on a regular basis in my English class, and her grades were quickly plummeting. She had bloodshot eyes, and her posture had changed drastically over the course of a month. Concerned, I decided to search MySpace and found her new profile. I came across ten snapshots of her and her girl-friends wearing skimpy bikinis and playfully spanking each other in increasingly sexual poses. A bit dismayed, I then decided to check her online status past midnight. Sure enough, Nadia was online at 1:00 AM on a school night. The next day she did not have her essay written, nor was she able to participate in class because of her exhaustion.

When I met with her parents to discuss her poor grades, they informed me that they, too, were concerned about her waning motivation, her lack of involvement with friends, and her declining physical health. But when I attempted to broach the subject of MySpace with her parents, I was met with stalwart denial. "Nadia has strict limitations on her access to the computer," they said. They were convinced MySpace wasn't the issue; her mother assured me that her daughter was in bed by 10:00 PM on school nights. In the end, I told these parents I would keep trying to motivate Nadia.

Teenagers like Nadia are not an anomaly. As a high school teacher, I am reminded each morning as my students trickle in just before the 8:00 AM bell rings that sleep deprivation is becoming a teenage epidemic. In an effort to explore the causes of their inability to function in the morning, I'd pointed fingers at satellite television, the proliferation of energy drinks, and even, much to my chagrin, my own teaching skills—to no avail. The latest studies on teen brains and sleep patterns tell us that our kids need more sleep. According to Dr. Mary Carskadon of Brown University, teens need 9.25 hours of sleep in order to be "optimally alert." As children become teenagers, the brain's circadian clock (a biological timing system) shifts forward, causing them to naturally stay awake later. Many school districts have altered their start times to accommodate these findings. The idea is that students are benefiting from sleeping in and are showing up for a 9:00 or 10:00 AM first period class much more refreshed. While I believe there is merit in this study and approach, I find the strategy only addresses part of the issue—it misses the proverbial mark. And that mark is MySpace.com.

Sixteen-year-old Aaron says that he spends up to four hours per night sending messages to his 149 friends, tinkering with his site profile, and surfing through other MySpace pages. MySpace is the teen medium of choice for getting massive amounts of attention. As Aaron says, "This website is pretty important to me and my friends' social lives . . . It's an unphysical way of hanging out." He adds, "It's probably the first and last thing I do each and every night." Aaron is most certainly not alone. Most teens I talked to said they spent anywhere from three to five hours online each day, and found it difficult to quantify how much time they spent communicating with friends since they seem to feel constantly connected and engaged in some sort of electronic exchange.

Across the board, teen Internet usage is on the rise. According to comScore Media Metrix, teens (age twelve to seventeen) spent an average of 1,233 minutes online during February 2006, up 19 percent from a year ago, and communication-related activities account for the majority of time spent online by teens in February 2006. Time spent using instant messengers ranks highest, with teens spending 489 minutes per month using IM, up 41 percent from last year. E-mail ranked second at 176 minutes per visitor (up 33 percent) and discussion/chat ranked third at 159 minutes per visitor (up 46 percent). In February, teens spent the most time on MySpace, averaging 368 minutes per visitor, up 22 percent from last year.

Take a look at these statistics taken from several research studies performed in 2006:

- Close to nine out of ten teens, or 87 percent of youth ages twelve to seventeen, are Internet users, and half of these teens go online daily.
- Nearly a third, or 29 percent of students surveyed, said their parent or guardian would disapprove if they knew what they were doing on the Internet.
- One-third, or 33 percent of online teens, share their own creations online, such as artwork, photos, stories, or videos.

- 64 percent of online teens say that most teens do things online that they wouldn't want their parents to know about.
- 82 percent of teens live in a home with Internet access, and 46 percent have high-speed Internet access.
- One-third, or 33 percent, of thirteen- to seventeen-year-olds and nearly half (48 percent) of sixteen- to seventeen-year-olds report that their parents or guardians know "very little" or "nothing" about what they do on the Internet.

Now, remove the word *Internet* from the above studies, fill in the blanks with the word *MySpace*, and read it back to yourself. MySpace has come to mean the Internet to the majority of teenagers today. According to fifteen-year-old Ruby, "I only use the Internet for MySpace. I mean, everything I want to do online is there: music, pictures, blogs, friends. It's actually my home page when I sign on." Her perspective is pretty standard among teenagers. Combine that attitude with the fact that roughly 25 percent of the reported 100 million MySpace subscribers are under the age of eighteen, and that amounts to 20 million preteens and teens logging onto this self-proclaimed "place for friends." Most Internet research studies declare an estimated 150,000 new members sign up on the site *every day*. These statistics actually seem low to me. My experience with teenagers in Los Angeles is a little different: nine out of ten of my ninth- and tenth-grade students in the 2005–2006 school year used MySpace daily.

A Psychologist Answers:
What Is the Appeal of MySpace?

I spoke with Jonathan Nadlman, a prominent Los Angeles psychotherapist, about why teens are so attracted:

CK: Jonathan, in your many years of experience with teenagers both in schools and in private practice, what have you deduced to be the psychological pull of MySpace?

JN: First of all, teens are in the midst of a healthy narcissism; they feel like they can handle the world, so they take it on in a very public portal. Second, issues of popularity are played out on MySpace. And finally, it provides a space for connecting with other teens during a critical time of separating from parents.

CK: Is it healthy for teens to have a private cyberspace to explore that separation?

JN: While it encourages self-expression on one hand, it does create a precarious dance between individuality and conformity on the other hand.

CK: Why are teens in particular so attracted to MySpace?

JN: Teens are not socialized to tolerate their feelings. Adolescents don't understand that how one feels will dissipate; they think it will last for the rest of their lives. This mind-set breeds addiction to something like MySpace. Ultimately, it comes down to how it makes kids feel. Do you remember Matt Dillon in [the movie] *Drugstore Cowboy*? Speaking of his drug addiction, he explains, "I do it because if I read the bottle of pills, it tells me exactly how I'm going to feel." MySpace is a place where kids can go and know exactly how it will make them feel. Essentially, it's a place where they can feel like adults.

Why Kids Love MySpace

"I love MySpace because it gives me a feeling of self-worth. When someone comes by and says, "wow u look hott!" it makes me feel good."

—Dan, 14

"MySpace makes my life interesting. Getting comments from friends and strangers makes me feel important, like I really matter. I don't feel like some kid that everyone ignores."

—Carolina, 12

The craving to feel like an adult makes teens ideal MySpace patrons. The early adolescent years are marked by developmental milestones that leave the typical child especially susceptible to influences. According to youth marketing experts Daniel Acuff and Robert Reiher, authors of *Kidnapped*, the seven key vulnerabilities of 13-to-15-year-olds are:

1. *Separation:* The first few years of adolescence are marked by a breaking away from parents and other adult role models; such a breach occurs both physically and emotionally. The result is an adolescent who, write Acuff and Reiher, is "on a tenuous path without the secure emotional anchors of earlier years." Operating without constant parental supervision or the well-defined social boundaries of days gone by can be overwhelming for young teens.

2. *Peer Influence:* Early adolescence is a time of transferring loyalties from family to their friends and peers, whose approval becomes all-important. "As many teens migrate from family to peer groups, they are often more influenced by the thinking, valuing, and behavior" of their friends and classmates.

3. *Role Model Influence:* Celebrities, musicians, pro athletes, and entertainers seem to earn the most attention and emulation from teens. The strong influence these entertainment icons have upon younger teens cannot be underestimated. More often than not, "in the teen's desire to be and act 'grown-up,' there may be many age-inappropriate enticements."

4. *Sex Appeal:* Bodily changes and hormone surges contribute to the growing interest in the opposite (or same) sex among teens; "boys and girls are far from 'yucky' anymore." Young men and women between the ages of thirteen and fifteen are naturally prone to sexual exploration.

5. *Independence:* A strong desire to be independent drives many young teens to "embrace different and perhaps contradictory values from parents, other authority figures, and mainstream society." A necessary and healthy developmental step, it is important to note that such independence can cause great upheaval in the established family structure.

6. *Experimentation:* Today's early teens are prone to experimentation at a far greater degree than in the years past, mostly because of the amount of time they spend home alone or unsupervised. Also, the current cultural trend of awarding teens excessive amounts of personal freedom opens the door to "often problematic, even dangerous activities involving sex, drugs . . . even illegal behavior."

7. *Need for Control:* An ever-growing awareness of self and a blossoming desire for autonomy are characteristic for the young adolescent. Teens want to make their own choices. Again, many times, this need for control causes conflict with parents.

Each of these vulnerabilities makes for an eager and loyal prospective member of the private MySpace clubhouse.

A Star Is Born: Brittany's Story

Social-networking sites supply the glamour for teenagers to fabricate their own temporary celebrity status. As University of Washington sociology professor Pepper Schwartz notes, MySpace "feeds peoples' desires to be a star." In this media-saturated culture where celebrity is coveted more than world peace, impressionable teenagers have ingested the myth that spotlight and billboard necessitate happiness and fulfillment. The most popular television shows viewed by teenagers are *America's Next Top Model, American Idol, Made*, and *My Super Sweet Sixteen*, and the bold messages of all are not falling on deaf ears. Teenagers are formulating their concepts of success based on the attainment of notoriety. While being present on MySpace is far from a significant level of fame, it simulates the experience just enough to lull young adults aching to be known into a false sense of stardom. In a sense, the personal profile page doubles as a type of public relations agent, displaying only what photos, blogs, and interview answers support the desired image. To continue the metaphor, the messages left by friends are like a watered-down version of *National Enquirer* or *Access Hollywood* gone digital: personal interactions made public all in the interest of creating a well-engineered image.

Fourteen-year-old Los Angeles high school student Brittany does an expert job of promoting her faux luminary persona on MySpace. She ushers viewers in with a photograph of herself dressed in a low-cut little black dress. Her page is rife with images of scantily clad Victoria's Secret models and current hip-hop artists, and she writes that "I plan to marry sexxxy Channing Tatum." Her wallpaper is hot pink with glittery icons of Playboy bunnies, while background music is an upbeat reggae remix titled "Give It Up to Me." She lists her interests as "dancing" and "getting crazy at parties"; she also lists her favorite music, television shows, movies, heroes, and the social groups she belongs to. Her latest blog entries consist of a call for everyone to "have crazy wild sex . . . come on, come on . . . (do it!)" and blurbs that essentially tell her life story and whom she'd "like to meet" someday.

This carefully crafted image is solidified by the comments left by her friends: Diddy explains he is "jus droppin by to show sum luv." Christine mentions she's upset that she has to go to "this party this kid is having for me" and for Brittany to call her even though she'll "probly be wasted!" And Brandon attempts to coerce Brittany to attend a party because "I really want you to come . . . you've got boobs and know how to use them!" This young lady has done an expert job at designing her party-girl image; any professional publicist would be impressed. Clearly, Brittany has managed to make herself feel like a star.

Cyber Therapy: Jaimie's Story

MySpace also provides an outlet for the angry teenager who feels frustrated and stifled emotionally. It's easy to vent pent-up rage in a virtual environment. At some point, almost every teenager feels crippled by disappointment, and this can fester into anger, even rage. Unfortunately, teens are ill-equipped for dealing with these intense emotions, and more often than not, do not have a healthy outlet for expressing their angst. An attractive aspect of MySpace is the freedom to emote, express, and share with the world those intimate and overwhelming feelings.

But there is no professional counselor there for guidance. At best there may be a sympathetic ear from another teen. And for some teens, MySpace may be providing a false sense of therapy. Fourteen-year-old Jaimie is angry that her parents have divorced. Although she's an incredibly creative young woman, Jaimie is undone by her rage and often resorts to cutting herself. She is ostracized by her peers at school and academically she is failing five classes. When asked why she spends so much time on MySpace, Jaimie replied, "It's all I have."

Sadly, in many ways she may be right. Her fictional name is "Bloody Rabbit" and her profile photograph depicts her at age eight staring at a Peter Pan figurine. It is here that this frustrated teen has found a way to express her anger and a longing to regress to the innocence of childhood. She posts her amateur poetry, some of which is titled "Betrayer" and "Smiles of Murder." In the "About Me" section of questions and answers, she claims that her main desire in life is "to be loved." Asked in a MySpace quiz how she wants to die, she declares, "in a crazy mosh pit." In a message from her friend called "Menstruate," she is informed that she has been "virtually bitch slapped!" Her other friend called "Creep" desires to see her so he can "devour [her] soul!" Jaimie is drawn to the attention she receives, however negative, but again she receives no lasting advice for dealing with her problems.

The Purpose-Driven Space: Dixson's Story

For teenagers who struggle with feelings of insignificance and diminished self-worth, MySpace delivers a sense of purpose and importance that is rivaled by no other source. Here, the popularity contest is taken to a new level. Accumulating friends and "hits" is a badge of honor. Proving that you know the latest slang terms and hot music ensures recognition. For fifteen-year-old Dixson, the ability to create an online persona of a popular, attractive, charismatic, and confident young man is too appealing to pass up. This boy puts little energy into schoolwork, while he plays football obsessively. He displays a "what, me worry?" attitude in the classroom and a dramatic sense of his own prowess on the field. His bravado and posturing are the first signs of typical teenage-boy insecurities.

Dixson has found, however, a powerful medium to generate his cocky playboy image. His profile photograph shows him in his football uniform drinking from a beer bottle. To supplement, he provides a prominent icon of two people humping and a tagline of "getting

A Space of One's Own

An Interview with danah boyd, PhD candidate, social media research, U.C. Berkeley:

CK: Why are teens flocking to MySpace?

db: Just look at the evolution of the high school as an institution—it really was born out of the need to keep teens away from the workforce during the Depression in order to ensure jobs for adults. It began as a restrictive measure to corral teens and essentially restrict them. Ever since then, teens have endured stricter and stricter infringements on their right to be in public. Today kids don't have a public space of their own: MySpace is the product of youth creating space of their own.

Teens are looking for a release from the control of their usually unstable homes. The middle- to upper-class teen suffering from anorexia, bulimia, cutting, or promiscuity is really playing the game of risk-creating. It is a control issue at heart. MySpace offers a prime environment to create and take risks.

laid." Dixson is intent upon creating the image that he is an athlete, sexually active, and confident. He claims that his interests are "flirting . . . babes . . . and, oh yeah my car," and in turn supplies pictures of a fantasy automobile, motorcycle, and woman, all of which he is pretending to own. And just for fun, Dixson includes his favorite maxim: "Rock out with your cock out!" The macho posturing continues.

When Dixson's mother is apprised of the content of her son's page, she responds: "It makes him happy, so I hate to just cut him off. I do limit the time he's on there." This boy is living a virtual fantasy life with no intrusions; he has created a sense of self-worth, and of course, that feels good to him. But what is the impact on his coming-of-age?

———

Brittany, Jaimie, and Dixson are experiencing normal adolescent cravings. The issue, however, is whether they are pursuing their desires in a healthy manner. And, to go one step further, not all adolescent desires *should* be fulfilled. But the quality of MySpace that makes it so appealing to teenagers is that it supplies a way to ease every insecurity. And parents are the only buffer between functional teenage strife and decadent teenage gratification.

Furthermore, it's perfectly normal for teens to want to spend lots of time with their friends. But for many, the excitement of signing in to one's MySpace page, receiving new e-mails, comments, friend "adds" and page views, reviewing responses to recent blog or photo postings, and checking other people's pages for mentions about themselves can quickly become a compulsion.

Fifteen-year-old Lainie describes the feeling of signing on to MySpace as "a high like no other. I can't wait to sit at my computer and take the day's drama in. I just don't feel complete until I've caught up on the MySpace juice!" Lainie receives a surge of stimulation from the experience.

Likewise, kids feel the effects when they can't access the site. Fifteen-year-old Arianna has observed the irrational behavior of friends who face the loss of their MySpace profiles; she reports, "I once was with a friend whose MySpace was deleted by hackers, and by the way she was acting, one could think that her family dog had died. She was utterly distraught and was going on and on about how long it was going to take her to get it back up like that again." Clearly, Arianna is insightful enough to be a bit concerned by her friend's behavior. But even this insightful teen "started to wonder if I were that addicted."

Addicted. That's also how Holly, a senior at a local high school, described her relationship with MySpace. When I asked her why, she explained the compulsion to spend hours every day on MySpace as a symptom of her generation's having "nothing better to do in our lives." She continued with the poignant observation that "technology is overwhelming for our generation. The past generation didn't have the Internet and now we are always on it." I can't help but think of Frank Lloyd Wright's warning that "[if] it keeps up, man will atrophy all his limbs but the push-button finger." One cannot underestimate the growing role the computer is playing in our kids' lives. Holly expresses the fear and confusion many teenagers experience as they enter, or are pulled, into the unregulated expanse of the Internet.

Is It Really an Addiction?

It is telling that Lainie labels her feeling a "high," a term usually indicating an altered state induced by an illegal substance. Is there a similarity? According to several psychotherapists, an addiction, whether to drugs, alcohol, or the Internet, creates both a physical and a psychological dependency. And this dependency is one that can result in negative outcomes—kids becoming more withdrawn, less communicative face-to-face and with adults, and more isolated from the "real world." Teens are especially vulnerable to addictive behavior; it is the high from MySpace that Lainie describes that brings teens back to the site again and again, eventually commandeering both the teen's physical and emotional life.

According to Serenity Online Therapy, addiction is not only an illness in which a person seeks and consumes a substance, such as alcohol, tobacco, or a drug, despite the fact that it causes harm; nor is it only a dependence on a substance (such as alcohol or other drugs) or an activity to the point that stopping is very difficult and causes severe physical and mental reactions. An addiction can also be an uncontrollable compulsion to repeat a behavior regardless of its negative consequences. Avid MySpacers Aaron, Holly, and Nadia admitted to me an inability to control their behavior, and Holly and Nadia even told me that it was causing problems in their lives. Another element of addiction is believing that something harmful is actually beneficial, and in extreme instances, that something harmful is vitally necessary. Exclaims sixteen-year-old Paloma, "What's the point of going to school each day if I can't discuss what's happening on MySpace?" Her day, apparently, would feel empty and pointless without it; Paloma views it as necessary to her happiness.

If something feels good, chances are a teenager will want to do it—even when they know it's not good for them. That's normal. But it's not always healthy. Most teenagers will claim that MySpace is lame, but hours later they'll be logging on. Fifteen-year-old high school student Samantha admits, "Most of my friends at school are on it." In fact, users claim the one downside of the site is too much MySpace. Pierce College student Travis estimates he spends up to six hours a day on the site and that "it pretty much is ruining my life because I'm constantly checking on it at work, at home, you name it."

As fifteen-year-old Christy explains, "MySpace and I have a love-hate relationship. It's one of those things I know I should really live without, but I can't remember what social life felt like without it." She equates her presence on the site with her presence in the social landscape. "It's superficial, dangerous, judgmental, unhealthy, time-consuming, and addicting." When I asked her if she was willing to delete her account, she replied with an emphatic "No!"

Symptomatic of any addiction are moments of clarity; a user

realizes the negative nature of his or her behavior but is thwarted from breaking free by the need for more. Millions of teenagers know, more than any adult, that MySpace is not good for them, but they can't resist.

Are these teens addicted, or at least approaching addiction to MySpace? I believe so. In recent years, Internet addiction disorder has been gaining acceptance in the psychological community as a mental condition. However, do note that the medical community has yet to acknowledge teen Internet addiction as a disorder, even though extensive studies have been conducted on the teen brain and its addictive propensity. The *Harvard Mental Health Letter* reports that "human brain circuitry is not mature until the early twenties and that the prefrontal cortex (the seat of judgment and problem-solving) is not sufficiently linked to the emotional centers of the brain resulting in a reduced capacity for 'self-regulation.'" In fact, the report identifies the underdeveloped "mid-brain reward system" as the center where addictive behaviors assert their control, explaining, "Brain scans hint at why most addictions get their start in adolescence." In short, teen brains respond more intensely to new experiences than adult brains, making those experiences all the more appealing.

Take a moment to use this important checklist to identify potential physical and psychological symptoms of Internet addiction in your child. The Computer Addiction Services at Harvard Medical School identify the following symptoms of computer addiction:

Psychological Symptoms
- Social withdrawal; problems relating to peers or adults
- Having a sense of well-being or euphoria while at the computer
- Craving more and more time at the computer

- Feeling empty, depressed, and irritable when not at the computer
- Lying to family and friends about activities
- Problems at school (academic, behavioral, or social)

Physical Symptoms
- Carpal tunnel syndrome
- Dry eyes
- Migraine headaches
- Backaches
- Eating irregularities, such as skipping meals
- Neglecting personal hygiene
- Sleep disturbances and significant changes in sleep patterns

If your child is suffering from any combination of these symptoms, please consult a professional. It's also important to note that Harvard Medical School describes the most at-risk teenagers as those who are "bored, lonely, and introverted." This statement worries me for several reasons. Having taught middle and high school students, I am well aware that many kids in that age range suffer from boredom and loneliness. I don't see many introverted kids, but I believe a MySpace compulsion differs from an Internet addiction in this way. My conclusion is that the extroverts are more drawn to the space because of the constant "social" stimulation.

The Horror of Being Without It

Call it withdrawal, call it freedom, call it torture, call it humorous. But whatever you call it, the idea of living without one's MySpace is a daunting concept for most teens. I decided to ask my students how they would react if MySpace suddenly disappeared. Thirteen-year-old Bakari stood up from his chair and exclaimed, "If

MySpace disappeared, I'd strangle someone! Seriously, I'd be so pissed. It would be as if someone died. Shit, don't even put that idea in the air." Once he calmed down, I was able to resume the interview, albeit with a new perspective on the importance of this site to many teens. Sixteen-year-old Brooklyn had a more mature outlook, and she ruminated, "Deleting MySpace is the biggest problem I see my friends deal with. Their lives are completely taken over by it, and no matter how many times they tell me they are going to get rid of it, they never do." Perhaps one reason it's so hard to imagine living without it is that it becomes the main source for socializing. Fifteen-year-old Daria explains, "Originally, MySpace wasn't that big of a deal to me. The people who I knew had a profile were addicted to the computer, and I knew I didn't want to turn into that. But this summer my friend was over and kept trying to make me one. I finally gave in, so she showed me how to upload pictures, leave comments, and decorate my page. Pretty soon, I too became addicted. MySpace has become my entire summer. And I love it." She even goes so far as to say that "[i]t's better than talking on the phone!" No wonder the image of a MySpace-free world is so frightening.

How and Why Some Teens Delete Their Profile

So what happens to teens who realize they may be a little too chained to their MySpace page? Read the following blogs (web logs) from www.43things.com, a website devoted to the things young adults really want to do (including, of course, quit the MySpace habit):

> *Jpwinder:* i deleted my account last night, and i got some peer pressure from Friends, but other than that . . . i feel like i have so much more time to do other things. of course i had over 150 friends, and some of them i didn't know . . . but

we'll see who stands the test of myspace and keeps in touch. thank god i still use face book :0)

Xsquare4x: i can't do it! i can't delete my account! this is like the third one i've had to make. (my loved ones (my bf, bff, and my own mother) have all at one time or another deleted me!) i have like 300 friends, nd i cant say no!! for gods sake its on the page right behind this one!! i'm bad mouthing it as i partisipate in its evil!! lol, wow . . . this is going to be RELE hard!

FireflyonFire: LOL My boyfriend accused me by saying myspace is your life. When he said that it hurt my feelings, mostly because I knew he was right. I'd been on myspace for a little over a year and a half and I was sooo proud of my profile. It was customized to the max. It screamed ME. I had spent a lot of hours and changes making it look like that. So, with my bf's eye opening comment I deleted my daily visited account. It was sooooo weird not having a profile there at first. I was so used to logging in as soon as I connected to the internet and so now I have to find other things to do online while I wait for my bf to get online. It's funny how a stupid site like that can rule someone's life without them knowing it.

Your Assignment

It is vital to understand why the site is so appealing to teenagers; otherwise, honest dialogue will never occur, and kids will continue to feel isolated, misunderstood, disconnected, and lost. Begin by taking note as to how much time each day your child is spending online or texting with friends. How late is she staying up? Is she really doing homework on the computer, or is Word masking an extended IM session?

In an effort to "detox" your child from his or her daily dose of MySpace, try the following experiment. Pack up the car, lock up the house, and drive—take a weekend trip away from civilization, perhaps to a state park, the mountains, the ocean. Leave all cell phones, laptops, iPods, and electronic toys at home. Don't even listen to the radio. The point is to get far removed from the influences of technology and consumer culture. Beware: your teenager may be furious and even have a strong emotional reaction. Assert your authority, but don't get into a yelling match; address his or her reaction and begin a dialogue about why it is so strong. When you return home, discuss with your teen how it feels to see billboards, signs, advertisements, and other consumer icons after a day or a weekend without them. It is this reentry into culture that drives the assignment—*what does it feel like to see it all after being temporarily "free" from it?* Write your findings in a journal.

A brilliant social critic, Mark Twain once said, "Habit is habit and not to be flung out of the window by any man, but coaxed downstairs one step at a time." One person who decided to coax his MySpace habit out the door is Rob Alderman, a graduate student from Chattanooga, Tennessee. He shared with me his personal narrative detailing how he came to terms with his MySpace habit. While he is considerably older than the teen and preteen MySpacers, he eloquently communicates a common inner turmoil.

Rob's Story

"I've been having trouble beating my addiction. I've tried and tried, but it seems like I will never be free. It's the first thing I do when I wake up in the morning, and the last thing I do before I go to bed. I do it at least twelve times a day, sometimes more. Curse you MySpace . . . I hate your guts.

"I remember when I was the guy who wasn't doing the MySpace thing. Not being much of a computer type, I just couldn't see what all the fuss was about. All of my buddies kept bugging me about it though, and so I thought to myself, 'Well, it wouldn't hurt to try it once.' I went through the process of making a profile, entering in all of my information in great detail, and then came the photos. Grabbing my phone, I quickly snapped a picture that looked just right for MySpace: black-and-white, not looking directly at the camera, with just a hint of melancholy. Perfect. Finally, a name. I had to be careful, because MySpace kept warning me that once I had chosen one, it couldn't be changed . . . ever. With that finished, I clicked 'Submit' and held my breath.

"It was a life-changing moment when I saw the words for the first time: 'You have a friend request.' Soon, I was adding friends and requesting to be friends with people I'd never met. As my list of friends grew, I quickly became aware that I would have to be very careful about who was in my coveted 'Top 8.'

"I was writing blogs, reading blogs, commenting on blogs, commenting on comments, joining groups, creating groups, posting bulletins, reading bulletins, taking top ten quizzes that told the world what I thought about my favorite CDs and movies, and what character I would be if I was living in the world of Buffy the Vampire Slayer! My greatest MySpace moment occurred when one of my blogs cracked the top ten most-read blogs on the site. Not bad, considering MySpace then boasted over forty-five million subscribers. Suddenly, people I had never met were posting comments about my personal life.

"But in the back of my mind there were faint alarms going off. What exactly is it that causes us to spend hours staring at a computer screen in the hopes that someone will post a supportive comment about the party we went to last Friday, or the fight we had Tuesday night with our girlfriend? Just three years ago, meeting someone on the Internet was worthy of being cast to the bottom rung of the social ladder. Now, thanks to MySpace, meeting people via the Internet is not only socially acceptable, but there is a certain level of coolness to having tons of friends on your MySpace page.

"Don't like a friend? Delete them. Don't want someone's opinion? Ban their input. Don't like the way you look? Simply change your photo. You can be who you want, when you want, with whom you want. In fact, it's so perfect and so addictive that it's easy to spend all of our time there, pouring ourselves into our own little MySpace kingdoms.

"I'm not certain how I finally realized that I was worshipping at the MySpace altar. Perhaps it was the fact that I was dragging in late to work as a result of late-night blogging. Maybe I realized I was spending more time talking to my new 'Internet' friends than my real-life college buddies. Perhaps it was the fact that the letters had begun to fade from my keyboard from the incessant typing. Whatever the reason, I am thankful. No matter how fun it is, an addiction is an addiction, and it is not a healthy thing. I knew that I had to do something before I lost my soul completely to the void of cyberspace, and so I hatched one final desperate plan. I've decided to quit MySpace for two weeks, cold turkey.

"I'm not proposing a ban on MySpace or anything like that. In fact, I'm not even deleting my own profile. I'm simply saying that things like MySpace are only healthy when done in moderation. Logging a hundred hours of Internet time on MySpace is nowhere near as fulfilling as spending real face-to-face time with a good friend.

"I posted one final blog advising the MySpace world that I was taking a bit of a 'MySpace sabbatical' to regain some focus. This has not been easy, but I figure that the new perspective on life will be well worth the time spent away from my Mac iBook. In the past few days since leaving MySpace, I've gone for a walk, watched *Hotel Rwanda* (something I'd been swearing I'd do for months now) and started a great book. Last night, I even spent some time with my best friend, sitting on his front porch and talking about life, work, and faith. He has a new job, and I'm happy for him. He began to tell me all about the great day he'd had and for a moment, I thought, "This would make such a great blog," before suddenly catching myself. I was wrong. This makes for great life."

Pimped Out

Anatomy of a Profile

"When I sat down with my daughter to see her MySpace page, she explained to me that it wasn't really her. I'm not sure what that means, but I definitely saw a different person in that profile. Is this just some kind of digital dress-up game?"

—*Marta, parent*

"I definitely was addicted to MySpace. I would spend hours sprucing up my page, commenting to people I see every day, and filling out worthless surveys."

—*Wanda, 16*

"MySpace is just an outlet for self-professed, self-obsessed teenagers. And that's fine. Better on MySpace than in real life. Plus they look a hell of a lot cooler on MySpace!"

—*Adelle, parent*

———

Last year, eleventh graders at a charter school in Palo Alto, California, devoted hours to their final advanced-placement English project. They studied an author's methods of characterization, specifically the creation of Holden Caulfield in J. D. Salinger's coming-of-age classic *The Catcher in the Rye*. This assignment included the standard dissection of rhetorical devices such as tone, diction, syntax, and figurative language; however, it was anything but typical. Under the expert tutelage of my colleague and friend, Caroline Hunt, MEd, these teens designed a MySpace profile for Holden. An adept instructor and teen mentor, Ms. Hunt recognized the presence of MySpace.com in the lives of her students. She realized that it dominated most of their conversations, and she wove her lesson on characterization and voice into this pop-culture phenomenon. Needless to say, the students embraced the project, and the results were impressive. Ultimately, these teens made the connection that the method of representing oneself via a MySpace profile is not so very different from the literary tools used by great authors.

I'm not asserting that FUBU-wearing, braces-gleaming, iPod-sporting Tommy next door is in some way as profound as Chinua Achebe (although both may feel just as marginalized). But Tommy's MySpace profile, replete with vivid images, distinct voice, friends' comments, and reflective blogs, has the same elements and the same appeal as the depiction of the Nigerian Ibo warrior Okonkwo, in the often-assigned Achebe novel *Things Fall Apart*. And that appeal is the power, as Joseph Conrad said, "to make [us] hear . . . feel . . . and see." As Henry James asked, "What is either a picture or a novel that is *not* a character?" In other words, the creation of an image—whether published in hardcover or found online by concerned parents—is the creation of a character.

Teens craft their MySpace profile to portray a cool character, their favorite persona, an invented self. A canvas-turned-collage expression of self; since teens are experimenting with who that self really is, the profile becomes the compilation of all that searching for identity. And just as some adults await the latest Oprah's Book Club recommendation in order to lose themselves in yet another intriguing fictional scenario, so too our teens yearn to surf the menagerie of MySpace profiles. We're all connoisseurs of the human condition; we're all voyeurs of the lives we don't lead.

Becoming a MySpacer

In this chapter, we'll take a tour through the MySpace labyrinth—including how to log on and set up an account—and explore just what goes into creating a profile. I recommend logging on and signing up to find out what MySpace is all about—all with the intent to teach your teen about the risks as well as to engage with them in this new and exciting form of social interaction. There really is no way we as parents can broach the subject of MySpace and its impact with our kids if we have never been on the site. And trust me, the media coverage of the site is driven, many times, more by what will sell than by what is true. Some teen and technology experts warn that neglecting to share in the MySpace experience with your child is a sure route to a disconnected teen or a damaged relationship; obviously, I take issue with this myopic point of view. I simply urge you to spend some time in the MySpace culture in order to better understand your child's social reality. Mind you, I do not advocate becoming a member of MySpace for more than a week or two, but neither do I believe that a failed foray into the space will result in a loss of contact with your children.

Be forewarned that you will feel a strong pull toward seeking out your own child's profile. I advocate restraint for several reasons. First, unless you have already spent time on the site, you may not be ready to see your child's or her friends' profiles yet; your familiarity with the terminology, the layout, the risks, and the benefits of a profile are too rudimentary at this stage. Think of it as excavating a cave—you need to get acclimated before you can venture deeper, and you don't want to stumble and bump your head by exploring the mother lode—your own child's space—first. Rest assured that in chapter 9 I will guide you through the sperlunking steps of entering into the cyber-cave of your child.

The reality is that MySpace is (and should be) boring to the average adult. No sooner would I choose to swap out my Springsteen songs for some Fergie or Beyoncé than would I actually make MySpace a regular part of my daily routine. At a ball game, I only have to taste cotton candy once to understand why children like it and, as the sugar headache subsides, why I'll stick with the soft pretzels. I do believe, however, that an initial, temporary immersion into MySpace is imperative for parents. I recommend creating a profile and logging in once a day for a week to get to know the site and gauge its appeal for yourself. As the helpful website ModernMom.com advises, parents should "be in the know" and "take the time to learn about the popular online communities. Keep in mind your child's perspective and . . . why they might find the site so intriguing." While I will be addressing MySpace specifically in this chapter, I also encourage you to follow the same game plan for Facebook, LiveJournal, and YouTube. Let's get started.

Creating Your Account

While it is not necessary to create an account to surf MySpace in general, it is necessary in order to look at teens' profiles. Therefore, I advocate doing so. The first step in understanding a MySpace profile is creating one. Let's get our own account.

1. **Open your Internet browser (Internet Explorer, Netscape, Mozilla Firefox) and go to www.myspace.com.** Take a moment to browse the content of the home page. Check out the format and what is being advertised or promoted.

Finally, locate the blue box on the right-hand side titled "Member Login." Click the bright orange "SIGN UP!" box. Your membership form will appear, the top of which uses that little faceless person icon to illustrate the three simple steps required: "create your profile," "upload your picture," and "make new friends." Are you getting a feel for what is encouraged of teens and tweens yet? In other words, share your personal information, let us know what you look like, and then start talking to strangers.

A Word from the Wise

"Remember that not everyone may be who they say they are. For example a person who says 'she' is a fourteen-year-old girl from New York may really be a forty-two-year-old man from California."

—*Adapted from the brochure "Teen Safety on the Information Highway," Larry Magid*

2. **Review the Terms of Use.** At this time, I encourage you to click two of the links inconspicuously perched at the bottom of the page: "Terms" and "Privacy." The Terms of Use page will inform you that you are required to enter only authentic personal information, and that falsifying age, name, or postal code is a violation of MySpace policies. However, it is an accepted practice that tweens, teens, *and* adults enter falsified ages, names, and postal codes, for various reasons. Some reasons are for personal safety and privacy, as I will discuss in more detail in chapter 10. Some reasons are less honorable. Nevertheless, for our purposes—to surf the teen MySpace landscape—we must falsify.

A Word from the Wise

"Make sure your children know never to divulge personal information on the Internet, whether through a blog, profile, chat room, e-mail, or instant message. Personal information can include their name, phone number, address, or birth date."

—*County of Los Angeles District Attorney*

3. **Enter an e-mail address.** You will also notice that MySpace requires an e-mail address in order for you to register. As of this writing, the authorities at MySpace neglect to authenticate your e-mail address; you can enter a false one if you please. It can be beneficial to enter an invalid e-mail address because then you are protected from MySpace messages and identity-exposure risks. However, in order to contact MySpace authorities about your site (if it has been hacked, if you have received inappropriate content, or if you wish to delete your profile), you must use that e-mail address in order to be recognized, so keep that in mind. So for our purposes, I recommend creating a free e-mail account from Hotmail or Yahoo to use specifically for this exercise; that way you are safe on both ends.

Blog Bites

Some MySpacers are a bit cynical about their experience; the following blog entry illustrates the evolution of a member who wanted to find old friends and ended up disgusted by the typical amateur self-portraits and immature surveys. For what his honesty's worth, he does admit to being interested purely in the voyeuristic pursuit of looking into strangers' lives.

Crullin4fuel: It all started with wanting to find my friends from middle school, and now I find myself scrolling through endless pages of random people who all have that same stupid "MySpace blurry camera picture" of themselves. . . . I don't care about your 3 surveys on what food you like, or what your pimp name would be, or even what type of drug you would be . . . I just want to pry into your life, read your comments from people I don't even know, then take a look at the pics you took of yourself!

4. **Enter your name—but don't enter your real, full name.** Even though technically you are violating the Terms of Use, it's best not to enter your full name if you don't want someone searching you out and contacting you, especially since you are simply experimenting here. In the same vein, you may choose not to enter your correct postal code (you may wish to select a foreign country to bypass this question). Again, providing this information is antithetical to every cyber-safety rule.

Sample Message Sent to a Fourteen-Year-Old Girl's Profile

Frequently, friends or strangers will send a chain letter message to other members' profiles. The purpose of these messages is nothing more than to generate some level of playfulness or simply fun among peers. In my experience as a teacher, these chain messages supply many giggles and whispers the next day at school. Here's an example:

TAG UR IT! THIS IS A SEXYYY TRAIN IF U RECIEVE THIS IT MEANS UR FREAKIN SEXY . . . IF U GET THIS BACK UR EVEN SEXIERR . . . SEND THIS TO 10 PEOPLE . . . IF U BREAK THIS CHAIN U WILL HAVE BAD SEX FOR THE NEXT 30 YEARS . . . GOODLUCK

5. **Select a birth date.** As you can see on this registration form, MySpace requires all users to provide their date of birth; however, age verification is nonoperative as of yet. As of now, users must be at least fourteen years of age (not too long ago, the minimum age was sixteen). If you set your date of birth to reflect that you are fourteen, this selection will give you the option of setting your profile to "Private," which means that only those people you have accepted as "Friends" or who are under eighteen have access to your page. If you'd rather not select the age fourteen, the other option is to select one hundred years old, as it will remove you from the range of any MySpace searches. *Ever think you'd choose to be*

Cause for Concern

Although many publications have reported that a privacy setting is automatic for a fourteen- or fifteen-year-old MySpacer, there is an alternative option when signing up: the underage user can elect to make his or her profile available to users under the age of eighteen. So, yes, a seventeen-year-old senior in high school could have access to a fourteen-year-old freshman's page. That is, of course, if everyone is being honest about their age!

one hundred? For our purposes, I recommend selecting a birth date that would make you sixteen, in order to enable you to view other teens' profiles. This falsification of age is common practice, especially among tweens who are clamoring to be on MySpace but aren't yet fourteen.

Congratulations! You are now a presence on MySpace (but not for long, remember?)

Here's What a Profile Setup Looks Like
http://www.myspace.com/candiegirlie

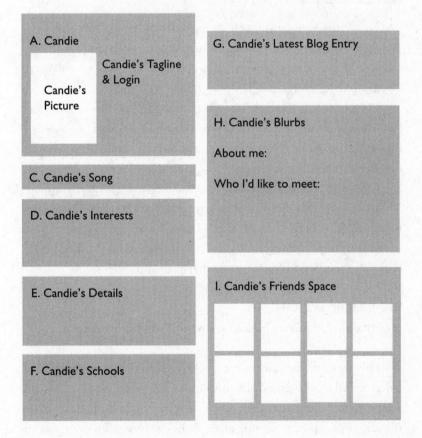

 33

A. Candie's Photo, Tagline, and Login Info
candie

"candie candie...sweet 2 ur taste buds"
Female
25 years old
SANTA MONICA, Cagliari
United States

Last Login: 11/19/2006 (Online Now!)

This virtual doormat welcoming visitors to one's profile supplies some of the most personal (and potentially dangerous) information. Using an actual photo is not wise (especially when you're obviously over thirty-five!).

The playful and somewhat seductive tagline of "sweet 2 ur taste buds" may encourage the wrong type of attention. Don't be fooled— log-in information is rarely accurate; Candie claims to be twenty-five but later establishes that she is a high school student. The older age selection ensures that she can be contacted by anyone on MySpace and that she can join any groups, adult or otherwise. I recommend Candie turn off the "Online Now" feature, as it could invite unwanted messages. It's also in this section that other members can view (and comment on) her pics and videos.

B. Contacting Candie
Email | Add | Chat | Invite | Share | Favs | Block | Rate

This section, standard in each profile, provides a sort of control panel for all the potential activities to be enjoyed: e-mail, add (send a request to be added as a friend), chat (meet in a chat room), invite (to join a group or a forum), share (send or forward this profile to another member), favs (save as a favorite profile to visit), block (block this user from accessing your own profile), and rate (self-explanatory).

C. Candie's Song

Choice of song sets the mood of one's profile. Candie is consistent in her self-representation as a scrumptious treat with her fitting selection of Fergie's "Fergalicious," the lyrics of which focus on teasing boys with how "delicious" and "tasty" she is. While anyone is viewing this profile, they will be getting an earful of Fergie.

D. Candie's Interests

Music
is a big part of my life, how bout u check it out? Rock an rap yo. RAP: OUTKAST. sleepy brown. rick ross. yung joc. da backwudz. Tupac, Biggie, Big Pun, NWA, Eazy E, Busta Rhymes, Ying Yang Twins, Ludacris, Akon, Bow Wow, Dem Franchize Boyz, Chamillionaire ROCK: Arctic Monkeys, AFI, Wolfmother, Taking Back SUnday, Brand New, Saves the Day, Rage Against the Machine, All American Rejects, Red Jumpsuit Apparatus, Anti Flag, Sublime (not really Rock), Kiss, Ozzy Osbourne, Slipknot

Movies
the break up . . . along came polly . . . legally blonde 1 2 and any other cute movie

Television
greys anatomy the OC!!! laguna beach . . . ANYTHING on MTV!

Books
yeah . . . right

Heroes
Mua! tom . . . thank you for making myspace.

The left-hand column houses more personal information. Many MySpacers use this opportunity to make a statement about who they are, based on what bands, movies, and television shows they love. Many times, potential friends will assess a profile's coolness factor from this section.

E. Candie's Details
Status: Single
Zodiac Sign: Sagittarius
Education: High school
Income: $250,000 and Higher

This smaller section really leaves room for fantasy play; most teens will choose "divorced" if newly broken up from a significant other or "married" if newly dating someone. Also, the income selection is usually over $250,000 since no teen fantasizes about making any less!

F. Candie's Schools/Companies
Concord High School: 2006 to Present
Santa Monica, CA
Graduated: N/A
Clubs: Art

Here's where some teens inadvertently set themselves up for trouble. Never should one reveal the high school of attendance, as it provides a reliable location for potential ne'er-do-wells. Candie makes the mistake of listing her school, its city, and what clubs or after-school activities she attends.

G. Candie's Blog

Here, since her profile is not set to private, and she claims to be over eighteen, anyone can access Candie's daily journal entries, or her blog. Users can also respond by commenting about what she has written. A new feature is the vlogging capability, or the use of video links to accompany a blog. This section has some danger potential if personal information is leaked out, or if highly incriminating information is published, not to mention the gossip potential.

H. Candie's Blurbs

Hey Yall mi name Is Candice and the boyz Call MI CaNdiE. I Am in High school. ? I LUV KISSES and HUGS. I used 2 pronise dat i wud never hav a myspace eva . . . but now lolz im addIcted. I love 2 Chill With my friends and ParTAYYYY ON TEH WEEKEND!!!! BuT look i love guys but . . . Im no easy girl, if youu thought so you were so off. if you Want me bad enuf, You are Gonna have 2 wurk. If you Know what I mean ;) . . . i love whip cream lol i love having fun and just being stupid and wild!! Hehe i luv 2 ShoP so Maybe one of you guys can take me shopping sometime! well if you really want to talk to me about me . . . ill be glad to tell you! call me 1-234-567-8910

TELL ME ABOUT YOURSELF—*The Survey*

Birthday:	June 8 fools
Birthplace:	L tothe A! lol hehe
Current Location:	dont worry ;)
Eye Color:	blue
Hair Color:	blonde
Height:	5'4
Right Handed or Left Handed:	both hehe
The Shoes You Wore Today:	my flip flops
Your Weakness:	boyz ;) hugs and kisses
Your Fears:	rats ew
Your Perfect Pizza:	i dont eat pizza
Goal You Would Like To Achieve This Year:	to get good grades
Your Most Overused Phrase On an instant messenger:	lol omfg
Thoughts First Waking Up:	noooooooooooooo
Your Best Physical Feature:	hehe my eyes and my legs
Your Bedtime:	whenever you put me 2 bed
Your Most Missed Memory:	preschool
Pepsi or Coke:	pepsi
McDonalds or Burger King:	ew
Single or Group Dates:	single...i like being alone
Chocolate or Vanilla:	chocolate
Cappuccino or Coffee:	frappacino!
Do you Smoke:	o:-)

Do you Swear:	hell no
Do you Sing:	in the shower
Do you Shower Daily:	yess!!! tht would be gross if i didnt
Have you Been in Love:	idk maybe
Do you want to go to College:	yes
Do you want to get Married:	YES!
Do you believe in yourself:	depends ask me tomorrow?
Do you get Motion Sickness:	whats that?

Who I'd like to meet:
Chris brown is soooo hott... orlando bloooommmmm lol
i love when in pirates of the caribbean his hair is always
wet ya know?! you know any cute guys... you maybe?

The "About Me" and "Who I'd Like to Meet" sections are utilized by teen MySpacers to best represent their online persona.
Here you'll notice the tendency to exaggerate desires and personality traits; the flashier you sound, the more interesting your online
self may seem to other members. The presence of mIsMatCHed
letters is just part of the mystique, and parents just aren't hip
enough to gEt It. Also, the abbreviated language may cause u 2
"lol" or at least 2 wanna sign off bad enuf. (More on this in the
next chapter.) Here Candie does a superb job of letting the
MySpace public know that she is boy crazy and willing to party.
Hopefully you cringed at the sight of her phone number. Other
than listing the obligatory teen heartthrobs, this girl takes her flir-
tation to the next level with her coy "he he" after claiming to be
ambidextrous and by inviting "you maybe" to be someone she
should meet.

I. Candie's FriendsSpace

There are eight slots allocated for Candie's top-ranked friends. The first one is usually reserved for a significant other or a best friend. It is this section that may cause the most drama for teens as it exploits the social hierarchy so integral to teen relationships. I will go into more depth about this issue in chapter 4.

Creating Your Profile

"This is MY page which I put MY time into. And it is an expression of me and who I am. No one can make me get rid of it."

—*Colin, 15*

Here comes the fun part—creating your own profile. The work inherent in this step is partly why teens are so enamored of MySpace. After all, many see it as a truly creative pursuit, spending hours, days even, "pimping" or "tricking" it out to impress friends and other MySpacers. Says fifteen-year-old Paulo, "The only reason I really like MySpace is because I can design and redesign my profile as much as I want." Teens get to digitally decorate their online room, in a sense, showcasing their computer skills and their personal likes and dislikes. Most common among teens is the inclusion of a musical selection, a photo, a tagline, quizzes, survey answers, "Who [they'd] Like to Meet," and the window display of their Top 8 (or up to Top 24) friends. Endless BTUs of energy are expended on these elements, so much so that many complain about their computers freezing from overload.

1. *Select and upload a photo to your page if you choose to do so.* The first step in creating your profile is the selection of your default photo. Note: you do not have to upload a photo, so you may wish to skip this step. If you'd like to include one, rather than uploading (transferring a digital photo from your camera to

your computer and dragging it to your MySpace page) the most recent photo of you at the Labor Day family picnic, I recommend using a cartoon image or some humorous clip art that communicates something you are comfortable with. Keep in mind that your default photo is displayed everywhere on the site, from search and browse functions to Friends Lists to comment postings.

A Word from the Wise

"Be very, very careful about using a webcam or posting digital or scanned pictures of yourself on the Internet. It really is the best thing to not put any pictures of yourself, in any way, on the Internet."
—*from "Online Safety Tips," Connecticut Internet Crimes Against Children Task Force*

2. *Select a display name.* The same philosophy goes for your display name—a fictional name that will accompany your photo and "you" wherever you go on the site. To keep it anonymous, do not use your name, but instead choose something random, like your favorite flower or favorite literary character. If you select a URL (a uniform resource locator, or simply a permanent link for a website), you can more easily access your page from the Internet: for example, you might want www.myspace.com/petunia (with "petunia" as your URL). Candie's profile can be found at the URL www.myspace.com/candiegirlie. Just type that into your web browser to instantly connect to your page.

3. *Invite—or don't invite—friends to join.* You will now be asked to "Invite Your Friends" to join. But it's best not to enter anyone

else's e-mail addresses to MySpace without your friends' permission. The text box that will appear on MySpace states the following: "MySpace uses the e-mails you enter on this form only to invite your friends and acquaintances to join MySpace on your behalf. MySpace will never spam, rent, or sell any e-mail addresses you enter for invitations."

MySpace will now again ask for your real name, "so that people can find you on MySpace," but I encourage you to skip this step for that very reason. Do not give out your real name because anyone searching for you will easily find your profile.

4. *Edit your profile.* Now close the page and go back to the www.myspace.com home page. Sign in with your e-mail address and the password you created. You will be delivered straight to your profile. Once there, click on "Edit Profile" and fill out *even more* personal information. Don't be surprised if you suddenly feel like you've joined an Internet dating site. The "Background & Lifestyle" questions along with the "Basic Info" and "Interests and Personality" inquiries will seem shockingly similar to those found on a dating service. If you'd like, go ahead and fill these in *as if you were a teenager* because, remember, you want to surf the MySpace teen scene for a week. How successful would you be if you listed your favorite movie as *All the President's Men* or *Fried Green Tomatoes*, let alone your heroes as Gloria Steinem or John Wooden?

Basic Info Form

Gender:	___Male _X_ Female
Occupation:	Teacher
City:	Los Angeles
Country:	United States
State/Region:	California

Zip/Postal Code: 90403
Ethnicity: No Answer
Body Type: _X_ No Answer
    ___ Slim/Slender
    ___ Athletic
    ___ Average
    ___ Some extra baggage
    ___ More to love!
    ___ Body builder
Height: __5__Feet __8__Inches
I am here for:

    ___ Dating
    ___ Serious Relationships
    _X_ Friends
    ___ Networking

Background & Lifestyles Form
Marital Status: ___ Swinger
    ___ In a Relationship
    ___ Single
    ___ Divorced
    _X_ Married
Sexual Orientation: ___ Bi
    ___ Gay / Lesbian
    ___ Straight
    ___ Not Sure
    _X_ No Answer
Hometown: Cincinnati
Religion: No Answer
Smoker: ___ Yes
    ___ No
    _X_ No Answer

Drinker: ___ Yes
                        ___ No
                        _X_ No Answer

In your travels you may notice the "Marital Status" option of "Swinger"; take a look at the "Body Type" inquiry, too. If you're like me, you may not understand why these options are included in profiles of under-eighteen users. Perhaps this issue is something that should be brought to the attention of MySpace. Now that you've finished the basic steps to creating a profile, click on "View My Profile" to return to your personal page and to see the fruits of your labor.

5. *Tom is now your friend.* Now we get to use the word we have always known as a noun, "friend," as a verb. We get to begin "friending"! And because MySpace makes its intentions very clear—that the purpose of the site is to encourage relationships between people who do not know each other but share similar interests—you may receive some friend requests, that is, people requesting to be added to your page and, therefore to have access to your profile, the first of which will be the ubiquitous "Tom." Tom, by the way, is the president of MySpace. He founded the site along with CEO Chris DeWolfe. Each MySpace profile is inaugurated with Tom as a default "friend," so he has quickly become known as the face of MySpace. (Therefore, don't respond to Tom; his welcome is just a formality, like the greeters at WalMart.) Now you may take advantage of the "Cool New People" displayed on the MySpace home page in order to meet new people; just click on one of their pictures and click on "Send Message" in order to contact him or her. Or, you may wish to enter a group of your choice; just select the tab at the top of the home page titled "Groups,"

and then select something harmless like "Family & Home" in order to select an existing group of members with similar interests. Once in, you can click on a member's profile picture and then click on "Send Message" to introduce yourself. Likewise, other members will be sending you messages and add requests, looking to become one of your friends. Be on the lookout! Proceed here as you like; you're an adult. But remember, your mission is *to experience the teen culture as played out on MySpace.* There's no need to try to become as popular as an Adirondack chair; you are an observer only, not a true subscriber.

Teen Talk

"Hey, all the teachers at my middle school have MySpace pages. Of course my math teacher's page is pretty bland. No one talks about school or homework with them or anything on there; we just say what's up. It's cool to talk to them about their pics and background and stuff during class. I'm not sure my parents would be too happy about that, though."

—*Josh, 13*

6. *Blog away.* At this point, you are now set up to play around with the options on your profile. Go ahead and post a blog entry. What should you say? Anything (except identifying details, of course)! You'll notice when you attempt to post a blog that you are given some privacy options; to access these, just click on the "Blog" tab at the top of the page, then click on "Manage Blog" and finally "Customize Blog." It is here that you can access the "My Controls" box: you are given the option of "showing" gender, status, age, sign, city, etc. To maximize

safety, I recommend selecting "No" for all options. Interestingly, with each blog entry, MySpace encourages you to describe *what you're doing* as you write your thoughts. A sampling of the choices are "playing music," "reading books," "watching a movie," or "playing video games." The value of this feature is puzzling. Finally, you are asked to reveal your current blog-writing mood, another puzzling feature. The choices include: "angry, bitchy, crushed, dirty, drunk, flirty, horny, hot, lonely, naughty, numb," etc. Yes, these are several of the supplied choices, and obviously a user with less than honest intentions could capitalize on a teen who expresses feeling "horny" and is visibly "online now" in myriad ways.

7. *Pimp it out!* Yes, "pimping" is how kids refer to sprucing up their page. The other phrase used is "tricking it out." Aside from the blatantly sexual implications, most teens associate these terms solely with the act of improving one's MySpace page with more pictures, better graphics, and funnier video clips. Next, click on some of the "Pimp Out" links to make your page, oh, how do you say it, "bling-bling"? A major part of the attraction to MySpace is the ability to customize a personalized profile page; this is done with hypertext markup language (better known as HTML and meaning simply the method with which images and words are displayed on a web page) and cascading style sheets (referred to as CSS and determines how the HTML document or image will be displayed). Even if you have no computer programming skills (which most teens do not), MySpace makes it easy to just cut and paste actual programming code into your profile page. Also, you may want to visit one of the various websites devoted to tricking out your MySpace page; here are three of the most popular:

- www.pimpmyspace.org
- www.ohmyspace.com
- http://my-space-templates.blogspot.com/2006/08/trick-out-your-myspacelayout-page.html

---

Teen Talk

"Most of the kids at my school use MySpace to pose as something they're not in order to be cool. There's the goth crowd, the player crowd, the ghetto crowd; you name it. But they're all a bunch of fakers. Any teenager that claims he is on MySpace to talk to his friends is a liar, it's only about showing off."

—*Jack, 13*

Cynic's Corner

A hilarious excerpt from Justin Rebello on www.pointsincase.com:

"This is my recipe for every single girl's MySpace profile:

- First, ensure the background is something real bright.
- Remember to add long sprawling poetry in there that nobody will ever read.
- Insert dumbshit polls nobody will ever take.
- Make sure your message board is populated by your equally vapid friends."

The Finishing Touches

And now for some fringe touches: you just *have* to post some snazzy quiz results on your profile. After all, what defines you more than displaying the results of questions like *How hot are you?* Or *What type of panties are you?* To do this, go to www.espinthebottle. com/quiz.phtml?trip=571 or www.quizilla.com.

Next, you might want to post your own polls or even your own tournaments; you can upload pictures and ask for comments about which girl is hotter at www.girlmadness.com. Maybe even add a humorous video clip now; after all, what would cause people to want to click on your page more than seeing footage of George Bush with no bones? Go to www.clumzy.com to see the best selection. Finally, for assorted tools in the tricking-out process (I'm definitely over thirty-five), go to www.myspacehumor.com; click on the "For Boys" tab on the left-hand side. Here you'll find plenty of "Cars, Hot Girls, and Cool Posters" (and the obligatory dancing skulls) for your profile.

A Day in the Space

Now we can look at what a typical day in the cyber-life is like. Let's explore our landscape and get popular! Because we are only interested in experiencing the digital reality of our children, try to imagine yourself as an anthropologist setting out on a somewhat frightening dig. Be prepared to see things you've never imagined, feel emotions you can't suppress, and make findings that may or may not be accurate. I caution you again here to stay away from your child's (or your child's friends') pages. Do not peek . . . for now. Seeing these pages will cloud your experience and distract you from your purpose. The first step toward an open dialogue with your child about MySpace is understanding the MySpace culture firsthand. To do that, you must restrain your curiosity and surf only random teens' pages.

1. *You need a good starting point, so I recommend doing a search.* Go to the home page at MySpace and click on the "Groups" tab. We have to jump off somewhere, so what better than to click on the "Fan Clubs" option? And what fan club is more popular with teens than the Paris Hilton Fan Club, or (gulp) porn queen Jenna Jameson's Fan Club? Sorry, but you will find most success tapping into teen profiles by beginning here, however uncomfortable that may be for you. (Another option is to try the fan club for an indie rock band popular with the sixteen-and-under crowd, like The Academy Is . . . or Arctic Monkeys.)

2. *Or, try visiting a chat room on MySpace.* Go to the section on Love and Relationships and click on "Dating." You'll get a quick "chat room" education. While this chat room is not specifically for teens only, it clearly has many young people chatting back and forth. Here's one snapshot sample (one minute) of a typical multithread conversation:

Tiny: hey people any 1 wanna chat
********** at 8:08 PM scott left the room

USC&.035;1: any horny ladies have msn

[]D [] []V[] []D: DO U HAVE MSN OR YAHOO

GUYS_DONT_LIKE_ME: Hello
********** at 8:08 PM Shawn left the room

Emily: well. unless maybe they are special ed

x-BeCky-x.: I have msn yes

Jason: Any ladies want to watch me explode on cam? Press 3434

Brandy: I'm not sure if they are, but they act "special"

Ian: hey girls. anyone want to trade pics with me?

Kia: any horny girls wanna trade pics?

As you can see, the landscape is not mine-free; an innocent teen looking for some interaction may be exposed to some unsettling content. In the above conversation, you may wonder who is talking to whom. It's actually "Emily" and "Brandy" who are trying to have some semblance of a conversation, but they are bombarded with salacious messages. In my experience working with teens, most will ignore the crass advances; nevertheless, the exposure to "Jason's" perverted inquiry could cause an instant loss of innocence for that twelve- or thirteen-year-old girl. How does she process that? The obvious danger, of course, is that your child will, for whatever reason, respond to "Ian's" request for pictures. The advent of the webcam (now available on most laptops) opens up some pretty scary doors for our teens typing away

Parent to Parent

"My son's prom date posted their prom pictures on her MySpace page, so he had to create an account in order to see them. Having stayed off of MySpace for the most part, he suddenly felt pressured to get on. I sat by his side as he created his page, and once we were cleared to proceed I saw more than I was prepared to see. Together we linked from one friend's page to another's and so on. I was surprised at what I saw; many of the pictures revealed beer cans, underage dance clubs, and girls wearing push-up bras. I was horrified to see these kids playing up to the MySpace image."

—*Becky, parent, from Tennessee*

behind closed doors. The temptation to e-mail digital pictures of themselves is real for most tween and teen girls; the thrill of risk-taking aside, most adolescent girls today are curious, if not downright desperate, for feedback about their appearance. The purpose of this authentic excerpt is to provide an average, random, early evening (8:00 PM) look at what's going on in a MySpace chat room.

Now that you're in the Paris Hilton Fan Club group (or really any teen favorite—try Ashton Kutcher), click on some of the profile pictures to begin your journey. You may encounter a few that are set to private—no problem. Just try another one. Eventually, you will be on your way to linking and linking endlessly and infinitesimally deeper and deeper into the cave. Don't worry if you find yourself linking to college-age users; in all honesty, their pages are not all that different from teen and preteen pages. All the while, you will be wearing your anthropologist's hat, making note of findings, and, most importantly, reaching a new level of understanding of your child's social reality.

Teen Talk

"I am able to check my MySpace at home, sometimes in front of my mother because I have nothing to hide. I even have schoolteachers as "friends." What attracts me to it is how I can create and re-create my page. When I'm on MySpace, the only thing I do is update my page. Some pretty impressive page design goes down on MySpace and to me that is the most appealing part."

—*Jackie, 16*

Don't just look at the front page of the profiles, either; access the blogs, read the comments, look at the pictures, notice the surveys, play the videos, and click on their friends' links. In the words of cyber-safety expert Michael Edelson, "It's not like you're stealing a key out of their drawer and reading their diary. This is public information." In fact, I have assigned a one-week stint of daily MySpacing as your homework in this chapter.

Also, be sure to check out the MySpace Videos section to get a sense of what sorts of music and images are being viewed and shared on MySpace. More a commentary on the music industry's harmful impact on teen culture than on MySpace specifically, songs like "Ms. New Booty," "Promiscuous," "My Humps," and "Shake That" rest their lyrics on the gyrating and vibrating rear ends of the female gender. And your child, whether allowed to listen to these songs or not, is free to download the virtual explicit video to display on his or her own profile page. I encourage you to look up the lyrics on www.lyrics.com or to ask your child to let you see the videos on MTV. Here are the most-downloaded videos as of September 2006:

1. *About Us* Brooke Hogan
2. *Ms. New Booty* Bubba Sparxxx
3. *Promiscuous* Nelly Furtado
4. *Snap Yo Fingers* Lil Jon
5. *Shake That* Eminem
6. *Stars Are Blind* Paris Hilton
7. *My Humps* Black Eyed Peas
8. *Tell Me When to Go* E-40
9. *Best Friend* Olivia
10. *Everything I'm Not* The Veronicas

Deleting Your Profile

Had enough? Let's get the heck out of the cave. You probably noticed in your wanderings that many profiles are defunct—either unused, abandoned, or (grimly) deceased. It's important to note that these profiles, especially when the user is only fourteen, will soon become public and visible to the entire Internet. That's a bit scary. Therefore, it is important to delete your account when you decide to sign off; for our purposes, that means no more than two weeks after registering.

Remember that I recommended you use a real e-mail address to log in? Well, this is why: in order to cancel your account, you must begin the procedure from that e-mail account. Just log in, click on the "Account Settings" link near your picture, click the red "Cancel Account" link in the upper left-hand corner, and click the red "Cancel My Account" tab. You are not out just yet, however. Make sure you go to the e-mail account you have used for your profile in order to open the "Account Cancellation Request" message from the MySpace authorities. From there, just jump through the various and never-ending hoops to cancel. They really want you to be sure, so don't log off until you have exhausted each step.

Congratulations—You're on MySpace!

Columnist and humorist Chris Erskine wrote that all he knew about MySpace was that it had a capital letter in the middle of it, "like LensCrafters." But because he is the parent of a teenager, he decided to dive right in and see what it was all about. Below are his musings on how he was able to "up his credibility" with his children by having logged in to MySpace:

> I'm glad I created a site rather than just sat back and passed judgment—which was my first inclination. It was also my right as a parent. But I think that by creating a site, I upped my credibility with the kids. I also, for the first time, really understood the attraction. For teens, it's got to be a great way to reach out and be heard.
>
> Such sites are amazingly habit-forming. The first couple

of weeks in particular were very time-consuming. I think these social sites play into our need for friendship and gossip, two powerful draws. Because I'm a father, I didn't see the sleazier side of things. In fact, people were very respectful. I was sure I'd get my share of adolescent, wise-guy comments. But there was hardly any of that. It even changed the way I think about the manners and decency of society as a whole.

In the end, I'd encourage other parents to dive into the new technology. It's much more mainstream and easy to use than five or ten years ago. It's also like catnip to our kids, and I think it pays to understand why and how.

And that's my point exactly. To write MySpace off as all bad, or even the opposite, totally harmless, is to do your child a disservice. The fact is that it is the most popular method our kids are using to explore their place in the world. And while the creative exploration is somewhat limited, the creation and maintenance of a personal profile has become a rite of passage for most teens, an endeavor worthy of the amount of time some of my students put into memorizing their Torah portion for their Bar Mitzvah.

Maybe Tolstoy would roll over in his grave if he read this, but I reiterate that for today's teenager, creating a MySpace profile is akin to the work of creative writers. The author of our sample MySpace character is quite adept at crafting a solid persona, regardless of whether or not you find it appealing. There's something to be said for the steps involved in identifying the image one wants to portray and then painstakingly going about making it come to life. I suppose my task as an English teacher is to get my students to "show sum luv" to the likes of Anna Karenina with the same fervor they do for the "candies" of MySpace.

And now that you've successfully participated in a profile dissection, it is here that I'll leave you on a musical note, with an excerpt from the lyrics of rap group DaCav.5's hit, "The MySpace Song" (misspellings and all):

Benofficial:
   "this track right here is the myspace song/ addictive from the minute that u first sign on... yall need to hurry up, quick, edit your profile/ but be original/ go and get ur own style..
   pimp ya whole page till its fresh to death/
   before you kno it ull be gettin friend requests (yes)...
   now ya hooked and you just cant quit / stuck on ur main page, tryin to upload pics...
   all the words are real witty that you wrote in the caption/
   but the servers to busy, so ur close to snappin/
   thats what happens when u r a myspace fiend/ can't sleep cuz ur top 8 is up in ur dream
   now it seems like tom is really a drug deala/ he's got u strung over of some tila tequila
   go to sleep-go to work-take ur ass to school/ and when u come back ur inbox might be full."

B-Roc:
   "hey baby . . . remember me from myspace. . . .
   when I sent you a request . . . to be my friend . . .
   you denied it! (why?)
   we could be friends forever"

To hear it loud and clear, please visit www.myspace.com/dacav5.

Your Assignment

I want you to create your own profile, perhaps saving the one we created together. Don't tell anyone if you feel embarrassed; in fact, get over feeling embarrassed. You are a parent and it is your duty to explore the places your child goes, physically or digitally. Sign on every day for a week for at least fifteen or twenty minutes, hop around to other profiles, join a group, read a blog, send a friend request, etc. Write about your experiences each day—maybe you'll even create your own blog!

Warnings:
- *Until you're familiar with MySpace, do not yet look for or visit your child's profile.* This may require some self-restraint, but it is imperative that you refrain from looking at your child's site until you have become acclimated to MySpace. I recommend viewing your child's page with him or her present.
- *As you tour MySpace, you will encounter some disturbing material.* Try not to freak out—don't react to each page you visit; just soak it all in and make mental notes. Essentially, get acclimated to the environment and immerse yourself in this aspect of youth culture. I recommend printing out pages that are particularly disturbing (or even funny), since you may want to reference them when you talk to your child. The teen MySpace glossary in the next chapter will help you with some of the unfamiliar subtleties of cyberspeak.

3
KPC
Keeping Parents Clueless and Other Cyberspeak Decoded

"I do feel terrible for words like 'probably' and 'someone' that are constantly bastardized into 'prolly' and 'sumone.'"

—*Michael, 23, search-engine marketer*

"I'm so over the posers who try to say things like 'What's your S/N?' and 'F'Shizzle!' They're trying way too hard."

—*Keika, 15*

"The thing I don't like about MySpace is the way the kids talk to each other. They use language that they would never use if they were face-to-face."

—*Tammy, parent*

"I have noticed that the language on MySpace is extremely different than what is used in real life. On MySpace a kid who never acts gangsta can say the "n" word all he wants, a kid who never swears can cuss it up, and a kid who isn't that bright can act all smart. MySpace is a shield against others where you can be all hard and curse people out, and they can't do anything about it at the moment."

—*Kip, 15*

"Since MySpace is accessed via the computer, the normal face-to-face contact is lost, and without those restraints, teens do not feel inhibited from saying stuff they would never say in person."

—*Armen, parent*

———

As an English teacher, perhaps I place an exaggerated value on both the written and spoken word. Nevertheless, I am always impressed by my students' love for the playful nature of language. When I introduce Oulipo exercises to my students (Oulipo is a literary technique of writing in constrained patterns to generate creative ideas), the room seems to come alive, and their writing becomes more invigorated. I see the same response when I teach Lewis Carroll's nonsensical "Jabberwocky" poem. (For fun, try translating it into standard English; you can find it at www.jabberwocky.com.)

Whether it's learning a new word while doing a crossword puzzle, giggling at a unique turn of phrase in a cryptogram, or competing at Scrabble, language is *fun*. I liken it to Play-Doh: it's colorful, it's meant to be manipulated, it can be molded into clever structures, it can be balled up and tossed at someone's head. So, while the purpose of this chapter is to alert you, in the interest of protecting your children, to the more alarming secret cyber-words and abbreviations, let me say that I do admire the ingenuity that goes into the creation of such a lexicon. And I encourage you to see it that way, too.

Language Codes

Baba, boppy, beedah, seeball, mowah. Baby talk? Well, yes. Those five words are a sampling of my daughter's blossoming tools for communication at age two (I'll save you the translations, but I'm sure you can figure some of them out). Even at a young age, children communicate their feelings, desires, and reactions in any way possible. Some toddlers even learn to use sign language. It's up to us as parents to decode those words. Most of us have exerted impressive efforts to decipher our kids' words during the toddler years, even taking some pride at times in being the only one who can understand the seeming babble.

Not much changes when that toddler becomes an e-teen; he or she uses language just as cryptic, but we somehow choose to tune it out. Writing off chat slang as juvenile, silly, or just plain boring is a mistake—in your preteen or teen's social world, it's very deliberate and meaningful language. The first step is knowing *what* your child is saying, but the second step is understanding *why* your child is saying it. In this chapter I hope to elucidate for you as best I can the ever-changing teen lexicon of cyberspeak, but more importantly, I hope to illustrate for you the important role language has come to play in your e-teen's world—essentially, why it matters and what it means. Today's teens are so enmeshed in the electronic world of texts, what with text messages, e-mails, blogs, messages, posts, and comments, that language is really more their tool of choice than the cell phone or the computer.

Clearly, images have grown to play a more prominent role in teen communication—via digital video cameras, cell phone still and video cameras, and web cameras—and they're played out on highly visual sites like MySpace and YouTube. Not only that, our teens have kidnapped language as we know it and created their own discourse. Simply put, if we have any desire to understand the how and why our kids communicate in their own cyber-language, we must be mature enough to treat it with a modicum of respect. Much of kids' Internet banter is harmless. Unfortunately, though, a substantial portion of "discussions" occurring among teens on MySpace covers topics that few parents would tolerate in front of them.

The idea of having one's own space combined with the faceless posting of comments and messages allows, even encourages, a certain bravado; what is written is drastically different from how teenagers talk in the non-cyber world. Thirteen-year-old Zach told me his "mother would freak out if she saw the language I use on MySpace." It is this total freedom of expression that adds to the appeal of the site. And teens crave nothing more in their social interactions than to be able to freely engage in any discourse of their choice; hence, the impact MySpace has on teens' social lives.

In addition, blocking porn sites and installing filters on your computer that alert you when your child is talking about sex or drugs are not always foolproof, as I'll discuss in the following chapters. Just try typing in "pron" and see what happens. What does it mean? It's cyberspeak for "porn," but I assure you that your monitoring system will not pick it up. And no, when you see the word "crunk" on your child's phone, the message being texted is not about a crink in the neck that has simply been misspelled; it means "crazy drunk." Now that's information you might want to have as a parent, right? I advocate tuning in, taking a crash course in IM-speak (that's instant message), and creating a crib sheet, however silly it seems.

In order to better understand the evolving language, or cyberspeak, your child uses in venues ranging from cell phone text messages to IMs to MySpace messages, please familiarize yourself with the following shorthand. There's no need to memorize each one of these terms, of course, but an effort as minuscule as scanning this glossary may make the difference between your being in the dark or in the know. Think of it as the Rosetta stone of the cyber-world and let it help you decipher high school hieroglyphics.

Screen Names

What do **juliaiscoolia, mAntrUmpEt,** and **artzyfartzygal** all have in common? Well, other than cramming a lot of letters together, they all qualify as actual screen names. A screen name or "s/n" is a name or string of letters, numbers, or symbols chosen to uniquely identify a user online—you may even have one yourself.

For teenagers, screen names are often treated as pseudonyms, frequently complemented by extra numbers, letters, or other characters to distinguish them from users with similar screen names on the same system. But most often, teens select their identifying screen name in a well-contrived effort to represent themselves in a particular manner. A screen name, not unlike a photograph, follows the teen wherever he or she goes online and accompanies all communication, so it is vital that the string of numbers, letters, and symbols best represent the image desired. A popular trend for teens is to use random upper- and lower-case letters in order to make it more difficult for parents or other adults to find them online. Another popular trend is to use various graphic symbols like an asterisk or a money sign to communicate either celebrity or "pimp" status. For instance, *****inmyeyes** is interested in sharing that she is starstruck or has stars in her eyes; perhaps she is trying to become an actress. In addition, **doinit4$$$** is expressing his love of money, perhaps bragging about how much he has. Some teens use their screen name as an opportunity to make drug connections, as I discuss in a later chapter, by selecting something that communicates an interest in illegal substances and paraphernalia, like **mjlover**. Some screen names are more straightforward and express a more innocent image, like **fairyprincess** or **unclefester**. Regardless, the screen name is an important moniker selected very carefully by your teen; I encourage you to take a look at your child's.

Slang Terms

The following slang terms may not be as common on a text message since they are not that short, but they will appear quite regularly in instant messages, blogs, and MySpace messages. These terms are used more often when a teenager is telling a story or describing a recent event, like a party.

Aight	Okay
Blazed	High
Boo	Girlfriend or Boyfriend
Cheddar	Money
Crunk	Crazy Drunk
F'Shizzle	For Sure
Fade	Fight
Fine	Nice Body
Hit Me Up	Call Me
Hyphy	Crazy
Krump	Dance
Lates	Bye

1337 Speak

1337 is the numeric formation of the word *leet*, or elite. It is a language used primarily by self-proclaimed computer hackers. Often it is used by gaming participants, but because of its remarkable simplicity, it has become mainstream among text messagers.

U	You
R	Are
O	Oh
M	Am
NE	Any
IMA B	I'm going to be
4	A
3	E
7	T

1	L
$	S
/\/	N
/\/\	M
13	B

Translation Quiz A

OK, just to make sure you've been paying attention, read the following IM sample. See if you can decipher it. In the event that you're not sure what this kOoLkiDD and msXXX business is, let me explain that these are simply the screen names of the two people instant messaging each other..

kOoLkiDD: 'Sup dog? U got NE cheddar 4 2nite?

msXXX: fshizzle. Ima B hyphy krumpin' and crunked, aight?

kOoLkiDD: Hit me up. Lates.

My Translation:_____

_____

_____

For more slang, please consult www.urbandictionary.com or www.noslang.com.

Translation Quiz Answer:
Quiz A:

kOoLkiDD: What's up? Do you have any money for tonight?

>   msXXX: For sure. I'm going to be crazy dancing and
>   crazy drunk, OK?
>
>   kOoLkiDD: Call me. Bye!

Symbols, Numbers, and Emoticons

A combination of the words *emotion* and *icon*, an emoticon is a
sequence of ordinary printable characters, such as ":-)", "^_^", "._.",
"XD", "X8", "-_-", "=D", "=p", etc., or a small image, intended to
represent a human facial expression and convey an emotion. Emoticons are commonly used in e-mail, instant messaging, online chat,
and blogs. Teens tend to rely on emoticons and other symbols,
including numbers, to more accurately express the tone of their message. The following list is incomplete, of course, and only presents
some of the more common (or alarming) symbols.

4AYN	For All You Know
4RL?	For Real?
4U	For You
4eva	Forever
4GM	Forgive Me
F2T	Free To Talk
G	Giggle or Grin
%\	Hangover
H8	Hate
^5	High Five
H	Hug
?	Huh?
143	I Love You
%*}	Inebriated
411	Information or Gossip
/myB	Kick My Butt

K	Kiss
420 4life	Marijuana
!=	Not Equal To
262	Old or Outdated
1CE	Once
?4U	Question For You
>U	Screw You!
53X	Sex
:-d~	Smoking/Getting High
3SUM	Threesome
T	Tickle
2U2	To You Too
2L8	Too Late
2MFM	Too Much For Me
26Y4U	Too Sexy For You
WOT?	What?
=W=	Whatever
W	Wink
#-)	Wiped Out, Partied All Night

Translation Quiz B

Feeling a little like Tokyo Rose? OK, now try this one. Be aware that the content is a little more mature. Again, the purpose is to alert you to the usage of these symbols and codes so that you can recognize a problem with your teen's texting or IM-ing discussions. Remember, I have provided you with the most disturbing words; many kids do not use terms like "H8" and "53X" regularly. But now, if you happen to see it, you won't be in the dark and you can address it with your child.

kOoLkiDD: 411! F2T?

msXXX: %\ but F2T. WOT?

kOoLkiDD: 420 4life & 3SUM? *W*

msXXX: 4RL? 143! *K*

My Translation:_____
_____
_____

For a more comprehensive list of symbols and numbers, please consult www.teenchatdecoder.com or www.sharpened.net.

Answers: Quiz B

kOoLkiDD: I've got some information. Are you free to talk?

msXXX: I'm hungover, but free to talk. What is it?

kOoLkiDD: I've got marijuana, and I want to do a threesome. Wink wink.

msXXX: Are you for real? I love you. Kiss kiss.

Acronyms

Acronyms seem to be the language of choice for most e-teens. The ease with which one can write a message, a thought, or an expression of emotion is appealing to a teen who has only a minute or two between class to type out a text message. Sometimes acronyms will appear in blogs or in MySpace messages, but not for necessity or the need to economize space. Usually, acronyms used in this manner are intended to either look cute, trendy, or cool, or to mystify parents who may be watching.

One of my favorite moments in the classroom involved a

sophomore I'll call Gareth. Upon hearing the night's essay assignment, he blurted out the acronym, "OMFG!" I looked at him in shock and demanded an apology for his crass language, at which point he tried to defend himself by claiming that he "didn't say a bad word!" He explained that he just used four random letters strung together. I offered to send him to the "HOS" (Head of School), but he finally apologized.

ASL	Age, Sex, Location
BOHICA	Bend Over, Here It Comes
BF	Boyfriend
BFF	Best Friend Forever
BRB	Be Right Back
CD9	Code 9 (or Parents Are Around)
EG	Evil Grin
EL	Evil Laugh
EWI	E-mailing While Intoxicated
FO	F**k Off
GNOC	Get Naked On Cam (webcam)
GRRR	Growling
GTG	Got To Go
GYPO	Get Your Pants Off
IDK	I Don't Know
KPC	Keeping Parents Clueless
LMIRL	Let's Meet In Real Life
LOL	Laughing Out Loud
LV	Love
M or F	Male or Female
MOS	Mom Over Shoulder
MUAH	Evil, Scary Movie Laugh
NIFOC	Naked In Front Of Computer
NMU?	Not Much, You?

OMG	Oh My God!
OMFG	Oh My F**king God!
P911	Parent Emergency
PAW	Parents Are Watching
PIR	Parents In Room
POS	Parents Over Shoulder
PRON	Porn
PRW	Parents Are Watching
S2R	Send To Receive
S or G	Straight or Gay?
TDTM	Talk Dirty To Me
WAN2	Want To
Warez	Pirated Software
W/E	Whatever
WTF!	What The F**k!
WYGOWM	Will You Go Out With Me

Translation Quiz C

Try the last one now. Warning: it's a bit unsettling. Internet predators have made a point of learning this teen-speak, both to win trust and to be able to communicate no matter who else is around. I have included a pretty typical exchange between a stranger and a teenager. I know you've seen all the *Dateline* stories on television, but take a look here at how it really can spiral out of control in seconds.

kOoLkiDD: ASL?

msXXX: EG. FO.

kOoLkiDD: WTF! Jus showin sum luv. MOS????

msXXX: don't freak me out lik 'at. BRB. CD9!!!

kOoLkiDD: u lonely lik me?

msXXX: not 2 lonely, jus bored

kOoLkiDD: u hav a webcam? We cud hav sum fun?

msXXX: how old r u? r u sum creepy guy?

kOoLkiDD: LOL, ima hs student lik u... frum cali

msXXX: ok , shuttin my door, *w*

kOoLkiDD: GYPO

msXXX: OMFG! U r sum creep, lates.

kOoLkiDD: wait... LMIRL!!!!!!!!!

My Translation: _____
_____
_____

For a more comprehensive list of acronyms, please consult www.noslang.com or www.lacountyda.org/pok/poklist.htm.

Answers: Quiz C:

kOoLkiDD: What's your age, sex, location?

msXXX: Evil grin. F**k off.

kOoLkiDD: What the f**k? Just showing you some love. Is your mom over your shoulder?

msXXX: Don't freak out like that. Be right back—parent emergency.

kOoLkiDD: Are you lonely like I am?

msXXX: Not too lonely, just bored.

kOoLkiDD: Do you have a webcam? We could have some fun.

msXXX: How old are you? Are you some creepy guy?

kOoLkiDD: Laughing out loud. I'm a high school student like you from California.

msXXX: OK. I'm shutting my door. Wink, wink.

kOoLkiDD: Get your pants off!

msXXX: Oh my f**king God! You are some creep. Bye!

kOoLkiDD: Wait, let's meet in real life!

Parent to Parent

I also decided to scour the MySpace blogosphere for some common motifs. I chose the top four members of the obscenity 4x4 relay team, *f**k, sex, nude,* and *porn,* and searched their popularity on MySpace blogs. To give you a peek at what is being discussed, take a look at my results (numbers have been rounded):

- *F**k* exploded out of the starting block at 13,749,000 hits
- *Sex* carried the baton in the second lap with a respectable 9,990,000 hits
- *Nude* held his own when the cowbell rang with 5,587,000 hits
- *Porn* took the last leg of the relay with only 2,442,000 hits

I don't think these blogs are medal-worthy, do you?

Basic Terminology

Finally, following are some basic terms specific to MySpace that describe the kinds of teens who use the site, the common terminology used by all MySpacers, and a little bit about the MySpace culture. For a hilarious, tongue-in-cheek take on these terms, please consult www.UrbanDictionary.com. At the very least, start throwing some of these terms around in front of your teenager and see how she responds.

- **Emo**—Initially a genre of soft-core punk music, this term is short for "emotional." It has come to mean a type of girl or boy who is highly dramatic, often depressed, and generally dark and disturbed. Often these teens wear black clothes, skull earrings, and tattered sneakers.
- **Ghetto**—Another category of teenager, usually indicating a style of dress, talk, and demeanor reminiscent of the urban or inner-city ghetto; this popular style crosses all race boundaries and is made popular by rap and hip-hop artists. Often, these teens wear the latest basketball

shoes, baggy jeans, and oversized T-shirts with crooked baseball hats—and it all matches perfectly.

- **Goth**—This genre of MySpace teen seems consumed with things gothic, or dark and supernatural. Often these teens will identify with morbid literature, music, and artwork. Some of the favorite goth bands are Limp Bizkit, Linkin Park, and Slipknot.

- **MySpace Whore**—A MySpace whore is not necessarily a girl who is particularly promiscuous in the traditional "whore" sense. She is one who has established a reputation for doing just about anything it takes to add as many friends to her page as possible. Sometimes that can mean posting revealing photos of herself in order to receive friend requests from as many guys as possible, but other times it just means accepting anyone and everyone who will be her friend. This is not a good thing, obviously.

- **Pimp**—As an adjective: if something is described as pimpin', then it is flashy, colorful, and decorative. However, as a verb: to pimp is to advertise (generally, in an enthusiastic sense) or to call attention in order to bring acclaim to something; to promote. To have a glittery, fabulous, high-tech MySpace page is to have it "pimped-out."

- **Poser**—The unkind term used to describe a boy or a girl who wants desperately to fit in with the cool crowd and will go to any lengths to do so. Many times this poser will buy excessive amounts of clothing or music to create an image, or to pose as something they really are not.

- **Scenester**—A person who tries very hard to fit the stereotype of a certain scene. Dresses and acts in a prescribed fashion. Image-focused. Vain.

- **Tila Tequila**—The Most Popular Girl on the Web. She's no doubt the most requested/visited/commented page in any MySpace account. Nearly everyone on MySpace knows who she is and has, of course, added her. She's definitely the first MySpace celebrity.

Other Helpful Definitions

Bulletin Board Systems (BBSs)—Electronic networks of computers that are connected by a central computer setup and operated by a system administrator or operator and are distinguishable from the Internet by their "dial-up" accessibility. BBS users link their individual computers to the central BBS computer by a modem that allows them to post messages, read messages left by others, trade information, or hold direct conversations. Access to a BBS can, and often is, privileged and limited to those users who have access privileges granted by the systems operator.

Chat—Real-time text conversation between users in a chat room with no expectation of privacy. All chat conversation is accessible by all individuals in the chat room while the conversation is taking place.

Commercial Online Service (COS)—Examples of COSs are America Online, Prodigy, CompuServe, and Microsoft Network, which provide access to their service for a fee. COSs generally offer limited access to the Internet as part of their total service package.

Electronic Mail (E-Mail)—A function of BBSs, COSs, and ISPs that provides for the transmission of messages and files between computers over a communications network similar to mailing a letter via the postal service. E-mail is stored on a server, where it will remain until the addressee retrieves it. Anonymity can be maintained by the sender by predetermining what the receiver will see as the "from" address. Another way to conceal one's identity is to use an "anonymous re-mailer," which is a service that allows the user to send an e-mail message repackaged under the re-mailer's own header, stripping off the originator's name completely.

Instant Messages—Private, real-time text conversation between two users in a chat room.

Internet—An immense, global network that connects computers via telephone lines and/or fiber networks to storehouses of electronic information. With only a computer, a modem, a telephone line, and a service provider, people from all over the world can communicate and share information with little more than a few keystrokes.

Internet Relay Chat (IRC)—Real-time text conversation similar to public and/or private chat rooms on COSs.

Internet Service Provider (ISP)—Examples of ISPs are Erols, and Concentric. These services offer direct, full access to the Internet at a flat monthly rate and often provide e-mail service for their customers. ISPs often provide space on their servers for their customers to maintain World Wide Web (www) sites. Not all ISPs are commercial enterprises. Educational, governmental, and non-profit organizations also provide Internet access to their members.

Public Chat Rooms—Created, maintained, listed, and monitored by the COS and other public domain systems such as IRC. A number of customers can be in the public chat rooms at any given time; they are monitored for illegal activity and even appropriate language by systems operators (sysop). Some public chat rooms are monitored more frequently than others, depending on the COS and the type of chat room. Violators can be reported to the administrators of the system (at America Online they are referred to as terms of service [TOS]), which can revoke user privileges. Public chat rooms usually cover a broad range of topics such as entertainment, sports, game rooms, children only, etc.

Usenet (Newsgroups)—Like a giant, cork bulletin board where users post messages and information. Each posting is like an open letter and is capable of having attachments, such as graphic image files (GIFs, for "graphic interchange format"). Anyone accessing the newsgroup can read the postings, take copies of posted items, or post responses. Each newsgroup can hold thousands of postings. Currently, there are more than twenty-nine thousand public newsgroups, and that number is growing daily. Newsgroups are public and/or private. There is no listing of private newsgroups. A user of private newsgroups has to be invited into the newsgroup and be provided with the newsgroup's address.

—from FBI Publications: *A Parent's Guide to Internet Safety*
(www.fbi.gov/publications/pguide)

Your Assignment

I really see no inherent problem with teens having their own paralanguage and actually feel it can be quite beneficial. However, if you begin to see acronyms like PAW or symbols like %, I encourage you to discuss them with your teen using some of the strategies discussed in chapter 9, "Taking the Tour." It's our responsibility as adults, teachers, parents, to be aware of how our kids are talking to each other, to attempt to keep up with it as best we can by consulting updated online dictionaries and engaging with our kids, and to continue to impress upon our children the importance of being safe online.

Using this abridged glossary and consulting the websites provided, try composing a note for your child in this language. Perhaps it's just a quick Post-it note reminding him to take out the garbage, or maybe it's an e-mail encouraging her to do her best in her volleyball playoff game—it doesn't matter. Although it is guaranteed to get a "freak out" reaction from your child, the effort on your part will communicate a willingness to enter into your child's social reality, a level of compassion and understanding, and an overall interest in your child's world. However irritated he or she may act, however many eye rolls you receive, trust me when I tell you your child will, deep down, feel validated knowing you've taken the time to communicate on her terms. And I guarantee it will be fun. Warning: most teenagers will tune out pretty quickly if they think you are trying to be too cool or trying too hard to act younger than you are, so be sure *not* to start using this IM-speak regularly. Let them have their own secret code . . . just make sure you have the decoding ring when you need it.

"Thanks for the Add"

Popularity, Gossip, and Relationships in the Age of Friending

"We hear constantly about cyberspace as a place of connections made between all kinds of people who would not have come together before. Perhaps. But every one of them has connected by being alone, in front of a computer screen, and this is a poor excuse for what community has meant for most of history."

— *Paul Goldberger in the* New York Times

"Don't want to see someone? Then call them. Don't want to call someone? E-mail them. Don't want to take the trouble of writing sentences? Text them. It's the ultimate social crutch to avoid personal communication."

— *Matthew Felling, Center for Media and Public Affairs*

"My favorite part of MySpace is how I can change who my friends are at all times. If I have a falling-out with a friend, I can delete them."

— *Thomas, 15*

"Some of my friends have MySpace parties. Basically, a bunch of kids get together with their laptops and all sign on to MySpace and start surfing it together. The party takes off when they start surfing kids' profiles who aren't present. You can imagine what a gossip scene it is."

—*Tara, 16*

"MySpace is how gossip travels. You can find out that your boyfriend is cheating on you because they post a bulletin about it—how sad. I don't have a MySpace, and I never will."

—*Lindsay, 17*

———

In middle school, my best friend and I had a silly habit of calling our friendship a "friendboat." I helped Debbie study for her Bat Mitzvah while she comforted me when I thought I must be pregnant, even though I had never so much as kissed a boy yet, since I could feel what I thought was a heartbeat in my stomach. (It turned out to be my pulse.) We were together often, made fools of ourselves regularly, and kept each other's secrets no matter what.

Although in 1982 the worst media influence on our social habits was the latest Stevie Nicks video, gossip was, of course, alive and well even then. I still have a box, a large box, filled with the notes we passed each other year after year; we would even fold them as creatively and securely as possible so as to ensure their privacy. Note writing was obviously an important aspect of our friendship, one that is just as important for teens today. Only today, these transpire substantially through text messaging, instant messaging, and the various features of online social networks. The Harrison Group's 2006 Teen Trends research reports that teens spend an average of more than *seventy-two hours per week* using electronic media like the Internet, cell phones, MP3 players, video games, and PDAs. Adolescent friendships today are frequently maintained electronically rather than through the face-to-face encounters or pen-to-paper exchanges that we once knew.

And while e-mail has become "so Stone Age" according to my sixteen-year-old interviewees, newer forms like text messaging (or "texting") and instant messaging have apparently ushered in the cyber age. The following percentages detail why teens text message each other, taken from a recent study called "IMing, Text Messaging, and Adolescent Social Networks" conducted by the Department of Telecommunications, Indiana University:

Keep in touch with friends	92.0%
Make plans with friends	88.0%
Play games with IM software	61.5%
Play a trick on someone	60.0%
Ask someone out	44.0%
Write something you wouldn't say in person	42.0%
Send non-text information	38.5%
Break up with someone	24.0%

What I'd like to first direct your attention to are the fourth- and sixth-most-popular activities being carried out via text messaging: *playing a trick on someone* and *writing something you wouldn't say in person*. At a respective 60 percent and 42 percent, each of these actions is pretty popular. Yes, kids will be kids; they will play tricks on one another; they are shy and often opt out of direct communication. However, the access to a technology like texting opens up a whole new medium for typical teen torment like gossip, rumor spreading, and tricks. And the anonymity afforded compounds the problem by removing the only thing that may keep a mouthy teen in check—inhibition. In other words, no longer is courage a prerequisite in confronting someone face-to-face, since now it can be done instantly, comfortably, and seemingly without an immediate consequence.

Once, during a school field trip, several of my students decided to play a joke on a rather shy boy. This junior boy made the mistake of sharing that he had a crush on a freshman girl (who did not return the affection). What ensued for the remainder of the trip was a barrage of false cell phone text messages appearing to be from the said girl to the boy expressing interest and downright flirting. I'm sure the perpetrators could be heard laughing each time this boy would be texting away on his phone, not realizing how cruel the prank really was. The other victim, the girl, had no idea this scenario was being played out and was a bit jarred when the junior boy approached her by putting his arm around her shoulder—an unwanted gesture to her, but an invited one to him according to the texts he had received from "her." Had this ruse been attempted through handwritten notes, perhaps it would have been easily deciphered by way of handwriting analysis and/or method of delivery; however, the anonymity of a text message aided in disguising any foul play. These high-tech high jinks are particularly mortifying to teenagers because not only have they been had by their peers, but also there is a trail of evidence for all to relish. This young man now had to sit there while the other boys read and reread his text responses. Ouch.

Friending

Let's look at the other statistics. Obviously, *keeping in touch with friends* could mean myriad things, from updating each other about the drama in their lives to something as minimal, but no less important, as just saying hi. After all, Debbie and I would never win a Nobel Prize for the contents of our notes; they simply provided a way for us to "gift" one another, or to "show sum luv" as it's said today. And for teens, this exchange, however seemingly superficial or juvenile, is vital in a friendship.

The other interaction technology at play in the evolving social reality of teenagers is of course the online social network. Being a MySpacer or on Facebook is sometimes enough for a teen to feel like she's part of the crowd.

"Friending" is a newly coined verb direct from the MySpace lexicon, short for befriending. It simply means *the act of accepting or being accepted by a new contact with the mutual intent of labeling one another "friend."* The result of successfully friending someone is having your photo and profile link added to and displayed on their Friends List on their profile page. There is a certain level of reciprocity involved; no one can friend someone else without their express approval. The steps taken to achieve friend status include sending a "Friend Request" to be "added," the results of which may be a denial, a block, or an acceptance. Once a friend has been accepted, a courteous "Thanks for the Add" message is usually sent in response—an almost chivalrous display of manners. However, the reciprocity usually ends there. True friendship assumes mutual motivations, and many of the friending exchanges that take place reek of social climbing, posturing, self-aggrandizement, or accumulation. Rarely do two people friend each other out of a sincere desire to relate, grow in intimacy, and strengthen a bond. As social media expert danah boyd explains, "The idea of actually meeting all your friends on your MySpace page is just strange; you wouldn't do that. These are just people you're connected to. And you connect to them for a ton of different reasons." Particularly for young teens, friending is merely a pragmatic way of restructuring one's position on the rungs of the social ladder, and there are as many motivations for a teenager to add a new friend as there are for a politician to court a special interest group.

Yet, don't underestimate the gravity of this process. Most teens are quite particular about whom they will add and whom they will reject, especially in light of the media frenzy over Internet predators grooming unsuspecting teens. In fact, during my research I attempted to friend several teens whom I did not know (and who did not know me). I was pleased to see that only one out of twenty-eight teens added me as a friend. I was rejected by 96 percent of my target group! Of course, either teenagers are getting the message that they need to be wary of unsolicited friend requests, or my generic profile was just not cool enough for an add. Regardless, most teens will investigate a potential friend before adding him or her. This investigation mostly consists of visiting the person's profile page (all the more reason for a well-designed page) to inspect the coolness factor versus the loser (or even creep) factor. The person's Friends List, music choices, pictures, and personal information are all fair game for consideration. In true *Wayne's World* fashion, these amateur sleuths are determining whether this potential friend is "worthy" or not.

Privileges of Friend Status

"As if I would ever add Kelly to my Friends List. I don't want people thinking I actually still like *Napoleon Dynamite*! She's so out of it. Why would I want to associate?" The decision to approve a friend is so important because benefits come with friend status. First of all, your picture will appear on this person's profile page (and vice versa), which can be a boost or a drag on one's social status. If, let's say, your son decides to "add" a friend whose profile is littered with references to his favorite history books or his favorite teachers, your son may pay the price. On the one hand, your son may not be added in the near future by a certain cool girl or a particularly hip older boy if there's a hint of his associating with someone who actually admits to liking history books. Also, at school your son may be ribbed a bit, or even excluded at times, if he demonstrates such a breach in MySpace social etiquette—the gaffe of adding a potentially uncool friend. On the other hand, your son could significantly boost his social status if he can earn that coveted add from the hottest new band, the sexiest girl in school, or the right brand-name shoe.

When other MySpacers check out your son's profile to contemplate "friending" him, the likes of these social essentials will ensure his acceptance, which then leads to more inclusion at school and on the weekends. Of course, the fact that associating oneself with the wrong crowd can adversely affect one's social life is nothing new in the history of human relations. In fact, a Japanese proverb states, "When the character of a man is not clear to you, look at his friends." However, this truth takes on new meaning on the rungs of the MySpace social ladder. Seventeen-year-old Tracy explains that she has "a systematic way of assessing whether or not I will add a new friend, one that is designed to weed out any potentially harmful adds." Sounds more like immunizing than relating.

The size of one's Friends List is also a major factor in determining one's popularity, both online and off-. "If you go to college and you don't have a full bunch of people on your MySpace or Facebook, then it's implying that there's something wrong with you," explains adolescent psychologist Susan Lipkins. She continues, "Listing your buddies and your friends is a way of establishing yourself, of feeling connected and feeling like you're accepted." And there's nothing like the rush of being added to a new person's Friends List. Olivia, a student of mine, described it this way: "When my add request is accepted, I get so excited! I mean, I just feel so validated, like this person thinks I'm good enough to be added."

Tom: Your First Friend

The MySpace that exists today went through its own metamorphosis, beginning in 2003 when UCLA graduate Tom Anderson and USC graduate Chris DeWolfe merged to created a nascent online social network rooted in the independent music scene. From their Santa Monica office, they gathered a small group of computer programmers in an effort to create a space for upcoming musicians to showcase, share, and promote their music. Internet-brand wunderkinds, Tom is now the current president and Chris is the current CEO of MySpace.com, potentially the most influential force in pop culture since the advent of television.

And yes, "Tom" is the guy wearing a white T-shirt and peeking over his left shoulder whose picture resides in every MySpace profile as your child's first "friend." Your child never has any contact with him; it's just an impersonal kind of greeting meant to retain the intimate feel of that "back in the day" era before MySpace mushroomed into well over 100 million users. In an interview with Forbes, Tom explains that "just one day, in particular, we saw this huge spike because of people telling each other. It just went crazy from there. We didn't have this big, long struggle behind it. We put [MySpace] up, and it got popular very quickly." Chris summarizes in the same interview, "If you have ten friends, and nine are on MySpace and you're not, you feel pretty left out. People end up joining sooner rather than later." Even the creators recognize the social pressure involved in the site.

How many adds do teens require? It takes friends to make friends, so once you sign up, you need to start adding as quickly as possible. "I would never add a person who had only, like, ten or eleven friends on his MySpace. I mean, he's probably a real loser!" declares fifteen-year-old Alla. The culture also has its own method of keeping members in check when it comes to the amount of friends one has—too many and you're considered a "MySpace whore." Seventeen-year-old Grayson explains that "MySpace whores make the world a nasty place. MySpace cuts out real communication between people. You cannot connect with someone by exchanging stupid comments like, 'Dude, love the layout. It's bomb,' instead of calling them up and hanging out. Since the communication is so meaningless, it makes relationships meaningless." How many is too many? There seems to be an unspoken number among teens; from my interviews I garner that anyone with over 250 friends is pushing the envelope toward "whoredom" and that anyone with fewer than 50 is slightly lame.

And, believe me, every MySpacer is well aware of how many friends they have at any particular moment. In fact, when I would inquire into how many friends a teenager had on MySpace, I never once received an answer like, "Hmmm, I'm not sure" or "I really don't know." Without fail, I was given seemingly exact numbers, and in the process a small treatise on why that number was just right. As in most arenas of life, balance is important for one's image, and these cyber teens are obsessively concerned with appearing well balanced when it comes to the amount of friends on their list. "I guess I would be kinda suspicious of someone who had two thousand friends, but at least I would know they have something to offer—and I definitely would want to be part of it," says Helen, seventeen. This game of friending, denying, and deleting is intense, and most teens are facing the pressures and pains of it every day.

On MySpace, the social coral reef is dominated by a new social order, and it's shark-infested. Any sign of a perceived weakness, and your child can be ostracized. Being rejected for not having enough friends on MySpace speaks to the larger issue of how a teenager is defined and categorized in the MySpace culture. Again, without the dominant presence of real-world intimacy, the most frequently utilized methods available to get to know someone are these shallow attempts—judging a person's social stock value merely by how many other people like him or her. This commodities-trading style of relating reduces our children to nonhuman entities and places an inordinate amount of pressure to represent themselves in whatever way will gain them more friends. And in today's culture, this can mean many unsettling ways, including but not limited to seeking attention by any means possible. For instance, the more shocking one's blogs are, the more visits and comments one's page will receive, and this recognition can only lead to more attention at school and online. Plus, if your daughter is trying to impress a certain clique of girls at school, and she knows they have a history of cutting or self-mutilating, she may feel more compelled to play up that angle on her MySpace profile. Whether she has ever participated in the behavior or not, your daughter may feel some very real pressure to represent herself in a manner that will get her ingratiated with this group of girls, and maybe even invited to one of their parties. For teens, the social stakes are high; it's about all that truly matters at this stage of life. And MySpace alters the playing deck in ways that cannot go unnoticed.

The odd thing about many of the teens I interviewed is that they recognize the absurdity of it all. But they also realize that it is a part of their social world that will not be going away soon, and in the typical teen fashion of rolling with whatever they've been dealt, these social pioneers mock, complain, and continue to participate. Fifteen-year-old Sharyn just can't be outside the social loop; she reports her experience with candor: "I first got my

MySpace in 2003, and I never really used it until my 'friends' started to increase. Over a year and a half later I had close to six hundred friends, and I didn't know who half of them were or why they were my friends, so I deleted it. It was nice at first, but then I started missing way too many parties." I can't help but think of Al Pacino in *The Godfather*: "Every time I try to get out, they keep pulling me back in!"

Top 8 and Ongoing Competition

Recently a close friend of mine was undergoing the (offline) torture of selecting which friends to include in her bridal party. She agonized over which friends had more of a role in her past as opposed to which friends she felt closest to now, and of course which friends did not include her in *their* bridal party the year prior. While this may seem petty to some, it's a very real decision for a bride whose wedding is not only a public declaration of her love for her husband but also a permanent statement of whose friendship means the most. Some brides, I have heard, will arrange their bridesmaids not by height, but by level of friendship. I can't help but see this practice as analogous to the controversial practice of the Top 8 selections on MySpace.

The "Top 8" is a feature that is prominently displayed on one's MySpace profile and allows the user to literally rank his or her top eight friends in descending order. Teens are encouraged to place close friends, love interests, bands, and the like in these positions of privilege in an effort, once again, to define who they are and how cool they are. It's also a way to jockey for higher social status; simply placing a good-looking girl from another high school in the top three or four slots will ensure kudos from male friends and possibly create some beneficial jealousy from female classmates. Interestingly, MySpace recently added a new option for the Top 8 ranking: now a MySpacer can have a Top 4, 8, 12, 16, 20, or 24. This feature will alleviate some of the social pressure, but issues surrounding who makes the first slot and who makes the eighteenth will not subside. And the reality is that not many teens select the Top 24 option; eight seems to be just the right amount to convey selectivity.

Whom would you choose? What difficulties would you have in selecting, ordering, and neglecting your family and friends? Now imagine being fourteen and attempting to piece it all together without completely offending the two girls you like and the friends you've had since elementary school, let alone the popular boy who isn't sure if he's going to invite you to his party. As Billy Joel once sang, "Pressure!" The most common arguments I overhear at school revolve around the Top 8 feature. Female students especially have difficulty overlooking their status on other female friends' lists.

Top 8 rankings are the cause of many severed friendships. Twelve-year-old Michael shared this anecdote with me: "My friend and I got into a fight over a girl on MySpace. He was pissed that I had her picture on my page; he was just jealous that she gave me some love. The next day at school he hit me in the face. I hit him back, of course. She's still in my Top 8." The sting of the Top 8 is that it's not shielded from your other friends since the picture and headline of your choice eight are displayed prominently on your profile, and anyone who signs on can see whom you have chosen. Beyond the rush of being added, the benefit to being placed on a Top 8 list is a big ego boost. Conversely, being removed from a Top 8 is a definite dis. Kids repeatedly check their friends' profiles to see where they have been ranked. This feature magnifies the drama factor, which, of course, attracts teenagers even more.

A week after creating his MySpace page, twenty-four-year-old J. D. felt inclined to post a disclaimer about his Top 8 selections. He stated: "The first spot will always be my brother (for obvious reasons) and the second spot will always be my friend Katie . . . The final two spots are, to be perfectly honest, the two most attractive female photos from my list of friends." And he's an adult. For the average fourteen-year-old, the task is more daunting, more defining, and even more subject to irrationality. One of the most frequent arguments I witness between my students occurs when two people begin dating. This act opens an entire Pandora's box of issues, not the least of which is each other's placement on the coveted Top 8 list. If the boy puts the girl in front of another girl he still kind of likes, he'll lose any chance of dating her, but if he has another girl ahead of this girlfriend, he may be in trouble. She may not want her girlfriends to know that she's dating this boy, and putting him on her Top 8 would make it obvious. Plus, what if her brother sees it? The issues are endless. As media expert danah boyd notes, "It gets highly dramatic." And the stress our teens experience is substantial.

Top 8: A Pop-Culture Presence

The issues surrounding friending are so prevalent in the teen world that there has been a T-shirt craze taking over the newest "yo' mama" insult: "Your Mom Is on My Top 8!" Ahead of its time, the sitcom *Seinfeld* addressed such friend vs. acquaintance issues frequently; for example, the character Elaine was horrified at being asked to act as the godmother of her friend's baby, a faux pas she termed "level hopping." MySpace's Top 8 "is the *Seinfeld*ian speed-dial dilemma of our generation," explains Sarah, 22. Half-joking, she continues that she thinks there should also be "a Bottom 8, or a Bottom 20. A hall of shame of sorts."

Keeping Up with the Latest Gossip: Blogs

Sailors keep logs, companies keep logs, *Star Trek*'s captain even kept one. Except none of them were posted for all to see on the World Wide Web. The term *blogging* is an abbreviated version of *web logging*, or writing an online journal. As an English teacher, I'm thrilled by most anything that gets kids writing, especially journaling. To take a look at typical blogs, sign on to www.technorati.com and do a subject search; what you'll find will range from prepubescent rants about unfair Spanish teachers to ultracerebral posits on how to isolate enzymes. The purpose is threefold: to express whatever is on one's mind, to share it with the rest of one's network (which may or may not include the entire online world), and finally to elicit comments and reactions from readers. In the most academic sense, this medium has the potential to be quite productive. Many schools, churches, and political organizations host blogs in an effort to facilitate lively discourse among its population, and from what I've seen, many are quite successful. There's little wrong with journaling one's thoughts, ideas, and even rants. That is, unless the content is malicious, inappropriate, or incriminating—and on MySpace, there's plenty of that. Especially considering a blog is *a published document*, considered a public record by authorities including schools, police, and government officials.

Let me illustrate with a recent news story. In early September 2006, a mysterious and salacious blog entry appeared on MySpace. The anonymous writer posted a detailed list of sexual encounters among dozens of Georgia high school students, including their full names. Unsurprisingly, this blog generated a real-world eruption of bitter arguments, hurt feelings, and irate parents.

The good news is that the local officials took the blog seriously and pursued the writer to the best of their ability with the intent to prosecute. The offense? Slander and the distribution of obscene materials to minors. The lieutenant on the case put some of the onus on the school's principal, saying, "The school has the respon-sibility to take every action they can to help keep the slander down." And, in fact, the principal has declared that if the writer turns out to be a student at his school, he or she will be expelled for violating the school's conduct code. In addition, the person responsible for this malicious blog may face civil action from par-ents of the students who were slandered. Lt. David Kilpatrick con-cluded, "There's a lot of difference between writing on a bathroom wall and distributing it all over the world on the Internet where anyone has access to it." The bad news, of course, is that no matter what actions are taken by authorities or parents, isn't the damage already done? Imagine all of your friends, enemies, and acquain-tances (perhaps even teachers) reading a published account of your alleged sexual encounters, whether true or not. Pretty devastating for an adult, but even more so for a teenager.

As demonstrated by the recent Georgia incident, a blog is a powerful communication tool. Although it can be a healthy method of cyber journaling, it's also a blunt weapon if wielded by the wrong hands—especially for impulsive and emotionally driven teenagers who are still navigating the intricacies and subtleties of social situations. Just as you wouldn't want the driver who suffers from road rage to keep a pistol in his glove compartment as he heads south on the freeway at rush hour, neither would you want the typical fifteen-year-old girl who can't keep a secret and just heard about her arch-enemy's brother being sent to Utah for drug rehabilitation to have access to a blog late at night!

Gossip has been and always will be spread by word of mouth or notes passed under the desk, but blogs are changing the face of gossip. Essentially, a blog provides a new set of legs, to carry, deliver, and disseminate the message. While most gossip dies out after a few days or maybe a week or two, blog gossip lives on and on and on . . . it's published for the world to see, and it can be forwarded ad nauseum. Plus, gossip put in writing is much more menacing than that which is whispered here and there. As comedian Carol Burnett once stated, "Words, once they are printed, have a life of their own." There's a sense of permanence, legitimacy, and power in something that is not only written, but published online.

These issues don't just rear their ugly heads at school or at the mall; they have now migrated to the cabins of summer camps across the nation. A former student of mine, Veronica, shared her experience with me: "I'm currently working as a camp counselor for the summer. The majority of all my campers (from age nine to thirteen) have a MySpace. Normally, I wouldn't care much about what they do at home, but it disturbs me when I hear what they talk about on MySpace. I hear about whole friendships starting and ending on MySpace just because someone wrote a hateful blog or started a rumor." When I asked her about the campers who chose not to participate (or were forbidden to participate) in the MySpace drama, she replied, "I find that the campers who don't have a MySpace tend to have a more peaceful life because they are happily lacking the drama that MySpace creates."

Caught on Tape: Pictures and Videos

What can be done with blogs can also be magnified with pictures, videos, and bulletins. One teen, I'll call her Karyn, attended a weekend party where she got drunk for the first time. At age fifteen, she was pretty naïve to what could happen to her, plus she felt safe being surrounded by close friends. As excessive alcohol is wont to do, it escorted her inhibitions right out the front door. Apparently, after doing tequila shots with her girlfriends, cussing out her ex-boyfriend, and pretending to make out with the coat rack, she passed out in the host's parents' bedroom. A pretty typical first night of alcohol-induced teen behavior. However, what isn't typical is that it was all caught on video and promptly uploaded to YouTube.com.

I'm sure it comes as no surprise that this footage was also soon e-mailed, posted, and circulated via MySpace. Karyn's first experience with alcohol, as embarrassing as it was, can't be shaken off and forgotten about anytime soon; it's all but written in the sky at this point. One person who received an e-mail with a link to the footage from YouTube is her high school principal—some student's idea of a joke. After meeting with Karyn and her parents, the principal concluded that the school must draft and incorporate an addendum to the student code of conduct in order to effectively address such issues as they become more common. I echo this sentiment, especially since the absence of a set policy renders school officials virtually powerless in an age where the above situation is increasingly likely.

For many students, especially girls, there's no escaping a presence on MySpace. One of the most popular pastimes for teenage girls is posing for, taking, and sharing pictures. And this was fact prior to digital, cell phone, and web cameras. (It's in our genes. We may be missing the Y chromosome, but we certainly have the Kodachro-mosome!) No longer are pictures being sentenced to years at the back of your desk drawer or solitary confinement in a frame. No, once your image has been recorded in today's cyber-culture, it's for public distribution. There's no telling where it will be posted, by whom, and for whose eyes—not to mention the caption that may accompany it or the comments that will be made about it. I felt a significant amount of sympathy for sixteen-year-old Cheryl, who lamented to me, "It's hard not to be involved in MySpace. I purposely don't have a page, but my friends all do. And they keep posting pictures of me on their pages, so in a way I'm on there even though I don't want to be. But what am I supposed to do? Not take pictures with my friends?" I think sixteen-year-old Karina captures much of this generation's mind-set when she declares, "Everything revolves around MySpace. I mean, what's the point of taking pictures with your friends if you don't post them on MySpace?"

Getting Tagged: Bulletins

Another popular feature on MySpace is the sending of bulletins. A bulletin is usually a mass-communicated quip in the vein of "tag, you're it." But in the online world, this isn't always a game, it's also etiquette. It's considered a small gift presented from friend to friend, and surprisingly it makes up a large proportion of the content of messages on each page . . . especially for girls. Bulletins, however, cannot be immediately deleted by the person who receives them. The only way to erase a bulletin that has been sent to you is to wait for it to expire after ten days. Obviously, for this reason alone care should be shown in what types of bulletins are sent between friends. It's also reason to be discerning about whom your child adds to his or her Friends List. In light of the gossip and slander issues prevalent in most teens' lives, this bulletin feature is yet another powerful weapon.

A former student of mine was the victim of a cruel joke played out via MySpace bulletins. A mid-year transfer from the local public high school, Shoshana was an unpopular sophomore who seemed to attract the negative attention of both boys and girls in my class. One Monday morning the class seemed particularly rambunctious, but I had no idea why until I noticed that Shoshana's desk was littered with makeshift thank-you notes scribbled out on notebook paper. Fortunately, she was absent. Apparently, a few students had posted a MySpace bulletin the previous week announcing a huge party at Shoshana's house on Saturday night; the authors included her address, directions, parking information, and an encouragement to "send this to all your friends!" All unbeknownst to Shoshana or her parents, of course. Some thirty teens stormed Shoshana's lawn, the police were called, obscenities were flung, and a socially awkward teenager was mortified.

Clearly this incident could have, and probably has, happened without the Internet. However, the advent of such features as bulletins that can't be deleted, blogs for all to see, and posted images that make the virtual rounds from high school to high school have exacerbated the problems. When I was an eighth grader, several girls spread a rumor about me: supposedly, I was observed blowing myself a kiss in the locker room mirror after getting changed for P.E. For about two weeks, I couldn't shake the stigma of being conceited. But soon word got out that Alyson and Roger broke up because he liked Linda, and the rumor mill moved on. I wonder, however, how much longer and to what extent more I would have been ridiculed had a bulletin been posted about my alleged locker room ode to myself. I know of one boy who was so discouraged by rumors about his sexual orientation that he transferred high schools, only to realize that the rumors had been circulated via MySpace, and he was no better off at a new school. The family eventually moved out of state. Incredibly, this, too, was to no avail, because some classmate caught wind of the move and forwarded the "information" to the members of that school's MySpace group. Again, technology provides the legs.

Sample Bulletin Sent to a Fourteen-Year-Old Girl's MySpace Page

Bitches...........Look up to you.
Bitches...........Look up to me.
Bitches...........Envy you.
Bitches...........Envy me.
Bitches...........Don't like you.
Bitches...........Don't like me.
When....That Bitch tried to play you.
That.....Bitch tried to play me.
When....That Bitch hit you.
Guess what....I made that Bitch fight me.

What's the Extended Network?

On MySpace, the "Extended Network" is made up of everyone who is not on your child's Top 8 List or his Friends List. However, these members are able to visit, browse, view, and contact your child *unless* the appropriate blocking measures have been taken. If your child has selected fourteen or fifteen as his age, the privacy setting should protect him from some unsolicited invasions by people in his extended network—that is, unless he has chosen to allow anyone under eighteen to have access. In that case, any undesirable member who pretends to be under eighteen can access your child's profile features through the extended network. And if your child is sixteen or older and has not selected any privacy settings, he is vulnerable to everyone in the MySpace extended network.

This extended network translates to a large group of people who could be watching your child unbeknownst to you or him. Of course, in the real world, we all have an "extended network" of strangers—I liken it to visiting a local park, where there's always someone sitting nearby on a bench or a conspicuous automobile that keeps circling the block. And anyone can deduce some personal information just by observing carefully—overhearing a cell phone conversation, for example. The problem with your child's extended MySpace network is that much more essential private information is available and easily harvested just by copying and pasting.

Remember that on a MySpace profile, your child is encouraged to disclose her real name, e-mail address, age, high school, body type, and dating status, not to mention her intimate hopes and dreams. Going beyond the safety issue, this situation makes for a strange new social reality. No one likes to be watched, and it's even worse when you have no idea if you are or are not being watched. And this *is* the social landscape for teenagers today; they live in a world of perpetual surveillance, and I believe it is taking a toll on their concept of self, privacy, and community. Most of which is a strange comfort with being public, digitally or otherwise, a concept I address more thoroughly in chapter 6.

There's Friending Bands . . .

MySpace began as a site devoted to networking independent musicians. In many ways, the site has retained its music-centered appeal; most teenagers consider the exposure to new music as one of the reasons to be present on MySpace. And most up-and-coming bands realize that a presence on MySpace is integral to achieving a fan base and any modicum of success in today's youth culture. Perhaps the ultimate MySpace band success story, the British band Arctic Monkeys sent their debut single to No. 1 in the United Kingdom without so much as an album release. How? They marketed their music via MySpace.com. Other independent bands that have reached meteoric success through online social networking are the Hoodoo Gurus (popular in the '80s and making a roaring comeback with the help of MySpace), In Flames, and The Academy Is . . . . This is how it works. Musicians create a profile page for their band (taking the same care of their image as they would in choosing an album design or music video), they send out mass friend requests with links to sample their music, and they interact with their fan base through bulletins and blogs. MySpace has quickly become one of the most effective ways to market a product.

Which makes your child a potential consumer. While she is frequenting a site in search of social connections, she is also being bombarded by mock friend requests generated by fan-hungry musicians. My mock MySpace page received hundreds of requests per week, but at the time I had little to no identifying information on my page for a band to locate as a potential fan. Several teens shared with me that they've lost count of how many solicitations they receive, and many revealed that they don't even pay attention

Sample Message Sent from a Band "Friend"

"Hey Mama! Thanks for the 'add!' (smiles) Just stopping by to say hi and to show your page some 'comment' love. Now it's your turn! Get at me with a mailing address. I have a CD for you. Check your inbox for details. Speaking of music . . . If you haven't done it already, please visit our page and take a listen to our NEW SONG 'Let Me Go.' We think you'll LOVE it! Stay beautiful baby! —DJ Freddy 'Ya'll Ready Now' The New Album from DJ Freddy is COMING SOON!!!"

anymore. Savvy older teens and adults are cynical and jaded enough to write off these requests, but this blurring of the line between "a place for friends" and "a place for fans" can be quite harmful to the preteen and young teen MySpacer. Gone is the healthy real-time exposure to various musical genres; what has replaced it is an onslaught of rapid-fire musical samplings by bands aggressively vying for your child's loyalty to develop some semblance of a fan base.

While I would never argue that exposure to music is bad, I do believe that too much, too fast, and too insincerely is not in the best interests of our children. As they explore these "friend" requests and find new bands they like, many truly believe that they are friends with these musicians. The careful selection of musical groups in one's Friends List is a sure indicator of one's coolness factor; remember, whom your child selects to present as a friend on his page communicates volumes about his worth in the friendship stock market. In short, such encounters continue to water down the consistency of true friendship. If a young teenager is repeatedly forced to equate interpersonal relating with shameless marketing, the potential result is a generation of kids with low regard for the sanctity of an agenda-free, unconditional relationship.

...And There's Friending Brands

This leads me to the next type of friend request your child is certain to receive on MySpace—inanimate objects surfing for brand loyalty. In a *New York Times* article, Fox Interactive's president Ross Levinsohn said it best when he explained his plan to monetize MySpace by turning "advertisers into members of the MySpace community, with their own profiles, like the teenagers . . . so that the young people . . . can become 'friends' with movies, cell phones, and even deodorants." In the words of the witty columnist Simon Dumenco, "Yeah, great idea! My name is Bobby Thompson, and my best friend is deodorant!" Again, as adults we are able to process the absurdity of the friend request, but our social structures are in place. Not so for a fourteen-year-old.

Witness the recent promotion deal between *Seventeen* magazine and MySpace, a revolutionary breakthrough in print publication marketing. According to an article published in *Advertising Age*, "*Seventeen*'s MySpace page comes complete with quizzes and contests, a Friends List with comments, and plenty of links directly to the magazine's website." Under the promptings of former editor in chief Atoosa Rubenstein, the entire editorial staff was asked to create their own personal MySpace pages with the intent of reaching as many girls as possible. Levinsohn's plan is under way.

Again, MySpace is an attractive platform for marketers coveting a relationship with young consumers, but at what cost to our kids' value system? *Advertising Age* predicts that other major corporations, "including several Pepsi-Cola beverage brands," are forging relationships with MySpace. In fact, a summer 2006 deal with Walt Disney Pictures to build hype for *Pirates of the Caribbean: Dead*

Man's Chest, starring teen-girl favorites Johnny Depp and Orlando Bloom, proved quite lucrative. Again, advertising is not morally neutral—as sociologist Melanie C. Klein remarks, "It is not benign; it shapes our values and our selves." Unfortunately for parents, the cash cow for MySpace is marketers, and they are actively sculpting our kids into the materialistic consumers they so desire. And the insidious way they are doing it is by sneaking in under the radar as a "friend." The reality is that MySpace has morphed itself into "BuySpace."

Sample MySpace Messages from Nonhuman Friends

- Thanks for the add! I wanted to show you this awesome website that I came across. You can add funny pictures, everything that you've ever imagined: Profile-Tweak.com.
- Hey Sexy! I just wanted to tell you that I think your page is awesome! HOWEVER, it could be sooooo much better by adding a cool . . . Quiz or Poll or Survey! Talk to you later!
- Thank you for adding me to your circle of friends. Please get some coupons for your next purchase of your favorite flavor of me. Love, So Delicious (non-dairy ice cream brand)

These are only a few of the thousands of examples of products requesting to be your child's friend on MySpace. In addition to these inanimate objects, be aware that your child may be convinced he has friended Paris Hilton. Many a celeb has a PR manager who constructs a working MySpace profile and actively fishes for friends in an effort to gain publicity.

Our children are learning that if they add (or friend) the right band, product, or celebrity, they will gain popularity points—in a way, grooming them to use friendship as their own marketing plan.

Social Reality Redefined

As you can see, your child's social reality is quite different from what you knew as a teenager, and not merely because technological devices speed up the process and allow for multitasking. One parent I interviewed who recently got savvy to MySpace marveled at its all-encompassing appeal. "It offers something for everyone—the voyeur, the music guru, the serial monogamist, the intellectual, the techie. What it rarely offers is real friendship. Real friendship is not brokered through anonymity; it happens in the real world, person to person, *not* screen to screen."

Kids have always struggled with understanding and finding "real" friendships, but today that problem is compounded. The difference today is in *what* these social-interaction devices communicate to our impressionable and socially insecure adolescents. As culture and technology expert Sherry Turkle, PhD, author of *Life on the Screen*, explains, "For every step forward in the instrumental use of a technology (what the technology can do for us), there are subjective effects. The technology changes us as people, changes our relationships and sense of ourselves." This e-generation of kids is operating under the assumption that intimacy does not require a physical presence, privacy is not important, sound bites are better than meaningful conversation, relationships are disposable, friendships are conditional, and trust is an illusion.

Most teens I interviewed said that joining MySpace, Facebook, YouTube, and other networking sites helped them feel like they belong—a vitally important achievement during adolescence. But is it authentic? Experts disagree on the answer to this vital question. Essentially, authenticity is in the eye of the beholder. In other words, if a teenager has never known the form of social interaction that his parent experienced as a kid, how is he able to discern whether or not his relationships are on par or subpar? And, honestly, why should he care? As adults, however, we are programmed to care. And we want our children to be growing socially in healthy ways, so when we see what appears to be an insincere social construct taking on more weight than it should, we become concerned. One wise analysis I received from a child behavioralist explained that adolescence is the practice field, essentially, for all meaningful human relationships to come. However, the Internet seems to exacerbate the issues of normal social posturing for teens. The belonging that many teens experience online often comes from nothing more than "bridging"—a construct that connects Person A to Person B *without* any intimacy. A bridge does not bring two closer points together; it merely provides a means to get from one point to another. Real bonding, on the other hand, means coming together in a close emotional way.

Another type of relationship that is fostered via online social networks is that of, well, networking. For mature college students and young professionals, this type of relationship can be important for garnering valuable recommendation letters for graduate school applications or for getting one's résumé passed on to an important associate in a major law firm. But for the average preteen or teen who has become dependent on MySpace for a good chunk of her social interaction, networking can be an exciting venture at first, but ultimately one that results in loneliness. So Harry has met thirty-five other boys who really dig Shakira—a network of shared interest—and they send each other video clips, pictures, and bulletins about her recent escapades. Perhaps there's the occasional message about "how hot" she is. But the reality is that these boys are not bonding, but bridging, and there is no real networking occurring since the only result could be a shared desire to meet Shakira. Maybe if they were older and pursuing a career as a roadie, it could be considered networking. Maybe.

The most productive aspect of online social networks that I have witnessed from my students is that it can be a good conduit for teens to, again, "keep in touch" with other teens who do not go to the same school or who do not live in the same state. One of my students, Chanel, explained her frustration in not having a MySpace anymore; she said, "I just returned from camp, and now I really miss my MySpace profile. All of the friends I met live all over the country, so it's not like I can call them that often. And not all of them have AIM anymore [it's become a thing of the past since MySpace]. I could communicate a lot better with my new friends if I could leave comments on their pages every once in a while!" Clearly, this feature is a plus, and one sorely missed by Chanel. She has a sincere desire to stay connected to her new camp friends.

So why hasn't Chanel exchanged mailing addresses and ensued in letter writing with each of these girls? Too outdated? Not rapid-fire enough to be cool? No, I believe Chanel, and other teenagers who feel so dependent on MySpace to keep in touch with long-distance friends, are not interested in the *cultivating* of a friendship. Writing a letter and sending it in the mail via the post office is simply too intimate. It's not too slow or too uncool, nor is it multimedia-challenged; after all, it only takes a few days to deliver, it's exciting to receive a little surprise in the mailbox, and it's simple to include pictures, CDs, and DVDs. And there's no chance of jamming your computer because of too many graphics. My answer to Chanel would be to rediscover the lost art of the thirty-nine-cent stamp. But that would mean leaving the comfortable world of familiar strangers and experiencing an unheard-of level of intimacy for her generation.

Odd Man Out

The few teenagers I interviewed who did not have an online profile acknowledged that they felt like the odd man out. Fourteen-year-old Alex told me, "Yeah, everyone else has one, and people always treat me like I'm weird because I choose not to. It's kind of like an Xbox 360: if you don't have one, you constantly feel left out. I guess I feel embarrassed sometimes for not having a MySpace." And the result is an evolving meaning of the word *friend*. Youth commentator for *YO!* magazine Amanda Peters, explains, "The meaning of the word 'friend' has become warped in this new MySpace generation. A friend could be somebody who you can't be sure really exists. For all you know, a MySpace friend could be someone who is just trying to build up his friend count. On the other hand, a MySpace friend could be someone who has the same interests as you, even if you don't know them." She continues to explain the appeal of a MySpace friend as requiring "virtually no responsibility and very easy upkeep."

Our kids are not familiar with this from computers alone. Most of their lives have been spent in a pretty isolated culture. Just look at our nation's car culture—a car is a type of personal space in and of itself, isolating individuals within the shared environment of the road. What you drive provides a great deal of personal information or "About Me" snippets; the driver's side window allows just about as much of a peek as a MySpace profile picture; and just read those vanity plates! As a culture we have ensured that personal space is of utmost importance and that community is a distant second or third. I know I couldn't count on my neighbors, next to whom I've lived for six years, to watch my daughter for twenty minutes while I ran to the store for some soy milk. I don't even think they know her name. And that communicates a great deal to her as she grows into the social being she is meant to be.

Recent research finds that Americans are living lives of increasing isolation; a quarter of us claim to have only two close friends on whom to depend, but hundreds of acquaintances with whom to make small talk. How many times have we as adults been relieved that we reached a friend's voice mail rather than the live person when we didn't particularly feel like having a conversation? If you're like me, more times than not. And why is that? Are we antisocial at heart or do we all struggle with the occasional insecurities that can plague our social interactions? I believe it's the latter.

Your Assignment

Although you may not have much control over whom your child is friends with online, for safety, I urge you at the very least to encourage them to use the many "friends only" settings that the MySpace account allows. For instance, your child's account settings should allow only those members who have been added (approved) access to do the following:

- Post comments on your child's page
- Post comments about your child's pictures
- Read blog entries and/or post comments on blog entries
- Invite your child to join a group
- Instant message your child
- View your child's calendar

Urging your teenager to make these selections or changes on her profile is one thing, but actually getting her to do so is quite another. Remember that selecting "Friends Only" isn't a foolproof method of keeping undesirables off your daughter's page; your daughter may be the one letting them on simply by bestowing friend status on them. In a sense, once your child grants an add, they are unlocking the front door to that person. Don't be alarmed; the fact that your child is social and wants to branch out to meet new people and discover the next trendy band is a good thing. Pursuing MySpace friendships is completely normal for teens today, so do not begin treating your child like a social pariah if she seems to anchor all her socializing in MySpace. However, as her parent, you must be in ongoing discussion with her about whom she adds, how she meets new friends, and what methods of discernment she uses in screening unknown users.

I recommend walking your child through a twenty-minute tutorial of how easy it would be for a predator or a bully to find out personal information. Sit down at the computer with your child and surf his or his friends' pages, making a list on a notepad of all the identifiable information that appears. Then, explain to your child that if you were a stranger with bad intentions, you could piece each of these nuggets of information together and easily locate, contact, or approach him or his friends. Several parents I have interviewed have used this strategy, and all have felt that it was successful in communicating the dangers of indiscriminate friending or "adding" on MySpace.

I will go over these in more detail in chapters 9 and 10. Talk with your child about the damage that can be done by indiscriminately adding any random person as a friend. The fact is that MySpace, and most online social networks, are designed to encourage people to meet new friends, so it is common for your child to receive friend requests from strangers. The good news is that once your child decides he does not want a particular person on his Friends List, it is quite easy to remove that friend. But remember the wise words of Benjamin Franklin, who advised, "Be slow in choosing a friend, slower in changing."

Wired and Ruthless

The Rise of Cyber-Bullying

"I have never encountered this 'cyber-bullying.' It has never affected me in any way. Kids who get cyber-bullied usually deserve it. Nobody writes nasty things about another person for no reason at all. The 'victim' obviously did something to attract the insult."

—*Jamie, 16*

"You just have to watch your back. All the time. I mean, if someone's stupid enough to let their guard down for one minute, then they pretty much get what they deserve. Come on, everyone knows once you show a weakness, it's going to be all over MySpace!"

—*Kahlid, 17*

———

- In 2006, a brutal beating of a teenage girl by her Centennial High School peers in Bakersfield, California, was videotaped and circulated around MySpace.com.
- In December 2005, eighteen-year-old James Dungy, son of the Indianapolis Colts head coach, committed suicide; troubling clues were found on his MySpace page.

- In October 2003, thirteen-year-old Ryan Patrick Halligan took his life; he had been relentlessly taunted and humiliated by his peers via the Internet.
- During the 2005 school year, a fifteen-year-old girl was devastated to find her picture on a digital hate book. A self-proclaimed Christian, the tagline to her picture read, "Jessica, Satan's on the phone for you."

Many who are unfamiliar with the social landscape of e-teens have a hard time understanding the gravity of cyber-bullying and are unaware of the potential for abuse. One parent wondered why it was an issue: "In the real world it is difficult to avoid a bully. But in cyberspace you just stop reading." Many adults associate threats with a physical presence only: "I thought the whole idea of bullying is physical intimidation and fear. How can a bully make someone afraid if they can't physically reach them? I met lots of bullies as a child, but I would have laughed at one that e-mailed me," explained a friend of mine. What my friend fails to realize is that the e-mail bully is not some random faceless stranger, but many times a schoolmate who intensifies his taunts or carries out his threats during class and after school. Cyber-bullying is nothing short of social terror by technology . . . and it's not going away. When I emphasized that authorities now have a growing awareness of cyber-bullying and plan to prosecute severe cases, another parent exclaimed, "Oh wow, they're going to start prosecuting for cyber-bullying? Get over it. So someone's MySpace account was compromised. Big whoop!"

While most of the instances of cyber-bullying studied by researchers Justin Patchin and Sameer Hinduja in 2006 involved relatively minor offenses, over 12 percent of the adolescents were physically threatened and 5 percent were scared for their safety.

What Cyber-Bullying Looks Like

As adults, it can be hard to see how something that looks as frivolous as a MySpace page can be used to intimidate. Unfortunately, for children across the country, it's hardly that simple, benign, or easy to ignore. This chapter intends to illuminate the very real and growing impact of harassment and intimidation that has taken on a whole new depth via texting, instant messaging, and social-networking sites. According to iSafe.org, cyber-bullying is harassment that takes place during online interactions, including but not limited to:

- **Flaming**—Sending a threatening, angry, rude, or obscene message to an individual via e-mail or text message, or to an online group, such as a chat room
- **Harassment**—Repeatedly sending a person offensive messages, again via e-mail, text messages, or to an online group
- **Denigration**—Sending or posting harmful, untrue statements about a person to other people, including the creation of a website or page intended to mock a person
- **Impersonation**—Pretending to be someone else and sending or posting material that makes that person look bad or places that person in potential danger; this also includes using someone's screen name and pretending to be them
- **Outing and trickery**—Sending or posting material about a person that contains sensitive, private, or embarrassing information, including forwarding private messages or images; engaging in tricks to solicit embarrassing information that is made public
- **Exclusion**—Actions that specifically and intentionally exclude a person from an online group

Other terms for cyber-bullying are "electronic bullying," "sms bullying," "digital bullying," or "online bullying." Whatever you call it, there is no denying its growing presence in our children's lives.

A Problem on the Rise

A recent survey from the National Center for Missing and Exploited Children has revealed that the number of kids reporting cyber-bullying has risen from 6 percent five years ago to 9 percent today. Cyber-bullying involves technology-based taunting, and examples can range from the hurtful to the vicious—a girl sending nasty text messages to a boy after a bad breakup, several teens ganging up on a rival athletic team member via a deluge of ugly instant messages, or hacking a peer's MySpace page and placing pornographic pictures on it. According to L. Kris Gowen, PhD, MEd, Portland State University, and creator of the informative VirtualMysteryTour.com, "The downside to online communication is that conversations that are assumed to be private can be shared with others without all parties knowing about it." Almost on a weekly basis I hear about an argument or a breakup that originated from the unauthorized sharing of a text message or a comment on a MySpace page; secrets are hard enough for teens to keep, but these new technologies make it nearly impossible.

Another invasion of privacy that constitutes cyber-bullying is the use of digital photos, either by webcams or cell phones. According to a 2005 survey by the National Children's Home charity of 770 youth between the ages of eleven and nineteen, 10 percent indicated that another person had taken a picture of them via a cellular phone camera, consequently making them feel uncomfortable, embarrassed, or threatened. And once that photo is electronically transmitted, there's no telling where it will be posted, how it will be presented, and what will be said about it.

Kids have always picked on other kids, but throw technology into the mix, and you have a whole new animal to deal with. Essentially, kids can be ruthless toward their targets in person, and wired kids can take it to a new level—ruthless on a far-reaching scale. Sites like MySpace or Facebook can act as the epicenter for the misdirected impulses of angry teenagers. Typical teen vulnerabilities like impulsive behavior, extreme emotional reactions, underdeveloped sense of empathy, and ignorance of real consequences play into the appeal of bullying via the Internet. In short, it's easier to whip up a message that says "I hate you, bitch!" in the heat of anger and click "send" than it is to dial a phone number, ask the parent if your friend is home, and then engage in a discussion about why feelings of hatred exist. Also, having to hear your friend's voice crack or chest heaving in sobs might deter your further assaults. And the false sense of anonymity afforded via electronic communication doesn't help, either. "You can't see the reaction to it and you can't see [the other person's] facial expressions, or anything, and so, you're, like, basically talking to a computer screen," explains Lexxi, a teen participant in a recent ABC *Primetime* report on cyber-bullies. A school counselor I interviewed calls it "the coward's way of bullying because you don't have to have that one-on-one contact . . . you can do it without having that physical reaction." Technology has ushered in a new era of cruelty, and our teenagers are in the zeitgeist of it all.

Of course, teens don't call it "cyber" bullying; they don't really call it anything. It's just a part of daily life in today's youth culture. Remember, your teen has been raised in an Internet-centered environment. It's been a ubiquitous presence since they can remember, so, in your teen's mind, it's just another setting where harassment would logically transpire. "Kids are natives to the Internet, and adults are the immigrants," says Elizabeth Englander of Massachusetts Aggression Reduction Center. For our purposes, however, we will use the term *cyber-bullying* and define it as harassment or intimidation by way of hurtful images and/or messages spread or posted via e-mail, blogs, instant messaging, Internet chat rooms, online social-networking pages, digital cameras, and cell phones. Researcher Nathalie Noret says, "Teachers and parents need to realize that a child's mobile phone or computer isn't just a communication tool—it is also a way for a bully to reach children in their own home." The most disturbing aspect of cyber-bullying is the fact that no longer is the family abode a place of amnesty; attacks now extend into cars, bedrooms, and family rooms—wherever there's a computer or a cell phone. According to a study by iSafe.org:

- 58 percent of teens admit someone has said mean or hurtful things to them online.
- More than four out of ten of these teens say it has happened more than once.
- 53 percent of teens admit to having been mean or hurtful to another person online.
- More than one out of three of these teens have done it more than once.
- And, finally, according to the Department of Justice, only 18 percent of cyber-bullying is ever reported.

So, over half of our teenagers, in the throes of trying to make sense of adolescence, have fielded mean or hurtful comments via the Internet, and almost half of them have had it occur repeatedly. Our teens are facing a new phenomenon in social ugliness, one that we never encountered and certainly don't completely understand. What also strikes me in the above statistics is that a whopping one-third of those teens who do the harassing tend to do it repeatedly; they don't let up. It's hurtful enough to be mistreated once, but to suffer abuse on multiple occasions is really quite damaging, especially to a teenager whose social world is so important to his or her emotional growth. Finally, and most disturbing of all, is that so few of these instances are ever reported. Honestly, this fact feels like an indictment on adults: why have parents, politicians, civic leaders, school administrators, teachers, mentors, and coaches not taken a more active role in educating teens and encouraging them to come forward about cyber-bullying? Perhaps we simply don't understand what our kids are up against. Let's take a closer look.

Why Kids Bully

As a high school teacher, I've attended more than my share of seminars on bullying and learned from multiple experts. I've crystallized those hours of training into three main reasons why kids act out in a bullying manner. They are as follows:

1. *Bullies frequently target people who are different, weaker, marginalized in some way. Then, they seek to exploit those differences.*

   Fourteen-year-old Madeleine is different from her classmates. She's not the stereotypical nerd with her nose in a book, nor is she shy and socially awkward. An outgoing, average student who is always cheerful at school, Madeleine has a close group of friends who stick by her. However, the fact that her mother is not around and her father is a gay man who cohabitates with another man has caused Madeleine significant grief from some of her classmates. Because the issue of gay rights is at the forefront of our society politically, and because her school has a solid policy against harassment based on race, religion, gender, or sexual orientation, she has been relatively buffered from any outright hostilities while at school. After all, no one wants to be suspended for calling her dad a derogatory name. However, Madeleine is not safe when she gets home each night and logs on to her Facebook account. On several occasions she has been met with graphic gay male porn images with captions that read, "Your dad sucks dick!" and "Don't kiss Madi—she'll give you AIDS!" As if this trauma weren't bad enough, Madeleine then had to attend class each day not knowing who the bullies were and when they would ever stop.

2. *Bullies are usually victims of abuse themselves; abusing others is a coping tool for dealing with another difficult situation, whether at home, at school, or at work.*

Thirteen-year-old Joshua had difficulty making friends at school, and he was frequently excluded by his peers. During physical education class he would choose to sit out of the various games and activities in an effort to protect himself from any extra jibes. He kept to himself and rarely spoke to anyone, except a teacher on occasion. However, when he got home at night, he channeled most of his anger into composing invective after invective on his anonymous MySpace blog; he attacked each and every one of the kids at school who he felt were unkind to him. His tirades were ruthless and obscene.

3. *Bullies have low self-esteem; they seek approval, power, or a sense of control and attention by striking out at others.*

Many schools today have electronic grade-reporting systems that allow parents, and sometimes students, to log on and view the academic progress via the teacher's grade book. While this invention seems to be an answered prayer to some parents, to others it can be a nightmare. At a local high school in Los Angeles, one teacher became mired in the tangled mess of a student who had hacked into her electronic grade book and altered another student's grades from Bs to Ds and Fs. Fortunately, a good computer science instructor helped get to the truth. The student who hacked into the computer system was expelled, but not before admitting to having enjoyed the whole charade. This child clearly sought power and enjoyed wielding it, no matter whom he hurt or whose job he put in jeopardy.

Who Are the Bullies, and Who Are the Victims?

At the risk of alienating you from me, let me say that if your child has been actively socializing online (and chances are she has), it is probable that she has been involved in some phase of online bullying. Yes, your child has most likely participated in a cyber-bullying encounter in one of the following roles, as defined by the wonderful pro-kid group, Love Our Children (www.loveourchildrenusa.org). Take a look at the possible roles:

- **Entitlement Bullies**—the typical bully who feels superior and puts down those who may be different
- **Victims of Entitlement Bullies**—kids who get harassed because they are an easy target
- **Retaliators**—these are the "get-backers" who have been bullied or whose friends have been bullied and are using the Internet to retaliate
- **Victims of Retaliators**—most often, kids who have been bullying, but are now on the receiving end of the cruelty
- **Bystanders Who Are Part of the Problem**—those who encourage and support the bully or watch the bullying from the sidelines but do nothing to intervene or help the victim
- **Bystanders Who Are Part of the Solution**—those who seek to stop the bullying, protest it, provide support to the victim, or tell an adult

Chances are that the bully is actually a former victim; many bullies are really retaliators in action. If your child is acting out as a bully, it is worth your while to investigate whether he or she, too, has been a victim.

The fall of any school year is fertile for new high school relationships. And so it was for two of my students . . . until things turned sour, and technology provided some powerful weapons for the ensuing battle. He posted some nasty bulletins on his MySpace page detailing the sexual favors he had received; he even went so far as to claim that he couldn't "get that smell off my fingers." She was humiliated. To retaliate, she posted bulletins to all her "friends" warning everyone to "[b]eware of the pimple-faced freak lurking around our school!" She even attempted to tape up printouts of the signs in the school's locker area before she was caught. Why was MySpace the perfect venue for this retaliation? Well, each of these students knew what we're all just learning—almost every teen at your child's school is on MySpace on a daily basis. The most effective and concentrated way for the jilted lovers to seek revenge was to publicly humiliate each other, and nothing is more public for teens than MySpace. It reaches more peers than the bathroom wall or a hate book from years ago.

It Can Be Relentless

One of the most disturbing aspects of online bullying is how unrelenting it can be. Because communication is instant, a click away really, it is not so far-fetched to experience a barrage of insults. A rapid-fire succession of text messages could last for only two minutes but leave behind a multitude of attacks. The harassment is quick, faceless, and seemingly everlasting. Once someone posts a nasty comment or a vicious blog about your child, it's almost impossible to delete it. Such postings have legs, so to speak; once they take permanent residence on a site like MySpace, they get tossed around like the proverbial hot potato for all to see. And it doesn't stop online—it reaches into the classroom, the lunchroom, and sometimes even the faculty room. Because not everyone sees the comments immediately, the effects can last for weeks as each new person discovers the blog or the photo or the message. What once would have a short shelf life now seems to last indefinitely in the annals of online social networks and the like.

With so many electronic communication devices to choose from, there are any number of ways teens can reach another teen to torment them, even if one avenue becomes blocked. One of my former students, Carla, shared her story: "When I was in high school, there were two girls that didn't like me because of my boyfriend. They used to send me threatening e-mails, and when I blocked their names, they just made up new names and kept it coming. These girls and their friends then started making up chat rooms on AOL about me with titles like CARLA IS A FAT COW or CARLA IS AN UGLY BITCH, and even worse. They would even print out the whole chat room conversation and leave it on my desk at school the next day. One of the girls even made a fake MySpace profile for me saying things like "I like to have my fat ass f**ked" and "I like to eat my dad's d*ck!" It got so bad that I didn't go online anymore. Then they just started calling my cell phone, and eventually my little brother's phone—there was no escape." Carla began to feel helpless, depressed, scared, and angry. She contemplated retaliating and even devised an elaborate plan to seek revenge, but eventually she just got too tired of the negative feelings, so she began reading the Bible. Every night, she tells me, she would resist the temptation to go online or to turn on her cell phone, and she would just shut her bedroom door and read the Bible. Raised nominally Catholic, she was never one to just pick up some Scripture, but she felt this was her last recourse. And she tells me her decision, or God's prompting, as she says, saved her life.

She has learned to forgive her harrassers, and is actually thankful that they reduced her to such a desperate state that she ran "into the arms of the Lord," as she describes it.

It Can Be Controversial

Bullies are wordsmiths; they manipulate language in artful and sadistic ways with the intent to upset or inflame their victims. One afternoon, while I was grading in-class essays, two female students of color approached me quite upset. They were incensed to find several of their classmates' MySpace pages littered with the word *nigger*. Two or three boys, none of color, were throwing the controversial word around with excessive flippancy, and it really bothered these two young ladies. "Mrs. Kelsey, we don't feel comfortable sitting next to these guys in class when we know how they talk and joke online," they explained. They had already confronted the boys, who then called them hypocrites for using the same word among themselves merely because they are black.

The complaint proved difficult to handle. On the one hand, their very real anger warranted my attention, but on the other hand, these boys weren't using the word at school; it seemed to be moored to their respective MySpace docks. The only real action I felt I could take was providing an ear to these girls, reprimanding the boys, and, well, writing a book that might encourage parents and school administrators to take action. You see, because our school did not have a well-defined policy about cyber issues, no disciplinary action was taken, much to the dissatisfaction of these girls and their parents. Cyber-bullying is not always clearly defined or easily identified. Does the use of racist language on one's personal MySpace page constitute harassment? Did these girls have the right to expect disciplinary action for their classmates? The point here is that cyber-bullying and online social interaction for teens is an ever-changing venue, and we must be aware of the many facets that arise.

It Can Be Cruel

On another occasion, a ninth-grade girl came to me quite distraught over images sent to her MySpace page the night before. Known as "emo" and a "cutter," this student, who in fact did suffer from the increasingly common disorder among teenage girls known as self-mutilation, received an onslaught of disturbing images of razor blades from another classmate. This behavior, popular among distressed or depressed teenage girls, involves using razor blades or other sharp objects to cause pain or draw blood, usually on one's arms; psychologists liken the disorder to bulimia or anorexia in that the patient feels inadequate and even angry enough to inflict the pain they feel they deserve on themselves. This student was receiving psychological counseling but still struggled with her problem and shared her failures and successes with me openly.

Unfortunately, she also shared with some insensitive classmates. While she was in the school computer lab, she logged on with her secure password only to find her personalized screen saver had been altered to be a picture of a pile of bloody razors. Sitting at my desk in my office, she told me her story in tears. After listening, I inquired, "Why are you being attacked in such a cruel manner? Do you have any idea why they would do something like this?" Apparently, I learned, she had angered the wrong people. She described the details of the previous few days' events: she supposedly text messaged a boy under the guise of the girl he happened to like at the moment; she pretended to be interested in him and proceeded to ask personal questions. When this boy and the impersonated girl found out, their cyber-retaliation began. And they struck the jugular. MySpace was the ideal location, once again, to host their nasty attack because one's profile is so personal, and opening it up and finding it vandalized with psychologically abusive images is debilitating. Again, because of the anonymity of it all, there was little the school could do about it.

In some cases, severe acts of cyber-bullying have triggered depression, even suicide. On October 22, 2006, the *Columbia Tribune* reported a story about a high school teen who was so hurt and degraded by messages left on her MySpace page that she missed more than forty days of school the previous year. Called names like "whore" and "cunt," this seventeen-year-old girl would repeatedly receive messages that informed her she would "get what was coming" to her. But not only did she face the harassment on MySpace; she also suffered verbal insults at school, enough so that she began making excuses to stay home. Her grades plummeted from honor-roll level to failing. Only after involving the sheriff's department did this young lady and her mother curtail the harassment.

In June 2005, Debbie Johnston's fifteen-year-old son, Jeff, took his young life. After two years of cyber-bullying at the hands of a fellow Florida classmate, Jeff wrote that he would "never get over eighth grade" and hanged himself in his closet. Jeff's mom continues to lobby school administrators, parents, politicians, and other civic leaders urging them all to do something about kids using the Internet to push other kids around. She has created the Jeffrey Johnston Stand Up for All Students Act, which would make cyber-bullying a crime, but it has yet to pass. After feeling "so numb I couldn't do anything," Debbie and her husband are working tirelessly to protect other kids. She says, "I'm not the first parent to experience this, but my son had a purpose to his life. And I would like everyone to know that."

Ryan Halligan's Story

John Halligan, father of cyber-bullying victim Ryan Halligan, who committed suicide at age thirteen, shares how he learned of his son's harassment.

"At the start of eighth grade, Ryan seemed to be doing fine, but we came to find out after his death that we really only knew what he was willing to share with us. A few days after Ryan's funeral, one of his classmates approached me online and told me that a bully at school had spread a rumor through school on the Internet that Ryan was gay. Other classmates who corroborated this story described the teasing as a feeding frenzy. I also came to find out that one of the popular girls pretended to like Ryan and engaged him in instant message conversations, and then embarrassed and humiliated him by sharing their private correspondence with others. She later told him she would never want anything to do with such a loser. He told her it was girls like her that made him want to kill himself.

"Ryan's time on the computer had another dark side. I discovered after his death that Ryan was friends with a kid we never met in person, nor knew he was friends with, who seemed to be obsessed with death and even suicide. The two of them had a lot of anti-popular-kid conversations and questioned the worthiness of life. There was a short exchange between them just two weeks prior where Ryan said, 'Tonight's the night, and I think I'm going to do it. You'll read about it in the paper tomorrow.' And the other kid replied, 'It's about f**king time!'

"Nothing will ever bring back our Ryan. Nothing will ever heal our broken hearts. But we hope by sharing the personal details of our tremendous loss, another family will have been spared a lifelong sentence to this kind of pain. Please never forget Ryan's story and the fragility of adolescence."

At a Loss for What to Do

Many of the parents I've interviewed have seen the problems caused by cyber-bullying in their child's life, but feel at a loss as to what to do about it. I understand their frustration. Oftentimes parents will hear the verbiage that it's up to each parent to bring his child up right, with courage, integrity, and compassion. However, as Tonya, mother of two teens, laments, "What do you do to parents who don't raise their children properly? I agree that parents need to be parents and teach their kids not to bully, but when there are so many that aren't doing the job, the schools get left with it. This is wrong, but it's a reality. You can't force people to become responsible parents if they don't want to be." And she's right. Nevertheless, parents of the victims of bullies still feel frustrated. One parent, Harriet, relayed her young son's experience with Internet bullies. "My son is eleven years old. I monitor what he does while on the Internet. His innocent child's fantasy game was hacked into yesterday, and all his awards that he had earned by playing had been stolen, and his Friends List had been changed. The new user name that was put on his account was not one a child would use. Now that is true cyber-bullying!" A different, but nonetheless traumatic, experience, and one that again leaves a parent feeling at a loss.

Some Electronic Help for Victims of Text Bullying

- **www.Hotxt.co.uk**—British-based service that enables users to hide their real identity and also block people from sending texts; it can be downloaded to the mobile phone, and part of their profits will go to a center that helps bullied kids.

- **www.vodafone.com/au**—New Zealand-based company that has partnered with www.NetSafe.org to offer a safe place for those being bullied to call and talk. In addition, Vodafone is committed to canceling the accounts of those users caught inappropriately text messaging.
- **www.kidsok.net/company.php**—A company called Mtrack has developed a device called "PingAlert," which will send an immediate message to parents from the mobile phone of their child if he or she is being physically threatened or bullied. It also locates the sender's phone to within roughly a quarter mile.

The fact is that we cannot protect our kids from everything, but we can try. One of the most frustrating hurdles as a parent is dealing with our child's irrational fears and self-perceptions. What children perceive to be true might as well be true. And that is why the advice to just stop reading a bullying e-mail is unrealistic. It may work for an adult, but even if a kid does stop reading it, he or she is well aware that there is an existing attack and another one waiting.

As one mother of a bullied child told me, "I don't think many adults understand the extent of harm that can be done. We're not talking about some simple e-mails being sent. There's more to this than just a few lines of type and nasty gossip." A fake MySpace account can be set up with fake images doctored by Photoshop to look convincingly real. Jokes and lies can be printed about someone. And however it's conveyed, the damage is the same—when read or seen by many students from the same school, these assaults can make that child's life miserable. One child psychologist who spoke with me advised, "Educating children is good, but will not be effective due to the nature of exploration/risk-taking of kids. Educating and motivating parents to take responsibility to monitor their children's online activity is best. And despite what people believe, children do not need video cameras, cell phones, and computers in their bedrooms." Essentially, kids are just as tempted to test the boundaries as adults, only kids are a little more daring and lack the maturity and life experience that helps to curb most adults from misusing electronic devices. The reality is that teenagers must be given consistent limits, especially in regard to access to such tools as video cameras, cell phones, iPods, and computers; otherwise, they are exploring and experimenting late at night in an unsupervised environment.

Signs Your Child May Be a Victim of Cyber-Bullying

1. Your child suddenly shows less interest in the computer, fails to check e-mails on a regular basis, and frequently "forgets" to bring his cell phone with him when he leaves the house.
2. Your child is not willing to talk about his or her online activities.
3. Your child often appears upset after Internet use.
4. Your child is often using the computer late at night and there is evidence that he or she is covering his or her online tracks.
5. Your child invents mysterious illnesses to avoid school.
6. Your child's grades are declining inexplicably.
7. Your child has trouble sleeping (including the onset of a bed-wetting problem).
8. Your child becomes depressed, withdrawn, angry, fearful, or irritable.
9. Bumps, scratches, or bruises are not telltale signs of this type of bullying, so don't confuse physical with psychological harassment;

however, these red flags could indicate an equally serious physical bullying problem!

How to Start a Conversation about Cyber-Bullying with Your Teen: Questions to Ask

- Do some kids you know get e-mails, instant messages, or text messages that are upsetting, threatening, or insulting?
- Have you ever sent an instant or text message to someone that you later regretted?
- When you feel angry at a friend or acquaintance at school, what do you fantasize about doing? What do you actually do about it, if anything?
- Are you ever tempted to play a joke on a friend at school by hacking his MySpace page or sending a fake text message?
- Who can be meaner at your school, the boys or the girls? How so?

Sample Bullying Messages Found on MySpace

In an effort to give you a firsthand experience with what can (and does) transpire on sites like MySpace, I've searched, found, and included two actual cyber-bullying messages that threaten physical violence. You may be shocked at the crass language and may even feel a bit uncomfortable reading them with your child, but rest assured that your child has seen his or her share of this language. The value of connecting with your child far outweighs a few moments of feeling uncomfortable. I guarantee your child will feel a sincere sense of relief to know that you are aware of the reality of his or her social scene.

I have included one message that deals with a friendship that has soured, perhaps from an angry teen who feels betrayed by a friend and uses violent and aggressive language, even threatening to know where her victim lives; the second is more inflammatory in nature as it accuses the victim of being a homosexual and ends with a threatening reminder about Matthew Shepard, the gay man who was brutally murdered by being dragged behind a pickup truck. Follow the steps I've given you below, and you will begin a fruitful discussion about real issues that affect your child:

1. I encourage you to sit down with your child and together read each of the following real-life samples of aggressive messages found on MySpace. Perhaps take turns with your child, or maybe read them silently together so as not to have to repeat the offensive language. Either way, you should approach them together.

2. Before discussing each one out loud, you and your child should both jot down some initial reactions, emotions, and even possible responses; be sure to have some pen and paper ready to do so. I also encourage speculating on the gender of the harasser, the situation at issue, and any other pertinent information that is apparent from the threats.

3. At this point, it is productive for you and your child to "share out" or read to each other what you have written down; use these notes as starting points for your discussion. Productive phrases or introductory words may include: "Why do you think this is a girl?" "What is the strongest emotion she is feeling?" "What could she be so upset about?" "What specific words does she use to intimidate or insult her victim, and are they well chosen?" "Is this message something that should be reported to MySpace, to a parent, or to a school official, why or why not?" And finally, "Have you ever received anything like this or have any of your friends, and if so, how did you handle it? Would you handle it differently the next time? Could I have been of any help?"

4. Finally, work together to devise a plan of action that each of the

respective victims should have taken to achieve the most productive results. Spend some time on this, think it over, sleep on it, even come back to it in the next day or two. This step is the most important, as it forces your teen to work with you on a common (and relevant to her) goal, and it models for her how to deal with hurtful and difficult situations in a healthy manner.

Sample One:

Hold the f**k up, u know what lil bitch, i dont even f**k with your dirty ass no more. your lil ugly ass wanna act funny toward me when i am supposed to be your friend, you start acting funny and acting like you dont know me. f**k you bitch. before i leave yo gay azz page lemme tell you dis...ima get you!!! I no where you skinny ass lives...

Sample Two:

Hey bitch y u such a homo? Huh? I know u want 2 kiss me u sick little f**ker. The bible sez homos will burn so cum near me, im a light u up good. Don't forget that shepard dude in tx!

Helping Your Child Deal with Cyber-Bullying

The worst thing your child can do in response to a cyber-attack is probably the most tempting and most appealing option to your child—to fight back. The national KidsHealth KidsPoll revealed that 46 percent of the children surveyed who admitted to being bullied respond by fighting back. In the prehistoric pre-cyber days, the victim of physical bullying was typically unable to retaliate because he or she was smaller physically. But now, in the age of MySpace and the like, retaliation doesn't require any muscles—or guts, for that matter. There's no built-in deterrent stopping a rapid-response touché.

Cyber-bullying escalates much quicker than the typical

school-yard incidents because both parties have endless technological gadgets at their furious fingertips, and no one hesitates to use them. Your archenemy posted a digital picture of you changing into your gym clothes on MySpace and it's being forwarded to everyone at school? Just set up a faux MySpace account under her name, post some incriminating information on it, and forward the URL to all the teachers and parents at your school. Then, sigh a vindicated, "Take that!"

It's our job as parents to put out these embers before they explode into full-fledged forest fires. The key to helping your teen refrain from retaliation, regain a sense of dignity, and recover damaged self-esteem is to counsel him or her to do the following:

1. *Express the anger in private* or at home; just don't let the bully or bullies know that they've hurt you or made you angry. The whole point of cyber-bullying is to have control over your emotions.

2. *Never retaliate* or give the bully a taste of his own medicine; returning the harassment guarantees only one result—that the harassment will continue, only meaner, uglier, and more aggressive.

3. *Ignore, ignore, ignore* the e-mails, text messages, or the like. Doing so will communicate to the bully that you just don't care. Sooner or later, the bully will get bored and move on.

4. *Walk tall and proud at school* and participate in class more than ever; by refusing to sit low in your chair, act depressed, and skulk around the hallways in fear you will demonstrate to your bully that you are unfazed by her attacks.

5. *Feel sympathy* for your bully—yes, sympathy; someone who feels comfortable enough to mobilize an all-out cyber-assault on you is probably a pretty jealous or unhappy person.

6. *Talk about it.* Encourage your child to tell you, teachers, school counselors, and administrators. Don't think of it as ratting anyone out, since cyber-bullying is really quite public. And,

keeping it secret is exactly what your bully wants you to do. Take notice of what one parent, Sherry, did to help her cyber-bullied niece. "The bully would send all sorts of nasty messages and e-mail her nasty threats. Fortunately, he was not the brightest and left his IP [Internet protocol address—an identifying router number that can be traced] on all of them, so I was able to track him down and find him. We presented his parents with all the evidence and said if we heard one more peep from him, in real or cyber-life, we would go to the cops and get him on everything we could. He stopped." While it may not always be that easy, the point is to create a safe enough environment for your child to come forward about what he is facing.

What If My Child Is the Bully?

So you received that dreaded phone call from the school principal: your child has been caught creating a hate group on MySpace in order to lead the cyber-charge to harass a classmate. *Is my child capable of being that mean?* The answer is yes. Most teens are capable of being mean (and aren't most adults?). Remember, cyber-jockeying for a spot in the social hierarchy is all but a rite of passage for most teens today, and it's likely your child was engaging in a power play.

However, don't ignore the fact that your child *is* engaging in an antisocial, harmful, and cruel behavior that needs to be stopped immediately. If your child has been caught, you now have the evidence needed to engage in an important character-building conversation. Keep in mind that excessive bullying is usually a symptom of unhappiness, insecurity, or some unresolved anger. (Perhaps your child has also been a victim of bullying, cyber- or otherwise, and is retaliating or acting out unresolved angst.) It would be wise to look into your child's emotional well-being, and I recommend arranging an appointment with a psychologist or a counselor. Even if your child doesn't have a history of bullying, the fact that you take the incident seriously enough to enlist professional help will make a huge impact on your child. And isn't that what it's all about—impacting your teen to make better decisions?

If you find out your child has been involved in harassing another student through technology, aside from officially apologizing either in person or in writing or both, is to apply very real consequences that restrict technological privileges. Take away the cell phone if it was used to text mean messages, take away the keyboard if it was used to type vicious instant messages, and by all means, have your child post an official apology on his or her MySpace page and forward it to everyone in his or her network of "friends."

What MySpace Has to Say about Cyber-Bullying

MySpace has recently updated their "FAQ" (Frequently Asked Questions) tab at the bottom of their home page. Please take the time to browse through this helpful section as it does a good job of addressing many relevant parental concerns. In the "Reporting Abuse" section, the following questions are asked:

- Someone on MySpace is bugging/harassing/threatening me—what can I do about it?
- Someone is pretending to be me—what do I do?
- How do we remove a teacher/faculty member's false profile?
- I think someone compromised my account, I can't log in, and things look different!

For example, the answer MySpace provides for question No. 1 is to "simply ignore" the harasser, "remove the person from your Friends List," "delete any Comments they leave on your Profile page," and go to their profile and click "Block User" to prevent them from contacting you. MySpace continues by encouraging you to "contact law enforcement immediately" if you are threatened. Finally, if someone has created a nasty profile about you, you can "contact customer service" and send the link to the profile.

What Can Schools Do to Help?

"Cyber-bullying is a problem that did not creep up on us, but rather swept us away. As technology will not disappear, neither will cyber-bullying," explains journalist Chris Nickson. More and more schools across the world are addressing these issues, but unfortunately not all schools see it as a valid issue. With a step in the right direction, in 2006, a school district north of Chicago made national news when they declared that students will be held accountable for what they post on blogs and on social-networking websites like MySpace. The school board voted unanimously to require that all students participating in extracurricular activities sign an oath agreeing that evidence of illegal, inappropriate, or harassing behavior posted on the Internet may be grounds for serious disciplinary action.

Many students are incensed about such an approach. Sixteen-year-old Paul reasons, "Although MySpace is a public site, when it comes to school administrators intervening with a student's private life *away from school*, it should be none of that administrator's business." He even goes so far as to explain that "once kids know that an administrator is monitoring their page, they are going to be more inclined to rebel and post more vulgar material." Nevertheless, many school districts are making it clear that while they will not monitor students' sites, they will take very seriously any tips or complaints.

Policies and Procedures from School Administrators

The following interview with an Ohio school principal not only details the limitations inherent in a school's jurisdiction, but more

131

importantly offers some real advice for how a principal can handle the situation.

From the Front Lines

An Interview with Brian M., a middle school principal, Ohio:

CK: What is the most important strategy for a school administrator to use regarding MySpace and its impact on campus?

BM: Parent education is extremely important. The PTO gave a presentation to our parent population in the spring; they used a projector to show the site and surf through it. Most parents were shocked. Because the online problems present such murky waters, we rely on effective parent education.

CK: What are some of the unique issues that MySpace places on your desk?

BM: The problem we see with MySpace and instant messaging is that the kids are more willing to say nasty things than if they were face-to-face. However, when an argument erupts in the cafeteria that originated on MySpace, it presents a very difficult, very sticky situation for a school administrator.

CK: What is the stickiest aspect of it?

BM: The question is what is in our jurisdiction to control. Ohio state law limits discipline measures to things that occur on campus; those are the only behaviors we are authorized to address.

CK: So what is your strategy if cyber-bullying occurs among your students?

BM: My strategy is to contact the parents of the aggressor first, to make sure they are aware of the MySpace account. I also want them to understand how the content on the page is spilling over into school. I want the parents to become partners with the school.

CK: What if said parent is uncooperative?

BM: If I have an oppositional parent, my next step is to explain to them that I am willing to turn the incident over to the local authorities to investigate the incident as a possible case of "telecommunications harassment." In fact, I recommend that each school administrator look into their state's policy on telecommunications harassment; it is a very useful tool with kids and parents. Once parents understand that their child will be subject to prosecution for his or her Internet activity, they usually will partner with the school to solve the problem.

CK: What do you do if a student reports being harassed by another student on MySpace, but the behavior has not spilled over into the school environment?

BM: In the event that I learn of cyber-bullying or the like, but my hands are tied because it does not reach the school environment, I am able to use the report as leverage. While I cannot implement any discipline action at school, I can inform the faculty to watch the respective students carefully, and 99 percent of the time, it eventually carries over into the classroom or the lunchroom.

The following sample letters and excerpts from codes of conduct illustrate a variety of ways that schools can hold their students accountable for their Internet behavior. I include these samples not to claim that they are the best or the only viable approaches, but to give some guidance to be looked at closely by both school administrators and involved parents.

A Sample Letter to Parents from a Private High School

May 6, 2005

Dear Parents,

The school year is winding down filled with many great activities, events, and ceremonies. However, there is one area of concern that I need to share with you. As I am sure you are aware, many of our students use technology for social purposes. The most popular site used by our students is MySpace.com. Students post profiles of themselves that include photographs and personal information for the World Wide Web.

This site and others have a large following that may include people with less than virtuous intentions. I encourage you to look into this site and sit down with your son or daughter to engage in open and honest communication regarding the acceptable use and associated potential dangers of such a site.

Sincerely,

Assistant Headmaster, Private High School, Los Angeles

A Message from a Public Middle School's Principal

Excerpted from the June 2006 Newsletter

When students engage in inappropriate behavior online, it inevitably creates conflict, drama, and hurt feelings here at school. At least 40 percent of the peer-conflict issues that our counselors handle originate on the Internet. We've even had a recent incident where students took inappropriate pictures at school and then posted the photos on one of these websites without the knowledge or permission of some of the students in the photos. Needless to say, we have strict rules against the inappropriate use of cameras on campus, but we have little control over where students post photos outside of school. I strongly encourage all parents to become knowledgeable about their child's Internet habits, to talk with their child about Internet safety and etiquette, and to closely monitor their child's Internet usage. If your child uses MySpace.com or other networking sites, I strongly encourage you to regularly go online and look at your child's web page along with those of their friends (links from your child's page).

Excerpt from Florida Public School's Code of Student Conduct
Harassment and Bullying

Sexual harassment or bullying of students or staff is an extremely serious violation of the Code of Student Conduct, as well as a violation of criminal law. It will not be tolerated in schools, school buses, or at school-sponsored activities. Any such offenses may result in severe disciplinary action when such behavior disrupts the learning process.

It is harassment when a student
- *Writes comments about a person, e.g., on a bathroom wall, on a website, via instant messaging, or through text messaging*

It is bullying when a student
- *Torments, threatens, taunts, ranks, degrades, targets, harasses, or humiliates a student or staff member using the Internet, interactive and digital technologies, or mobile phones, or inviting others to join in these acts.*

The School Board reserves the right to regulate, review, investigate, and discipline students for cyber-bullying, or for other disciplinary violations when such Internet statements, postings, or acts are made while on school campus, or while made off-campus and such statements, postings, or acts threaten violence against another student or otherwise disrupt the learning environment or orderly conduct of the school, school business, or school activities.

If Your Child's School Does Not Have a Policy

If you are concerned about your child's school not having a clear-cut or well-communicated policy addressing cyber-bullying, I encourage you to join with other proactive parents and get the ball rolling. Most schools will be happy to formulate a policy, but they're just too busy with the multitude of responsibilities involved in running a school, so don't label your administration as insensitive or unaware. The best approach is to partner with other committed parents, meet several times to brainstorm, determine your vision and define your mission, and create a calendar-based plan. Once you have formulated the above, it is time to meet one-on-one with the assistant principal or assistant headmaster. Remember, schools are like any business, there is a proper chain of command to follow, lest you step on some important (and powerful) toes. Present your vision, mission, and plan while emphasizing your love and concern for the school's young people. Chances are you will be heard, and the school will be excited to support your efforts. Remember to focus on the following points in your presentation:

- Even if cyber-bullying happens outside of school, the repercussions spill over into the classroom; bring newspaper and magazine articles about recent incidents of cyber-bullying that impacted campus life.
- Computer ethics must be part of the technology curriculum in this day and age, and that includes issues surrounding cyber-bullying. In addition, the school must update its computer laboratory's Acceptable Use Policy (AUP) to specifically prohibit using the Internet for bullying.
- Parents want to partner with educators to stop cyber-bullying; it's not all on the school's shoulders, but we must work together.

- Present sample cyber-bullying policies and codes of conduct from local schools; you may even photocopy the pages provided above—most school officials would be grateful to have a template from which to work. Most importantly, the school's existing bullying policy must be amended to include harassment via cellular and Internet technology, and there should be serious consequences for anyone who doesn't follow the guidelines.
- Ask the school to add such a policy into its handbooks and to address the issue of cyber-bullying at an assembly and at Parents' Night or Back to School Night; perhaps even arrange to host a Technology 101 night for parents who feel intimidated by all the new devices.

Once you have approached your school's leaders, be prepared to put your ideas into action. And remember, the ultimate goal is to create a united front against the unnecessary cyber-abuse our children often face.

Ideally your child will never be bullied and will never bully another child, but the reality is that your child's social world is now predominantly online, and cyber-relationships are highly susceptible to bullying. In the event he or she becomes ensconced in this aggressive behavior, either as a bully herself or as a victim, I urge you to use it as a teachable moment. That is, after comforting your child and dealing with the other party and his or her parents. As adults we know that we must deal with aggressive colleagues, drivers, sports fans, and Target shoppers; they, unfortunately, are a fact of life in today's high-stress culture. And, whether we will admit it or not, we sometimes are the perpetrators. So what saves our sanity? The fact that we've experienced it and *learned* how to deal with it.

From the Front Lines

As a high school guidance counselor, I have made it my business to become familiar with teenage issues. I am very lucky that I am computer literate, as it has become an important tool in dealing with adolescents and young adults. Much has changed in the past ten years concerning how teens communicate with each other.

Many of my students use MySpace.com as a way to keep in touch with friends, express themselves with a particular layout, and meet new people. Problems always arise among friends and enemies. Teenagers make friends and enemies so easily that the line often gets blurred between the two. Many times during the year, girls will enter my office carrying a paper copy of the comments exchanged on MySpace. It seems like these social-networking sites are just another way in which teens verbally abuse each other.

There are so many instances of harassment using the online site. It has been a useful tool for us in the guidance and dean's department since we have actual proof of teasing. I am always warning students to save any threatening conversations that they may have online. Parents are often clueless about their child's online activities until they see the actual proof on paper. Educating both parent and child on the dangers of these sites has become priority one. The difficult task remains ever changing, since teens always seem to be one step ahead of adults concerning the Internet.

—*Anonymous school counselor, Private High School in New York*

"Bullying has value. It is a quick path to learning the ropes of gossip mongering and backstabbing, and surviving; it equips one with necessary social skills in adulthood," says media expert danah boyd. Her advice to parents who face this trauma with their kids is to instruct them in "how to survive bullying" instead of focusing so much on the usually vain battle to stop it. While this approach seems a bit hard to swallow for many parents, myself included, there is a valuable nugget of truth to be savored. As parents we must stay involved in the emerging social stratosphere of our kids, we must be literate in the technological devices used by our teens, we must be organized and vocal in our local schools, but most importantly, we must educate our children in compassion and teach them how to deal with hurt. We may not be able to protect our kids from every instance of cyber-bullying, but we can focus our love and our wisdom on preparing our children to handle the hurts of our world in a healthy and productive manner.

You Show Me Yours

The Unique Sexual Pressures Girls Face Online

"A Texas teacher lost her job in 2006 when school officials found she had appeared topless in a photo posted on www.flickr.com, a popular online photo journal."

—Times Online, *July 23, 2006*

"Girls on MySpace are always trying to 'sexy it out.' My ex-girlfriend is wearing a bikini in her picture. It works. I mean, it makes you want to click on her page, ask her out, and, well, you get the point."

—*Jeremy, 13*

"As a parent of twelve- and fourteen-year-old girls who were representing themselves as older and using MySpace in a raunchy manner as expressions of their sexuality, my wife and I were shocked. We have terminated their total Internet access. Other parents on their Friends List have either closed the sites or insisted that they have access to their profiles. The worst part: letter to the site from us went unanswered!"

—*Dennis, parent*

"Redheads do it better."

—Teen profile headline with provocative picture on MySpace

———

Heard of Swiffergate? No, it's not another political scandal. Swiffergate is the name precocious teens gave the social scandal involving a middle school girl, a Swiffer mop, and popular online social network Friendster. In the winter of 2004, an eighth-grade female student at a well-regarded private school in New York digitally recorded herself performing fellatio on the handle of said Swiffer mop, culminating in her dramatically masturbating. Why? She had a crush on a boy and wanted to entice him with these images of her irresistible sexuality, or at least to prove to him that she could be as nasty as any other girl about whom he may fantasize. She e-mailed the amateur sex file to the boy, and before she knew it the clip was posted on Friendster.com, a site similar to MySpace.com, for all the world to view. And did it ever circulate.

If you're like me, your first response is horror, your second is poor girl! But don't be so quick to pity. While it's impossible to know whether this was a mortifying mistake or a deliberate attempt at fame, she apparently became increasingly popular and achieved something of celebrity status at her school as a result. According to related news stories, this young lady was barraged with invitations to parties, dances, and other social gatherings. Whether her newfound popularity was worth the price of her dignity is another issue, but clearly the days of ostracizing the school "skank" are long gone. This young girl simply joined the likes of Pamela Anderson, Janet Jackson, and Paris Hilton, all of whom gained more notoriety when videos of their own sexual misadventures were distributed on the Internet. According to Pamela Paul, author of Pornified, "Pornography has not only gone mainstream— it's barely edgy." Today women who bare all are lifted up as brave, free-spirited, and daring-minded—and this public approval has not been lost on our tween and teenage wired daughters.

Wait a minute, you say. Eighth grader? Blow job? Amateur video? *That she had the nerve to send to a guy she might sit next to in class?* Although the above may not be a common scenario, as a teacher, I can tell you that middle school ain't what it used to be. While most studies about preteen and teen sexual activity indicate a decrease, they tend to focus on sexual intercourse only; the reason there is a decrease in sexual intercourse is because this generation of kids has been well educated about the risks of AIDS and pregnancy. Frankly put, kids today, especially middle schoolers, have personalized the message, and they steer relatively clear of it with an "anything but intercourse" approach. But they're not abstaining from sexual activity. A recent UCLA study on teen sexuality reveals that while 47 percent of teens are virgins, 35 percent of these virgins are actively engaged in oral sexual relations. What most sex surveys fail to report on is the rising trend of oral sex among preteens and teens. Patricia Hersch, author of *A Tribe Apart: A Journey into the Heart of American Adolescence*, ruminates, "To me oral sex was more intimate . . . kids today absolutely don't see it that way. It's done commonly, with a shrug." Even middle school girls who have been well counseled in the values of abstinence and purity are engaging in oral sex as an alternative to losing their virginity. "It's now the expected minimum behavior," says Michael Schaffer, supervisor for health education in Prince George's County, Maryland.

In fact, the phrase "friends with benefits" is the latest category of middle and high school relationships; it means that two people are friends, are not dating, and are sexually involved. Essentially, it's casual sex on a whole other level. Whether it's at a party, in the school bathroom, or behind the local 7-Eleven, boys are requesting a casual blow job, and girls are complying. Evidence of this rise in the oral sex craze among preteens and teens is the incredible increase in the amount of STDs found in adolescent girls' throats. When a child comes in with a sore throat, Dr. Meg Meeker, a Michigan pediatrician, reports that "you can't just think mono and strep; with dramatic increases in oral sex [among young people] you have to think herpes and gonorrhea." The activist group Concerned Women for America reports that 12 percent of teens are involved in oral sex while only 15 percent of parents claim that their child is involved in a physical relationship beyond kissing. That's quite a disconnect on the parents' part. In addition, while 85 percent of parents surveyed claim to talk to their teens about sex, only 41 percent of kids corroborate. Parents seem to be out of touch on this issue. It seems apparent to me that a very real discussion about sexual behavior, including oral sex, must occur between parents and their children, maybe even prior to middle school. The reality is that our kids know about it, are talking about it, are seeing it, and may be doing it. We don't want our kids simply Googling or blogging on this topic, right?

The role MySpace plays in this emerging sexual landscape is prodigious. The site can be an extremely toxic environment for young girls, especially preteens who are searching for self-worth, as it shines a premature spotlight on the sexual stumblings and fumblings of our daughters. To have one's various sexual curiosities recorded on YouTube and circulated around MySpace certainly alters the outcome of that girl's experience. Perhaps she didn't like flashing a few boys at that party, but now that the whole MySpace school community has seen footage of it, she almost has to become that girl, become comfortable with it, and begin to allow the technology to define how she is received. As mentioned above, girls are ferociously searching for boys' attention, and MySpace is the ideal platform for achieving this goal. The sexier the photos, the taglines, and the screen names are, the more male MySpace friends a girl will earn. In this chapter, I will chip away at the marble exterior of

MySpace as merely "a place for friends" and reveal to you how the site exacerbates the above female adolescent issues. I will also provide you with practical advice for how to approach these issues with your daughter.

May I Have Your Attention . . . Please?

Adolescent girls have always craved attention from boys. It's a normal, healthy, age-appropriate desire to seek the approval of the opposite sex. Teen girls are in the aftershocks of puberty, sexually aware of their own bodies, and eager to carve out their individual value by way of trying on various identities. Essentially, ages twelve to seventeen are in what I call the "flesh age." These six years mark a Sisyphean attempt for most girls to define themselves—and find self-worth—either by way of their physical attributes or by how sexual they can appear to be.

A recurring battle I faced when teaching sixth-grade girls was the proliferation of Playboy bunny necklaces and belt buckles. One student, eleven-year-old Jill, felt comfortable wearing these emblems in front of her teachers, her parents, and her peers. While Hefner's marketing team has done a bang-up job mainstreaming his emblem, I will never find its presence in my classroom to be even mildly acceptable, especially for a sixth grader. After meeting with Jill in my office in private and explaining the connotation of the bunny to her (because in my naïveté I actually thought she must not know what it really means), she refrained from wearing it for about four days, at which point my eye caught it sparkling, almost winking, at me from behind her hot pink Juicy sweatshirt. When I spoke with her again, she was more bold and informed me that she wants boys to know that she is "sexy" and "not uptight about sex." At that point I let her mother know about our conversations and pulled the dress code policy card—"no inappropriate symbols on clothing." Her mother didn't seem to understand the weight of the issue and asked me to stop singling her child out. Nevertheless, she did manage to get her daughter to respect my rules. I may have won the battle, but I certainly didn't win the war.

"Just a year ago I wasn't even wearing a bra and now I've got a push-up with extra padding and a drawer full of thong undies; I kind of don't know how to handle it all," says thirteen-year-old Zania. Unfortunately, for many of these young women, there comes a time when, highly aware of their newly blossoming bodies, they become confused and seem to lose the faith in their nonsexual abilities that once guided them. Recently, *Newsweek* reported that 39 percent of girls in fifth through eighth grade were on a diet, and that 13 percent of these girls admitted to having binged and purged as a method of weight control. Body-image issues begin to take over while the pressure to look increasingly sexual dominates the messages being received by these girls. Because most girls are struggling with these issues, the topics of conversations naturally revolve around makeup, hair, diet, clothing, and—at the risk of sounding like a fried chicken commercial— breasts, thighs, and skin.

It's no secret that during adolescence, girls' friendship often turns competitive. Girls share, they compare, they copy what's "in," they mock what's "out," they vie to be prettier and more popular than the others in their social circle. Remember that one of the seven teen vulnerabilities mentioned in chapter 1 is that of *peer influence*, and studies have shown that the most powerful peer influence on a teenage girl is other teenage girls. So what we end up having is a veritable petri dish of body-central thought and behavior. Girls tend to perpetually compare their bodies with other girls' bodies, sizing up breast shape, leg length, waist width, and hair volume. Watch virtually any young woman when a group of boys and girls enter the room, say at a crowded restaurant, and you'll notice that the girls check each other out first and foremost, before even noticing the guys. Why? Because we've been conditioned to consider how we stack up physically against other women. Boys, of course, play their own role. Just as it doesn't take long for teenage boys, in the maelstrom of puberty, to begin noticing the female chest, it doesn't take long for girls to become aware of the power of their bodies. Suddenly, now, it's earning them quite a bit of attention from the guys.

One of the most startling things I have noticed about boys and girls after working with teenagers for years is the discrepancy in how each gender perceives the other. We rightly teach our daughters that they have the same voice as men and encourage them to speak their minds. But in my observations, it simply doesn't play out that way in the adolescent years. At the ninth- and tenth-grade level, although girls are by and large more mature and aware of their feelings and their surroundings, and certainly have just as many viable things to say as the boys, they simply aren't taken as seriously by their male peers.

My husband, Kevin Kelsey, is also a teacher. During his four years of teaching a human development class that focuses heavily on gender relations, he often polled ninth graders about their perceptions of gender roles and sex. The one heartbreaking fact consistently confirmed is that fourteen-year-old boys admit they listen to what their female counterparts say *based on what the girls look like.* Girls who are more attractive are overwhelmingly considered more worthy of boys' attention. Now, why does this happen? Boys say they listen to "good-looking girls" because they would want to "get with them." The next question is, are they really listening to these attractive girls? That is, is he listening in the same way as he would listen to what another guy is saying? He usually responds, "No."

Our culture has been flooded with hypersexual images of women, in music videos, print ads, commercials, and the ubiquitous Internet content—and apparently the less clothing the better.

My husband has polled hundreds of teenage boys, and without fail they say that they can't just turn off or compartmentalize these suggestive images in their heads. For the time being, the girl in their algebra class is being measured just like the adults around them have taught them to—by her physical attributes. And this is where MySpace comes into the mix.

How Girls Are Learning to Market Themselves

"My daughter and her friends have MySpace," says Dasha, an Alabama parent. "When I saw their pages, it blew me away. They are posing in thong underwear and squeezing their breasts together to look sexual." Elisa, fifteen, poses with friends in bikinis. She's topless and her arms are draped over her breasts. Jennifer, sixteen, sits in skimpy undergarments with her knees bent and hugged tight to her chest. Darren, a Nevada parent of a fifteen-year-old son and fourteen-year-old daughter, is equally concerned: "I have reviewed both of their pages, and those of some of their friends. I don't like what I see, as MySpace is a way to provoke otherwise shy teens into expressing themselves sexually."

On networking sites like MySpace, which are built around the posting of images and personal desires and exploits, girls are encouraged to wield the perfect weapon to conquer the attentions of boys their age (and older, for that matter). Young girls are now able to market themselves like a super-glossy ad campaign to reach hundreds of potential "customers" interested in their "product." Tamyra Pierce, a mass communication and journalism professor at Fresno State, recently surveyed three hundred high school students and randomly searched seven hundred profiles; she found that 59 percent of the sites included photographs with sexual poses. Several female MySpacers I've interviewed are proud of receiving hundreds of add requests by guys, and even more alarming, are fully aware of *why* they are interested in having them as MySpace friends. Fifteen-year-old Nadine explains, "It only makes sense why so many guys would like to have my picture on their page; I look hot. I'm trying to look as hot as possible and get as many adds as possible." After all, once you've been added, your picture appears on that person's profile page, nothing short of a badge of masculinity for the teenage boy MySpacer who has a bevy of hotties on his page. As Taylor, age fifteen, told me, "Everyone loves my page! I have the hottest girls as friends, so everyone wants to add me, too. It's pretty easy to collect them—I just surf until I find one and then link to all her friends and request them to add me, too. Usually you just have to act sweet and compliment them or something and they'll accept the add." Most teenage MySpace girls I interviewed considered the appeal of her pictures very important to receiving add requests from boys.

As discussed in earlier chapters, the other way girls have learned to get attention on MySpace is with a provocative screen name or personal quotation/tagline (located to the right of their profile picture). The careful selection of a name or quotation communicates a precise message to all who see her page, and this is particularly important when requesting to be added to someone's Friends List. Remember that wherever your child travels on MySpace, her photo and chosen name follow. A search for display names that simply said "sexy" or "sexygirl" turned up over fifteen thousand MySpace users, and this does not include the tens of thousands of variations. I've compiled a sampling of particularly striking screen names and taglines from actual profiles, and to emphasize the impact of the antigirl MySpace culture on our young teens, I've included only those who claimed to be fourteen. They are as follows:

- I want HIM 2 N O T I C E ME♥
- I like 2 party and when I shake it da boys go ooo mammy!
- U got mi name N UR mouth lik a dick

- They say nothin' last forever—can I be UR nothin?
- Shake YO $-money$-maker!
- B!TCHZ A!NT SH!T
- Suck it slo, ho!
- My bf getz it n u don't
- Wut do u want 2 be dun 2 u?
- koteMYthrote
- s3xy aSS bitch, ya'll
- u PaY—ill SwaLLow

The Personality Test

The second element at work on MySpace is the emphasis on baring it all, not necessarily physically (although that applies as well), but emotionally and psychologically. Teenagers who are shy or reserved seem to transform once they cross the threshold of MySpace: blogs are intensely personal, messages reveal intimate information, pictures expose secret behaviors. But it is the personality surveys and quizzes that broadcast intensely private hopes, dreams, and desires . . . among other intimate details.

While girls have been participating in surveys and quizzes for decades via teen magazines, the nature of the MySpace quiz is quite different. Certainly there are harmless quizzes that inquire into what type of pet you are best suited to own, but the reality is that most teens are not posting these on their profiles. The purpose of the MySpace quiz is to engage a person, usually a teenage girl, in the process of revealing extremely intimate information, confessions she might hesitate to share face-to-face.

The end of each quiz asks which online social network site the results should be sent to (of which MySpace, Facebook, and the like are included). Once the quiz is "tallied" and the determination is made, it shows up in all its glittery glory on the girl's profile for all to see. This common practice among teen girls preys upon the adolescent desire to find one's identity while, once again, defining these girls in a limited way that they may not be comfortable with at all. And, of course, the pressure to represent oneself as sexually progressive and "cool" plays out on these quizzes, as they can become increasingly inappropriate. Let's look at three popular quizzes:

1. *Who is your celebrity boob twin?*

   A bit different from most quizzes, this one asks only one question: What is your bra size? It then matches you up with a celebrity who supposedly has the same-shaped cup. When it appears on your MySpace page, you get a nice image of said celebrity's breasts squeezed together in all their glory.

2. *What kind of panties are you?*

   The following quiz asks ten straightforward but highly personal questions, all in an attempt to determine what type of panties you are. Apparently, the information garnered from below can be useful in labeling you either "lacy," "crotchless," "spandex," "thong," or "granny."

   Do you think your butt is too big?
   Do you like to dance in your underwear?
   Do you like to wear miniskirts?
   Do you use tampons?
   Do you like to skinny-dip?
   Do you tend to flaunt your butt when wearing a skirt?
   Do you wear short shorts alot?
   Do you like your boyfriend to feel your butt?
   Do you like to wear really high heels?

3. *Who's your soul mate?*

   While the initial question posed seems harmless enough, further exploration into the types of questions used to determine this said soul mate reveal quite an unhealthy approach. Questions include: How often do you masturbate? What are your favorite sexual positions? What size are your breasts? What does it take to get you off? Do you prefer being fingered or toed? What is your least favorite anal sex position? Do you like the taste of semen? Remember, the purpose of this quiz is to determine the person's soul mate, formerly known as a romantic ideal. And many MySpace girls are posting the question-and-answer results on their profile pages.

As we've seen, one thing to pay attention to is how MySpace ensures that it receives personal information from its users. On MySpace, teenagers can augment the appeal of their personal page by identifying with certain celebrities and products; they do so by taking any number of corporate surveys offered, the results of which are then displayed on the individual's page. Teenage girls are most prone to taking these surveys in an effort to help create their MySpace image. Because these surveys are interactive, teens are attracted to the gamelike quality and suspense involved in finding out their results. The surveys don't just offer another distraction for the bored teenage girl; they also feed into four of the seven key vulnerabilities identified in chapter 1: *peer influence, role model influence, experimentation,* and *sex appeal.*

Most of the surveys are enticing because they offer whimsical queries such as "Who's your celebrity style twin?" and "What's your signature makeup look?" What most young people are unaware of is the subliminal message being sent in questions such as these. Identifying with a celebrity in terms of style begs the follow-up question, "Whom *should* I idolize?" Queries like, "What's your signature makeup look?" demand a young girl wear makeup; whether she wears lipstick now or not, according to this survey, she better start right away.

One of the most popular surveys is the one that inquires, "Which Victoria's Secret Angel are you?" Young girls are urged to identify with a lingerie model; again, whether they are sexually active or not, this survey all but mandates they better at least dress like they are. Below are the questions that follow the Victoria's Secret inquiry on MySpace:

Which Victoria's Secret Angel Are You?

1. Forgetting your real ethnic background, what do you think you look like?
   - A mix of ethnicity
   - Eastern European
   - Latin American
   - African/African American
   - Western European
   - Southern European

2. What best describes your gaze?
   - Mysterious
   - Seductive
   - Innocent
   - Sassy
   - Dreamy
   - Friendly

3. And what's your sexiest body part?
   - Your butt
   - Your boobs
   - Your legs
   - Your stomach
   - Your shoulders
   - Your curves (all of them)

4. What best describes your look?
   - Sexy and natural
   - Sex kitten
   - Sultry and exotic
   - High fashion
   - Girl-next-door pretty
   - Hot yet approachable

5. What type of lingerie would you most like to model?
   - Silky panties
   - Not lingerie, but a bikini
   - A skimpy G-string
   - Expensive bras
   - Stockings
   - A see-through chemise

If you read the questions posed above with a careful eye, you will notice that they grow increasingly more personal and more sexual from No. 1 to No. 5, with the ultimate question assuming that the girl would "like to model" lingerie. Young girls are coerced right out of any sense of modesty, slowly exposing more and more intimate information about themselves until all the world can view it and, of course, comment. This survey cleverly mainstreams and promotes the idea of teenage girls being sexual exhibitionists and enjoying every minute of it—or, at least, the idea that they *should*. And what else does this survey communicate? Not only that girls are expected to be sexy, but that to get that way, they must shop at Victoria's Secret.

Before your child can take any of these quizzes, he or she is bombarded with various related advertisements. On a "What style of jeans are you?" quiz, websites and ads for trendy designer jeans pop up; in fact, in order to even begin the actual quiz, teens must scroll down to wade through the swamp of denim marketing. On the "What kind of a girl are you?" survey, a prominent ad for *Teen Vogue* magazine pops up. And let's not forget that corporations like Victoria's Secret and Abercrombie & Fitch garner and utilize all the information offered during these surveys. Remember what Ross Levinsohn, president of Fox Interactive, was so excited about? I believe it had something to do with the free personal information teenagers so willingly offer in the name of creative expression.

Going Wild: Everybody's Doing It

"Pussy only—no f**king guys," screams the MySpace screen name of one girl whose tagline declares, "I'd f**k me," and displays a photo of two women embraced in a sexual manner. Reads sixteen-year-old Jenny's profile, "Sixth grade girls blow kisses at me," and her profile picture shows two blonde girls French-kissing. Another young girl's profile features a photo of her hand on her crotch, with the screen name "lick it good, girlfriend," and the tagline "I love girls." Fourteen-year-old Betty's tagline simply commands, "Finger me, Bitch!" next to a photo of her standing, arms crossed defiantly, above what appears to be four or five female concubines lying beneath her.

Unless you've been living on a secluded boat without any media intake, you're probably ultra aware of the proliferation of "lesbian" culture. I put lesbian in quotation marks because, of course, the word *lesbian* really only applies to two women who are sexually attracted to one another. However, the media's version of "lesbian" is not about female attraction at all, but girl-on-girl play with the sole intent of stimulating men. The porn-generated fantasy of two girls making out in wild abandon has gained mainstream popularity, and not a day goes by that I don't see a billboard, an advertisement, or some reminder that in order for a woman to be sexy she must perform sexual acts with another woman—in front of a man!

It has become a mass-market badge of femininity—both online and off-. One widely spread bulletin I received on MySpace.com reads, "We've just added a separate MySpace page for our Lesbian Clicks Online Store! We've added a ton of new designs and products to the store. :) Please add us as a friend and spread the word!!!" Why did this advertisement reach my page? It was randomly generated.

I am reminded of a time when this male fantasy was literally in the face of me and roughly eighteen twelve-year-olds. For about two months a huge billboard advertising a show on Comedy Central was perched on Sunset Boulevard just outside the windows of my sixth-grade English class—windows that had no blinds or curtains. The billboard showed two large-breasted cartoon women making out and groping each other in a pool. Now, I definitely have sympathy for teachers whose classrooms are short on desks and books, but try teaching in *that* environment!

Unfortunately, the result of this cultural onslaught is that teenage girls today are learning to equate feminism or female liberation with the power of their sexual organs to satisfy male fantasy and thus gain approval from boys. Just look at Joe Francis's multimillion-dollar video property called *Girls Gone Wild*, built on the topless backs of everyday girls who choose to flash their G-strings, make out with each other, and masturbate on camera—and all for a trucker hat and some applause. As journalist Adam Sauer defines the phenomenon, "It's a video. It's a state of mind. It's grammatically incorrect. It's a reason to hope for sons. But more than anything, *Girls Gone Wild* is a brand." And the brand is making millions. With over a hundred titles in circulation at last count and doing over $40 million in business last year, Francis is ready to branch out into the restaurant business, following the likes of Hooters. This soft-core empire has become a pop-culture icon; Snoop Dogg is actively involved in the advertising of its merchandise, and female role model Jennifer Aniston reportedly purchases *GGW* hats for her friends. The message our daughters are hearing is that this behavior is acceptable, and while the fourteen-year-old girl in my freshman English class hopefully never comes in contact with Francis's crew, she's able to act out the glorified exhibitionism on the annals of MySpace. Writes *L.A. Times* journalist Claire Hoffman, "Nursed on MySpace profiles and reality television, many young people today are comfortable with being perpetually photographed and having those images posted on the Internet for anyone to see."

In 2006, a school district in Florida had to amend their student code of conduct to include specific rules forbidding "the flashing of underwear or the willful flaring of skirts" on school campus and at school events. Recently, while chaperoning a school prom,

I witnessed a blatant display of *Girls Gone Wild*–style behavior: on several occasions I had to break up girls in the process of giving lap dances to their female friends, and all to the cheers of their seemingly content male dates. The party culture of exhibitionism is sweeping our girls' social reality faster than Joe Francis's private jet plane is sweeping the beaches of Miami.

"A baseline expectation that women will be constantly exploding in little blasts of exhibitionism runs throughout our culture. *Girls Gone Wild* is not extraordinary; it's *emblematic*," analyzes Ariel Levy, author of *Female Chauvinist Pigs: Women and the Rise of Raunch Culture*. Girls fear that if they do not push the envelope of sexual exhibitionism at every opportunity, they will be ignored. One way to push that envelope is to engage in faux lesbian acts, from kissing one's girlfriend to putting one's hands up her skirt. The images of teenage girls on MySpace engaged in faux lesbian acts are endless; in fact, out of forty-five random fourteen-year-old MySpace profiles I searched from one local high school, I found twenty-eight photographs with girl-on-girl poses.

I spoke to several teens about this sensitive subject, and most of them agreed that they just act this way to outdo one another and to get a boy to think they're cool. Sixteen-year-old Alannah explained, "I'm not a bisexual . . . I'd never do that to a girl *really*. My pics on MySpace are just a show. I know guys like it, and I want them to respond. I've added more guys 'cuz of those shots!" Fifteen-year-old Anne concurs. "[Some girls] hook up with other girls because they know the guys will like it. They think, *then the guys are going to want to hook up with me and give me a lot of attention . . .*" But one boy I interviewed about the same topic had an interesting response, one that Alannah and Anne might want to hear. David, a fifteen-year-old from San Antonio told me, "What girls don't understand is guys *always* want girls. If every girl dressed casually, you'd still like girls. It's like, you don't have to exhaust yourselves."

157

Yet the pressure on teen girls to exhaust themselves is pretty strong. According to most of the young ladies I have consulted, the expectation at many parties is for girls to show up ready to perform. It's no coincidence that the girls with provocative MySpace photos and taglines are the same girls who receive all the coveted party invitations. Nineteen-year-old Pedro explains that he and his friends spend hours poring over MySpace profiles within their zip code radius in an effort to find the wildest girls possible for their mega-parties. "We want people to start spreading the word that our parties are the hottest, and the more crazy we can get the girls, the faster that reputation will spread!" Teenage girls know these facts, and they've been effectively indoctrinated enough to exuberantly participate in the game. "People know to come to me to find out what's on for the weekend," boasts sixteen-year-old Layla, whose MySpace photo shows nothing but her ass cheeks poised high in the air with a flimsy G-string and the tagline, "Slap me for free . . . weeeee!"

The million-dollar question for some is whether or not teenage girls are acting out these representations in real life, whether they pursue the lifestyle of promiscuity that they seem to emulate with their MySpace identity. In the words of Dr. Roger MacDonald, child psychologist, "A child's job is to test her boundaries; a parent's is to see that she survives the test." It is normal for girls to experiment with both the technology of the day and the mainstream messages of society; however, we must be cognizant of both and willing to escort them through the fires. Teen expert and author of *Queen Bees and Wannabes* Rosalind Wiseman says that teenage girls "have come to the conclusion that they're on their own and can't depend on anyone but themselves. However, this doesn't mean they don't romanticize love and sex. They're still girls caught up with wishing someone will rescue them and see them for *who they really are.*" When I asked psychotherapist Jonathan Nadlman whether the "real" kid is the MySpace representation or the everyday representation, he clarified that neither is real—"they haven't found who they are yet, so everything you see is a trying-on of a possible identity."

We as parents must be more aware of the expectations, subtle and overt, we communicate to our preteen and teen girls. So how do we teach our daughters to crave respect, not attention?

The "MySpace Girl": Does MySpace Empower Young Girls or Manipulate Them?

An interview with Melanie C. Klein, professor of Sociology, California State, Northridge:

CK: When you first explored MySpace.com, what was your initial reaction?

MK: I was struck by the glaring gender issue present—and what these MySpace girls wanted their peers to know about them.

CK: In my experience as a high school teacher, I have noticed that many girls consider being sexually active, if not outright sexually loose, a sign of their gender equality. What do you make of this mind-set?

MK: Girls today are highly sexualized. Once, on a final exam, one of my female students declared that she is "a powerful woman because of my [vagina]." Girls on MySpace generate ostentatious displays of sexuality. Clearly they are not empowered, but they really think they are. I term this "falsely empowered." Essentially, these girls are giving the culture exactly what it wants. Unfortunately, the result is a generation of depressed, disconnected, self-mutilating, anorexic young women. It's not a healthy place for girls.

CK: Let's talk about the MySpace girl. What are your thoughts regarding the trend of exhibitionism and girl-on-girl poses being posted?

MK: This trend of young girls posting pictures of themselves kissing their girlfriends is not a new proliferation of lesbianism; it is merely an extension of heterosexuality. These girls are savvy enough to figure out that this is an important part of pleasing and entertaining men today. The girls are not engaged in a sincere exploration of their sexuality or another female's body; they are performing for the male gaze. This is the same generation of girls who are so programmed to please men that they engage in "chicken-head parties" and "rainbow parties" (as you can imagine, a chicken-head party gets its name from the repetitive motion a girl's head makes while performing oral sex on a boy; rainbow parties get their name from the multicolored lipstick marks left on the boy's penis after receiving multiple oral favors).

CK: But haven't these behaviors existed since the sexual revolution? Is it really so different today?

MK: Behavior that may have existed twenty years ago was never talked about or as flaunted as it is today; promiscuity in teenage girls is glorified by the media, and, therefore, girls are more and more flamboyant about their behaviors. Many teenage girls consider their sexual activity a manifestation of being empowered sexually, a type of feminist feather in their caps. Unfortunately, they are defining themselves in a highly mediated patriarchal culture.

CK: Can MySpace be beneficial as a place for girls to come of age and explore their sexual identity?

MK: There is a huge difference between girls experimenting with their blossoming sexuality in a natural way and girls acting out of insecurity and a quest for validation from boys. On one hand, sexual exploration is natural and important at twelve or thirteen, and it shouldn't be stifled. However, the level of visibility and exposure these girls are accessing is frightening.

CK: Are the girls to blame, is it entirely MySpace at fault, or is there another culprit?

MK: Absolutely there is another culprit. This behavior is merely a symptom of our schizophrenic culture where women are considered either a whore or a mother (and as a teenager, the choice of motherhood is not too appealing). Simply put, the MySpace girl is the product of a culture that teaches girls to be available and disposable.

CK: What does all this mean long term for these teen and preteen MySpace girls?

MK: What concerns me is that these girls are trading intimacy, love, and community for power and conquest. These girls are unaware that a female community is so important to their coming-of-age process. They need to commune with other girls, not by kissing each other at parties or in posted photos, but through real-life friendships.

Your Assignment

Some of the most productive conversations I've had with teen girls were born out of months of listening and, eventually, a set of questions I like to throw their way. These questions came to me after teaching a predominantly male class of sophomores a fascinating utopian novella called *Herland*, written by early twentieth-century feminist Charlotte Perkins Gilman; a group of male explorers make a crash landing in a foreign land populated only by women. While it's quite humorous, the observations these men make are poignant and revealing about our society. I asked my few female students to pretend to be anthropologists who had just landed in our society. Let me share these questions with you in the hopes that you may be able to employ them when the time is right (I recommend discussion rather than journaling for these):

1. *What holidays are celebrated or held to be important in our culture, and what do they all have in common?*

   Overwhelmingly my female students focused on civic or religious holidays; they found the common thread to be the honoring of a national or holy event, often violent in nature. What they quickly realized is not many female experiences are celebrated or lifted up as important enough to be considered holidays. These teen girls began to question why the passing of the Nineteenth Amendment in our nation's history wasn't commemorated with any fanfare, a concept I have to admit never having considered. On a more personal level, some girls wished there was some mother-daughter ritual surrounding the purchase of a training bra, almost an ushering into womanhood, turning the shame usually associated with it on its head and embracing the experience as a bonding moment between mother and daughter.

2. *List three social behaviors that are acceptable and three that are unacceptable, and explain why.*

   Without fail my female students focused on the social graces or manners as acceptable behaviors, as girls are wont to do. What I found interesting is that many homed in on the issue of physical space in public; apparently, teenage girls are aware that when they are in a room, at a desk, or on a bus, they are expected not to take up too much space. Boys, on the other hand, they observed, sit with their legs spread wide, taking up as much space as they desire. It certainly led to some spirited discussion on society's gender expectations.

3. *What are the traits, both personality and physical, necessary for a woman to be considered important? Answer the same for a man.*

   The most relevant answer from this question is that girls believe it is imperative for them to be the "cool" girlfriend or friend. Upon further discussion, I learned that this meant not judging, criticizing, or standing up for anything in any way that may make a boy uncomfortable. Fifteen-year-old Nikki explained that her boyfriend "likes to look at Maxim magazine, so I look at it with him. I'm not that crazy about it, but I would never tell him that. He thinks it turns me on, too."

4. *What body types are considered ideal, and how is that message communicated to you?*

   The answers here are pretty standard, but the value of the discussion is anything but. Discussing body image and media is never a futile endeavor, especially with teenage girls. If anything, it will give you, as the parent, a better insight into how your daughter views her place in the world.

5. *What rules must you follow as a female that males do not seem to have to follow? And what are the consequences, spoken or unspoken, if you break those rules?*

    Overwhelmingly, my students complained that boys get to dress however they wish, and that they don't have to worry about their appearance to the extent that girls do. The consequences, as understood by these teens, are total social isolation and ridicule. The pressure to dress and carry oneself in an acceptable manner is so intense that total ostracization is the perceived (if not real) risk.

It is imperative for girls, especially in light of the blatantly sexist and harmful messages being sent to our daughters, to see *through the motives* of such an assault. Only when girls can step outside the madness can they recognize the absurdity of it all and, therefore, establish an inner resistance to it rather than participating in it. The following blog I read on MySpace was written by a fifteen-year-old girl: "It's been so crazy. I can't sleep and I feel like shit. I'm feeling a little sick on my stomach and all I can think about is how I just wish I were someone else. It's like everytime I look in the mirror I find something I want to change I change my hair color all the time, but it's just never enough. I've never felt like I've met anyone's standards for being pretty because no one ever tells you it's ok to be imperfect."

The Importance of Male Role Models

Several years ago I taught my ninth-grade students Sylvia Plath's *The Bell Jar* as part of my unit on the coming-of-age experience. We also looked at her poem entitled "Daddy"—a painful, raw ode to her father. I'll never forget how moved one of my female students became—one of the fiercest partiers. She churned out a few poems of her own detailing the pain surrounding her own fractured relationship with her dad.

Many times, a father or father figure's behavior helps shape what a girl will find acceptable in her relationships with boys and, eventually, men. In an effort to better understand the importance of father–daughter bonds, especially in light of the ubiquitous culture of MySpace, I interviewed Joe Kelly, author and founder of an organization devoted to the strengthening of father-daughter relationships called Dads & Daughters (www.dadsanddaughters.org). Here are his words of advice:

- Spend time with your daughters and interact with them, whether it's shooting hoops, going for hikes, or washing cars together. Encourage your daughters' creative, intellectual, and physical capacities. Praise her and share positive attention.

- Dads have more information about guys than anyone else in their daughters' lives; so, they have a unique influence on their girls. You are the first man in her life and can contradict the harmful messages of a sexist culture.

- Communicate with your daughters about their sexuality and coming-of-age experience; you must talk about it with your daughters. Tell her when she represents herself in a provocative manner that you wish we lived in a world where girls could safely celebrate their bodies, but unfortunately we don't live in such a place. Let her know you understand how unfair it must feel.

- It is never too late to reestablish your relationship with your daughter. Repairs won't happen overnight, but as the adult you must keep making the effort.

I also consulted L. Kris Gowen, of the Virtual Mystery Tour, a program dedicated to understanding the influence the Internet has on teen sexuality (www.virtualmysterytour.com). Here is what Dr. Gowen has to say about talking to your teen about MySpace and sexuality:

- Help your teens think critically about how they choose to represent themselves online. What are the implications of choosing a screen name such as "seXygirl" or "hottie92"? What sorts of people are names like that going to attract? Are these the people that they want to communicate and become friends with?

- The same lesson can be used for selecting MySpace photos. I have seen teen girls provide photos of themselves in a bustier, a bikini, or even represent themselves through their bodies or cleavage—not bothering to show their faces at all. Girls need to understand that although they may have a strong desire for attention and approval, it is equally important to get that attention and approval from people they care about and respect.

- Knowing that your child is representing herself in a sexual manner online may feel very threatening. As parents we got so excited about having a baby, but we never bit our lip in rapt anticipation of a teenager struggling with her emotions and exploring her sexuality in a brutally raunchy culture, right? The reality is—if you have a daughter—you will have to face her sexual maturation. She needs you to guide her through the madness.

Agrees psychotherapist Nadlman, "Parents are too intimidated to discuss things like oral sex and lesbian experiences with their prematurely sexualized daughters, so a whole generation of girls is looking for answers online." Our first step in helping our daughters understand and navigate through this exhibitionist MySpace kingdom is to get in touch with our own sexual baggage; only when we as parents are ready and able to talk with our children can we truly have more influence than popular culture on their choices.

How to Support and Positively Influence Your Sexually Maturing MySpace Girl

- Gently but firmly explain to your daughter that this, unfortunately, is the culture we live in, but remind her that she does not have to take part in it. Assure her that she will still be attractive to boys even if she remains outside the exhibitionist whirlpool.
- Tell your daughter that she is a real person with feelings, hopes, dreams, and desires, and that she does not need to create any secondary personae.
- Reinforce with your daughter that her main focus of energy should not be exploring what turns a guy on, but that her main project right now should be exploring what she wants to be, what she thinks about, what excites *her*.
- View your child's MySpace page without criticism. Ask your child why he or she wants a MySpace page, and whether their current screen name and profile help them achieve this goal or not.
- Search the profiles of other MySpace members (not your child's friends, but pick another geographical location and go from there) and talk about them with your child. Ask your child what he or she thinks that person is like and why they think that way. Ask your child if he or she

would like to be that person's friend and why. This exercise may help your own child understand the messages inherent on their own page—sexual or otherwise.

- Encourage them to visit sex education websites that are accurate and that fit your family's values. A good place to start might be Sex, Etc. (www.sexetc.org), a site written by teens for teens but fact-checked by adult experts in health and sexuality.

Logging On, Lighting Up

The Drug Connection

"Why is it drug addicts and computer aficionados are both called users?"

—*Clifford Stoll, author of* Silicon Snake Oil

—

- In September 2006, two New York college students died of heroin overdoses. Both girls' MySpace profiles contained several drug references.
- In May 2006, a high school student was arrested on numerous drug charges; authorities were tipped off by his MySpace photos, which showed him smoking marijuana.
- A MySpace group called "sXb—straight bud" is devoted to uniting people who smoke marijuana; their headline is "a group of mother f**kers who say . . . weed is good . . . join if u feel . . . and keep shit real." They currently boast over 5,500 members.

Generation MySpace

Your fourteen-year-old son seems withdrawn, and his grades are slipping. Suddenly he has a whole new set of friends, none of whom you ever see. He's stopped playing basketball, although he likes to play in Yahoo's online fantasy basketball league. In fact, the one thing that seems to keep his interest is his computer. *At least he has something meaningful in his daily life*, you think. Maybe his new friends are techie types who like to chat about new computer codes and the latest online games. Maybe that's why he's at the keyboard all evening and sometimes all night. *Could he be doing drugs? Not our son.* Besides, a recent drug test confirmed his innocence. Unfortunately, what you don't know is that your son learned how to beat that drug test by doing a simple search on the Internet one night. In fact, he has worked his way through marijuana, Adderall, and OxyContin through his Internet connections. And now he's struggling with a secret addiction.

Teens have always been vulnerable to drug and alcohol abuse. However, in recent years the face of such experimentation has undergone intensive plastic surgery—the teen drug culture of 2006 bears little resemblance to the teen drug culture of the '80s and early '90s. Besides the consistent popularity of marijuana, the majority of kids today are no longer seeking to score cocaine, heroin, LSD, or even crystal methamphetamine to the extent of days gone by. Not unlike the studies in the previous chapter about teens and sexual activity, we can find bliss in the surface statistics, thinking that teens are having less sex and doing less hardcore or "street" drugs. However, lest we be fooled, the reality is that kids are simply substituting oral sex for intercourse and, likewise, teens are substituting prescription drugs for street drugs. It's called "pharming," or getting high off pharmaceuticals. Take a look at the following data from the University of Michigan's "Monitoring the Future" study for the National Institutes of Health:

Percentage of Twelfth Graders Who Said They Had
Used Certain Drugs Over the Past School Year

	1999	2002	2005
Marijuana	37.8%	36.2%	33.6%
Cocaine	6.2	5.0	5.1
Ecstasy	5.6	7.4	3.0
OxyContin	—	4.0	5.5
Vicodin	—	9.6	9.5
Ritalin	—	4.0	4.4

Notes the study, "Of special concern today are the high numbers of young people using *prescription-type drugs*. . . . we now see significant proportions reporting psychotherapeutic drug use without medical supervision. If amphetamines are included, about one in four [high school] seniors (23.5 percent) report such use at some time in their life; while one in six (16.7 percent) report such use in just the past year."

This generation of teens has grown up with a great familiarity with prescription drugs; according to a recent study, over five million teenagers take medication daily for behavioral disorders. In addition, these youth have witnessed an ever-growing population of adults who rely more heavily on prescription answers to mood, physical, and sexual dysfunctions. It's rare to attend a baseball game without being bombarded by Viagra advertisements, and an evening of prime-time television leaves one wondering how we functioned for centuries without mood-altering substances to solve our problems. Our children have come of age in an era where almost any problem can be prescribed away, and it has definitely affected their outlook on self-medication.

The most prevalent drugs used today for behavioral disorders in the teen population are Ritalin and Adderall, both stimulants, similar in effect to speed. With millions of our teenagers carrying these medications around in their backpacks each day, it is no wonder that the temptation to sell, share, and abuse them has shot through the roofs of most American high schools recently. A 2005 survey by Partnership for a Drug-Free America revealed that 19 percent of U.S. teenagers, that's 4.5 million youths, had taken Ritalin or Adderall to get high. The same survey illustrates that three out of five teens admit to being able to get prescription painkillers from their parents' medicine cabinets.

At the same time, there has been a remarkable metamorphosis in the topography of teen culture over the past ten years. As we've seen, the widespread use of personal electronic devices has contributed to a teen social reality organized around private communications and uncensored information. One result is that today, many teens are utilizing cell phones and online social sites to facilitate their experimentation with or addiction to drugs. The Internet specifically is integral in the growing ease with which teens have access to drugs, both illicit and prescription. For instance, in September 2005, the U.S. Drug Enforcement Administration shut down roughly 4,600 Internet "pill mills"—or illegal online pharmacies. Most of these sites indiscriminately supplied millions of teens with the drugs of their choice.

Carol Falkowski, director of research communications for the Hazelden Foundation, says young abusers of prescription drugs also have begun using the Internet to share "recipes" for getting high. "Some websites are so simplistic," she says, "that they refer to pills by color, rather than their brand names, content, or potency." That, Falkowski says, may explain why emergency rooms are reporting a remarkable increase in the amount of teens overdosing on odd mixtures of pills. In fact, according to the federal Substance Abuse and Mental Health Services Administration, in 2004, one-fourth of the 1.3 million drug-related emergency room admissions were due to overdoses of prescription and over-the-counter drugs. The fact is that teens are on to something—it's pretty easy to get ahold of drugs over the Internet, it's pretty easy to get a nice high off mainstream prescription drugs, and it's pretty easy to operate under the parental radar.

"Parents hear 'computer' and they think they're so good for teens," says sixteen-year-old Edward. But "technology absolutely allows kids more access to drugs. There's no authority on the Internet, no one watches your every move, nobody is all up in your business." Edward's parents knew he spent a lot of time online. What they did not know was that he had found doctors online who would sell him prescription drugs and send them right to his home. Edward returned from school before his parents arrived home from work, so he was able to pick up his mail undetected. How did he locate these doctors? It was easy, he says: "Through friends I met on MySpace."

It's impossible to monitor your child's every move online—nor should you. There's no way to truly shield our kids from the images and temptations being shot their way at warp speed. (We're also too tired to be sure they're not up all night surfing these sites or chatting with late-night strangers.) But there are ways you can make a difference. This chapter will help you to recognize whether your child may be just beginning to get involved or is already deeply involved in the world of drugs, as well as talk to your child successfully about the Internet and its relationship with drug access. But first, let's take a look at the many ways teens are using new technologies to access—and glorify—illegal drugs and alcohol.

Sean's Story

"Many kids have their first encounter with drugs and alcohol through someone in their family or a close friend. That's how I got started. I was twelve and hanging out with some older cousins during a family vacation. I wanted to be cool like them, so when they offered me a hit of marijuana, I took it. For about three years, I only smoked pot when I was with my cousins. But then I started high school and found myself smoking pot every day. I could make a simple cell phone call and instantly have access to drugs.

"My parents didn't have a hard time figuring out I was regularly smoking weed . . . my clothes, my hair, my room all reeked of it. They immediately had me meeting with counselors and often screened me for drugs. It was when the screening began that I started going to the Internet to find ways to pass a drug test. Guess what? If you type 'how to beat a drug test' into Google, you can get a ton of websites!

"From that point on, the Internet became my first source of drug information. I found out about 'smoking herbs,' how to grow marijuana, make crack, recipes for LSD, how to make pot more potent, you name it—I found it! I stumbled onto a site called Erowid.com through a Google search. It was a mecca for pro–drug information! Eventually, I linked my IM [instant messenger screen name] to the site so my friends could access the information, too. We would order drugs online, even prescription drugs. All we needed was a credit card or billing address. Pretty easy. I had a MySpace profile . . . Of course, everything that was in my profile was about getting high. My friends and I would post pictures from parties—one friend even had instructions on how to make drug paraphernalia.

"So, how did I keep circumventing my parents? We had four computers in the house, and I had a personal laptop. Because of my drug habit, I also had messed-up sleep patterns, so I'd log on when everyone else was asleep. During the day hours, anytime my mom walked by me, I'd close out all my screens or have a new game of Solitaire up. While I was buying drugs online, my mom was on the Internet looking up ways to help me with my suspected addiction. But she hadn't learned how to monitor where I was going online.

"Now I'm seventeen years old and in treatment. I'm doing much better now and getting my life back in order."

Cherie's Story

"At first, I never made the connection between MySpace and drugs. They weren't exactly opposite worlds, of course, but I had never realized how MySpace is like a teenage black market. I only started noticing after I was deprived of the one thing I was never without: my cell phone. With all the drugs I have been doing, my attitude at home had worsened and the cussing didn't fly with my parents. The only thing they could think of doing was take away my cell phone. I seriously thought I wouldn't be able to survive. I didn't even remember what life was like without my cell phone! Drugs were less accessible and 'delivery' was slower. I needed to find a better way.

"One day a friend, who was a dealer, told me she mostly uses MySpace [for dealing]. The minute I got home I put all my time into making my profile. I put things like 'Anyone who wants to have a session' in my "Who I'd Like to Meet" section and soon enough, I was part of the drug community on MySpace. Every time a dealer would get a new pound of marijuana or a new amount of coke, it was first come, first served. I even saw a couple of people selling paraphernalia. I also realized it was *much* easier to sneak on to the computer at night and ask people to give me a ride rather then sneaking on to the phone and calling.

"If it wasn't for MySpace, my parents' punishment could have worked. I could have been forced to stop using drugs. I could have lived on without ever having to be informed of the new E parties or raves; I could have stopped at fifteen. MySpace didn't let me."

Recently I attended a roundtable discussion in New York City with recovering teen drug addicts and their parents, hosted by the nation's drug czar, John Walters, and in partnership with several drug recovery institutes like Pathway Family Center. It was the second in a series of gatherings that the Office of National Drug Control Policy and TheAntiDrug.com arranged in an effort to understand the emerging role of texting, IM-ing, and the Internet in youth drug culture. Sean and Cherie are two of the teens I met who are now in recovery and who shared their stories with me. They and their parents told me how their stories are not anomalies, that they are the lucky ones who ended up in treatment before destroying their lives or overdosing. Apparently, many of their classmates are traversing a similar path, but have yet to be helped. The sad fact is, these teens told me, that most kids are not addicts, but thousands nationwide are using technology to experiment with drugs.

Obviously, one appeal of the Internet is the ability to find information about almost any topic desired—who hasn't benefited from its vast database? However, one major drawback of the Internet is that it is unregulated; there are no checks on what can be accessed or by whom. Preteens and teens are particularly vulnerable. As Walters says, "In one click of the mouse, teens can enter a world of drugs; recipes for meth are as easy to find on the Internet as recipes for barbecue chicken." And he's right. In my simple Google searches, I found out how to beat a standard drug test, how much cough syrup I could take based on my weight in order to get a good high, and how to mimic the symptoms of ADD so that I could get a prescription for Adderall. And considering the Pew Internet and American Life research findings that few parents supervise their kids' online activities, the opportunity for kids to explore this underbelly of our culture is ripe. But even if your child isn't one to be searching for pro-drug information, be assured that bogus pharmacies frequently flood e-mail inboxes and MySpace pages with spam pushing prescription drugs. You may even have received some of these spam messages yourself—they're hard to avoid. Walters explains, "The pusher has moved to the PC; drug dealers lurk in these chat rooms just like pedophiles, targeting teens with pro-drug messages and offers of drugs." And don't delude yourself into thinking these e-dealers are necessarily older strangers—often they are other teenagers.

In fact, a study by *Pediatrics* found that the Internet leads adolescent drug users to try new drugs and drug combinations. The following case study comes from an article by Paul Wax called "Just a Click Away: Recreational Drug Websites on the Internet": an eighteen-year-old male college student undergoing a seizure admitted to having ingested several tablets of "blue mystic," the street name for a hallucinogenic amphetamine similar to mescaline. "The student stated that he had been using blue mystic sporadically but on this day decided to increase his dose." An Internet search revealed extensive information about this drug on the annals of the popular teen drug hookup websites, Erowid.org and Lycaeum.org.

The Internet and Prescription Drugs

- 55 percent of Internet users say they have received an unsolicited e-mail advertising a prescription drug.
- In September 2005, a DEA investigation resulted in the arrest of eighteen people operating more than 4,600 rogue Internet pharmacy websites.
- Pro-drug websites commonly include descriptions of the preparation, dose, administration, and psychoactive effects of drugs, as well as recommendations for managing the adverse effects of illicit drugs.

Cheyenne's Story

"I'm fourteen years old right now, so you can only imagine how young I was when I started drinking alcohol and using drugs. I was eight years old when I had my first drink with my dad. He was going to jail the next day and thought it would be 'one last hurrah' to get me drunk. From that point until I was twelve, my drug of choice was alcohol. I had a certain negative perception of drug addicts, and therefore had no interest in doing drugs.

"What changed? Well, I met an older guy—a 'druggie,' who asked me if I wanted to get high one day. So I did. We hung out regularly, and as you'd expect, my drug use became more frequent. Pot replaced alcohol as my drug of choice.

"At the time, I was visiting a lot of chat rooms, meeting druggie guys, and they would IM me asking if I drank or got high. I didn't think too much about giving them my cell phone number. We would end up meeting to drink, get high, or mess around with prescription drugs.

"When I wasn't hanging out in chat rooms, I was posting stuff to my MySpace profile. I lied about my age and posted pretty seductive pictures to attract guys. Most were between sixteen and twenty-five years old. Of course, I attracted the druggie types because my profile page was filled with talk about smoking and drinking. I dug the attention and acceptance! But the drugs really took a toll. I was rushed to the hospital three times for drug and alcohol abuse. I couldn't stop, though. I would skip school for fear of missing out on something. I equated fun with drugs, and drugs with meeting people. And I loved meeting new people!

"I started buying drugs online and would have them delivered to my home mailbox. In 2005, I switched schools and heard about a website from other students where drug users posted messages talking big about getting high the night before. I got on the site, lied about my age again, and began making drug deals online.

Because my mom was working all the time and my dad was out of the picture, it was pretty easy to get away with a lot of the stuff. It wasn't until I refused to go to school that my mom put me in treatment. I'm . . . glad to be recovering."

It's Just as Easy for Girls

According to a recent analysis about drug and alcohol use trends among girls released by the White House Office of National Drug Control Policy, *Seventeen* magazine, and teen medical experts, "Despite commonly held beliefs that boys are at higher risk for using illegal substances, data indicate that girls have caught up with boys in illicit drug and alcohol use and have actually surpassed boys in cigarette and prescription drug use." In addition, there appear to be more girls than boys who are new users of such substances. Walters explains that he is "urging parents to become aware of the unique risks that make our daughters vulnerable to substance use and to talk to them about why it's important to stay drug-free."

Studies show that teenage girls abuse substances for dramatically different reasons than boys. While boys are usually seeking a thrill or taking a risk, many girls are attempting to feel comfortable in their adolescent bodies. The teen girl's dramatic physical transition during early adolescence results in a marked decline in self-esteem and self-confidence. Studies show that girls, in fact, are more than twice as likely as boys to report depression. According to the above study, "Young females tend to use alcohol or drugs to improve mood, increase confidence, reduce tension, cope with problems, or lose inhibitions." And after learning about the sexual pressures on teen girls in the previous chapter, it is not too difficult to imagine why girls would be more vulnerable to drug use. My experience as a high school teacher has afforded me many opportunities to watch young girls begin to abuse drugs for the sole purpose of weight loss. A few years ago, the drug of choice was crystal methamphetamine, and a handful of my students were wasting away to nothing at the claws of this monster.

So how is it different for girls to procure these substances? Most of the female drug users I interviewed were pretty candid (and, at times, proud) of how they were able to make connections with older guys. These drug-dealing men were eager to connect with younger females and often were quicker to trust them with their contact numbers. As discussed in the previous chapter (about the unique pressures on MySpace girls), many girls who are desperately seeking boys' attention, especially older boys' attention, do so by being willing to experiment with cigarettes, alcohol, and drugs. Girls have bought into the myth that they look cool hanging out with older boys, especially older boys who party. "Not all kids do drugs for the experience; they do it for the image and the social involvement it provides," say Sharon Lamb, EdD and Lyn Mikel Brown, EdD, authors of *Packaging Girlhood*. Teen girls who are curious about drugs and insecure about their appearance can easily fall prey to the damaging messages they receive via the media and online environments.

As sixteen-year-old Trina shared with me, she wanted the "excitement of Paris Hilton's life, with all the drama and the clothes and the mayhem!" Well versed in the publicity rags and pop-culture celebrity shows, this young lady swallowed the myth of Paris Hilton hook, line, and sinker; she believed that a daily dose of partying and clubbing would alleviate the boredom of her middle-class white world. Unfortunately, Trina's choices led to a serious cocaine addiction, one that became apparent when her nose began bleeding while talking to me and my daughter in the school parking lot. Fortunately, with my prompting, the school alerted her mother, and Trina has been in drug rehabilitation for a year now, apparently doing much better.

Why MySpace?

So you may be wondering how, exactly, a teen would go about using these virtual sites and other electronic means to score actual drugs or alcohol. It's really quite easy, thanks to the networking features. Remember, MySpace can be used by anyone fourteen or older, or at least anyone who claims to be fourteen or older. One of the great things about MySpace is that it provides a venue for teens to hang out—virtually that is. And where there are teens, there will be purveyors of mind- and mood-altering substances.

Soliciting with a Profile

As we've seen, the profile is the face your teen shows to the world; it is nothing short of a carefully constructed marketing tool. And as teens feel a sense of anonymity from authority on social-networking sites, those who use drugs or are curious about trying them are not shy about posting comments, discussions, and even photographic evidence of their habits—or about asking for the substances they want. It is not unusual to see background wallpaper on a profile showing fluffy green marijuana leaves or raining multicolored pills; nor is it rare to see explicit requests to "meet" others with a connection or hookup for drugs. Many MySpacers will select songs with pro-drug lyrics to play on their profile or even supply links to popular drug-paraphernalia sites.

Sixteen-year-old Ahmanda explains that "on MySpace it's better to use the messaging feature than the comments feature because it's more private. I have a better chance of getting phone numbers and drug contacts. I also personalized my profile to attract other drug users or potential hookups; I have a large marijuana leaf as my background and pictures of me lighting a blunt [a joint]. In my 'About Me' section, I make it clear that I'm interested in drugs. I've had about fifty people request to be added and then want to get drugs from me."

Joining Drug Groups

One of the more popular features on MySpace is the formation of
and membership in various special interest groups. (See one of the
main tabs on the MySpace Home Page, titled "Groups," to check
some out.) This feature allows for anyone to form any type of
group or club organized around a specific common interest. Not
unlike the chess club at school or the Young Republicans, this feature offers MySpacers a great opportunity to network, learn, and
socialize. One popular interest of MySpacers is drug use. Take a
look at the following sample posting from a marijuana group:

POTSMOKERS UNITED at URL:
http://groups.myspace.com/users6863123

Billy: I wanna kno somethings bout acid before i try it.
Also i wanna kno if it stays in your system and can
be detected thru a drug test ((piss test type))?
Juice: personaly, i love acid, its my DOC [drug of choice].
for your 1st trip, i would say try 1-3 doses
(microdots, blotters, jell caps) just so you know
what your dealing with. later on you can up the
dosage if you want.

I monitored some exchanges on MySpace recently and found
a group called "Pill Poppers Forever," where one user asked if it
was possible to get high off the prescription painkiller Darvocet.
One of the many replies suggested Vicodin for "a better high."
Where are these individuals getting the Darvocet? Well, assuming
this particular member of the group was not recovering from
recently giving birth to twins, clearly the inquiry into "getting
high" indicates he or she has either raided Mom's medicine cabinet or is intending to order some good stuff off the Internet. In

that same group, I came across a bulletin offering cheap, prescription-free Xanax, the drug used to treat anxiety and panic disorders. In another group, called "Drugsters," a fifteen-year-old MySpacer began a conversation about what everyone's drugs of choice were; answers included marijuana, crystal meth, cocaine, ecstasy, and OxyContin. All on MySpace. In fact, according to an article in the *Miami Herald*, Robert Roth, coordinator of adolescent behavioral health at Montgomery General Hospital in Maryland, says kids who come into his addiction clinic talk frequently of groups on MySpace, and it seems more popular among *middle school students* than among high school students. He goes on to say that he has noticed their parents "are usually completely unaware."

Recent studies show that one out of every thirteen sixth graders have smoked marijuana, and that the numbers increase by 300 percent for seventh graders at an alarming one out of five who have inhaled. And in a recent survey by the National Center on Addiction and Substance Abuse (CASA) at Columbia University, findings reveal that 28 percent of middle school students attend drug-infested schools—up from 19 percent of middle school students in 2002. That's 2.4 million middle schoolers. Pair this with the ease with which the Internet contributes to the problem, and we have a newly ripe environment for tween substance abuse.

Following Links

Of course, using search engines to search MySpace and the Internet in general to look for answers to specific drug questions is an expedient method for curious teens. However, one need not even search—many of these links also appear on pro-drug MySpace pages. Fifteen-year-old Ernie tells me that "while on MySpace, I found all sorts of good links to sites where I could order drugs."

Popular Pro-Drug Websites Teens Visit

www.erowid.org (the most popular, apparently; also includes links to other sites)

www.lycaeum.org	www.clubdrugs.org
www.dancesafe.org	www.legalsmokeshop.com
www.ravesafe.com	www.amsterdam.com
www.ecstacy.org	www.hightimesmagazine.org
www.bluelight.nu	www.totse.com
www.tripzine.com	www.marijuana.com
www.eztest.com	

Do a Google or Yahoo search yourself using simple terms like "marijuana" or "OxyContin" to see the myriad links that encourage and enable our teens to enter the drug culture.

Finding Real-World Parties

Today a popular method for advertising a party, one that promises to be large and out of control, is via MySpace or Facebook. Seventeen-year-old Anastasia explains that "making a ton of phone calls or putting up flyers on lockers is lame when all it takes is posting a bulletin on MySpace!" She continues to emphasize the value of a wide spectrum of friends on your Friends List in order to have the optimum exposure to the party scene. The more friends you allow to send you bulletins, the more assurance you have, apparently, that you will not be excluded from the weekend's calendar of teen gatherings.

Crystal's Story

"My friend introduced me to MySpace; she used it for meeting people around the area. We both used drugs and alcohol and MySpace.com was the best place to land a party.

"I went to a party with her and got wasted with people I didn't know, but that was normal for me. We drove an hour out of town, drank with these kids from MySpace, and drove home—drunk. That night I decided to get my own MySpace profile.

"My friend would post sexy pictures of herself on her page. My pictures consisted of me flipping off the camera or smoking. The two of us didn't attract the best crowd.

"MySpace finally became a place to not only find parties but to find the drugs that went with them. For me, it helped me create my living hell. To anybody who's still out there using MySpace.com, use it wisely."

References to party culture are everywhere on MySpace—one bulletin, called "Party Hard in MySpace's Party Room," is accompanied by an image of a cute kitten bagging marijuana. Another says, "Yeah, I drink Coors" with an image of a bikini-clad girl and a Coors Light sign. One "About Me" section from a group of friends' MySpace profile declares: "We love to drink and party—that's what we do best. So if you see us at the club don't be shy, introduce yourself and be a gentleman and buy ALL of us a drink. Thanks bitch!!!" But beyond hosting a venue for the posting of party pictures, MySpace offers connections for users to find substance parties in the real world.

It is this prevailing culture of "post every photo of yourself on MySpace no matter how revealing" that encourages teens who are either not savvy enough yet or who simply don't care to broadcast evidence of their drinking or drug use. As social networks expert danah boyd states, teens "go online to gloat to their friends about the stupid things they've done—or to embarrass the heck out of them. The number of teens who worry about their image with adults is very small." And that's obviously an indication of the reality of youth culture today—the by-product, I believe, of an emerging feeling among teens of invincibility and untouchability thanks to new technologies and out-of-touch adults.

However, the uniting of over 100 million people in an insufficiently monitored environment and an increasingly risk-encouraging culture is the recipe for a large-scale Haight-Ashbury effect. All over the country, schools are honing their discipline policies in light of the emerging MySpace drug/alcohol photo evidence epidemic. Recently, in Massachusetts, school administrators mandated a drug test for a group of students who posted photos showing them passing around what appeared to be a drug pipe. Incidentally, the ACLU persuaded the school to drop the demand. According to the *Boston Globe,* East Grand Rapids High School in Michigan "temporarily prohibited about twenty students from participating in extracurricular activities after seeing an online photo of the teens drinking."

The response of MySpace's safety czar, Hemanshu Nigam, as told to ABC News, was: "Teens will do what they do. What we are doing is looking at sites that go up, and identifying them. When somebody tells us about a site, we very quickly determine if our members' rules are in violation or not, and then we take it down."

Popular Trash Drugs Advertised on the Internet

These common household items are used as inhalants in a variety of ways. Each one yields a different result, from a marijuana-like high to a mushroom-like hallucination. Information about how to prepare and ingest these can be found with a simple Google search on the computer.

- Nutmeg
- Peanut shell
- Morning glory seeds
- Banana peel
- Sage seeds
- Devil's trumpet (flower)

This list is not comprehensive—no list could be. However, it was composed with the help of drug-savvy teens willing to assist parents in becoming more aware.

The Cell Phone Connection

MySpace isn't the only way teens score drugs. Just five years ago, most teens didn't have a cell phone. Now, that's all changed. According to teen expert Peter Zollo of Teenage Research Unlimited, teens are using technology all the time, everywhere. He states that "almost 90 percent of twelve- to seventeen-year-olds use the Internet; half of them use it daily. About nineteen million teens instant message, and 60 percent of teens have their own cell phone." The appeal of the cell phone for a teen who is interested in making plans or sharing information is that text messaging allows for succinct and private messages to be sent from a phone to another phone or to an e-mail address. It is extremely private. Also, cell phones now offer extensive contact list storage capabilities, which comes in handy when organizing one's drug-hookup connections.

Unfortunately, that cell phone capabilities allow teens more secrecy about their contacts and their plans means parents now have their work cut out for them. Of course, a possible sign of cell phone misuse is if your child rushes to answer his or her phone and then hides out while responding via text message. I recommend taking advantage of the itemized cell phone statements that list incoming and outgoing calls and text messages; if you don't recognize any numbers, ask your child about them.

One student, Amy, told me, "Keeping up with my drug contacts is the whole reason I got my cell phone." Amy admitted that her cell phone became "the most important tool for me to get drugs."

So what's the difference between a land line and a cell phone in terms of facilitating drug usage? "I kept all of my drug dealers' names in my phone book on my cell phone and would sometimes put them under other names so nobody could find out." She also has total access to her phone every hour of every day, and she can place the ring tone on vibrate or silent so as to keep her communications private. No one can accidentally pick up the line and hear her conversations, a common fear when most of today's adults were teens. Finally, there's the ability to text message, send e-mail messages, and send Internet links. "If a new drug contact wanted to send me the latest recipe for a trash drug or the steps to beat a drug test, all he would have to do is text me the link."

Another of my former students, I'll call her Johnna, approached me in tears during her lunch period one day in January. She confided in me that she had been sneaking out of her house each night and partying with friends from another school until it was time to come home, shower, and go to school. She explained that she had been able to survive each day only because she was snorting excessive amounts of cocaine. She asked me to help her. After meeting with her mother and devising a solid treatment plan, I was confident that she was on her way to recovery. But Johnna didn't seem to be doing any better. She told me that the crowd she partied with wouldn't leave her alone; they kept calling her cell phone and leaving messages on her MySpace page harassing her to come out and get amped with them one last time. She gave up one night and met them on the roof of her apartment building, but her dad caught her.

On several occasions I kept her on the phone for several hours late at night in the hopes that I could keep her from being in contact with the drug crowd. Finally, I told her that if she were serious about breaking free of her addiction and old way of living, she would *have to* get rid of her cell phone . . . or at least change her phone number. She reacted quite vehemently; the idea of losing her cell phone was too much for her to process. When I inquired into her strong reaction, she explained that her cell phone was her connection to drugs and that without it she would *really* be quitting; she didn't want to lose the ability to maybe get high one more time. She equated her cell phone with her access to drugs. Johnna and Amy would have been doing drugs with or without their cell phones, I am sure, but the convenience and networking features of their phones clearly contributed to their falling deeper into that culture.

Nineteen-year-old Nick takes issue with the idea that new technologies contribute to teens' drug access and addiction. While he admits to learning how to "cook up hash, how to make up different bongs and pharmaceutical drugs" on the Internet, he blames himself, not the technology. "MySpace and cell phones don't make addicts." This is true, but what they can do is make it much easier for a teenager to become enmeshed in the drug culture. Could Nick have found out how to create trash drugs from common household products had he not searched a site like Erowid.org? Probably. But he would have had to do some serious research, including contacting experienced drug users and/or dealers, people who are more difficult to reach without a cell phone or a computer.

Parents to the Rescue

As a parent, I realize that sometimes trying to be vigilant about all the dangers in your child's world can feel like you're trying to plug leaks with tissue paper. No matter what method you try to keep your child safe, there always seems to be another way for your child, or some bad influence on your child, to seep through the cracks. It can be discouraging, I know, but the first step to combating such influences is learning about them and understanding what your kids are up against. While it may be difficult to imagine your child sneaking around your rules, for instance, it is vital that you realize how easy and inviting today's technologies make it for your child. Teenagers are not bad or inherently dishonest. However, they are vulnerable, and the culture they now inhabit continuously facilitates that direction. As Dr. Richard Gallagher, PhD, a child and adolescent psychologist at New York University's Child Study Center, describes it, "Teens are incredibly fragile beings who are easily influenced. There are many toxic environments for teens in our world, including the latest technologies."

Whether your child is utilizing technology to do so or not, the indicators of drug or alcohol abuse are the same. Focus Substance Abuse Services lists these warning signs of teen substance abuse:

Physical
- Lack of interest in personal appearance
- Physical changes (e.g., persistent runny nose, red eyes, coughing, wheezing, bruises, needle marks)
- Change in eating/sleeping habits
- Smell of alcohol on the breath
- Sudden use of strong perfume or cologne
- Sudden, frequent use of breath mints

Emotional/Social
- Isolation, depression, fatigue
- Uncharacteristic withdrawal from family, friends, or interests
- Hostility and lack of cooperativeness
- Change in friends
- Loss of interest in hobbies and/or sports that used to be important
- Unusually protective of cell phone, especially forbidding a parent from answering it or looking at contact lists

Family/Home Life

- Increase in borrowing money
- Frequently receiving mysterious or seemingly normal packages in the mail
- Unaccounted-for cash, especially in small denominations
- Evidence of drugs or drug paraphernalia (e.g., rolling papers, eye drops, butane lighters, pipes)
- Use of incense or room deodorant
- Abnormal need or request for cough syrup, Sudafed, or other over-the-counter medications
- Evidence of inhaling products (such as hairspray, nail polish, and white-out) and chemicals used to get high (e.g., rags soaked in chemicals or gasoline, smell of chemicals on the person, more frequent need to buy household products)
- Watered-down alcohol in liquor bottles in the liquor cabinet
- Heightened secrecy about actions or possessions

Academic

- Drop in school attendance or academic performance
- Drastically different behavior or citizenship reports from teachers
- Reports of excessive tiredness and/or inability to stay awake during class

If you suspect your child is abusing drugs or alcohol, the first step is to take action! I recommend educating yourself about your teen's world as best you can. You can sign up for the AntiDrug "Parenting Newsletter" at www.theantidrug.com, for instance. The next step is to get past your fear of talking to your child about your suspicion; it is vital that you let them know that you are aware that they may be using drugs. In this conversation, make sure you are calm and that you are specific about what is causing you concern. The goal, remember, is not to find out how or where your child is getting the drugs, but to find out *why* your child is getting the drugs. Try the following phrases throughout the discussion:

- I love you, and I am concerned that you may be experimenting with alcohol or drugs.
- I want to listen to why you are making these decisions.
- I want to help you move away from these choices.
- I will do whatever you need me to do to get you clean.
- I am willing to stand by you while you break away from this lifestyle.

In addition, I recommend consulting a physician to rule out physical causes of the above warning signs as a good precaution. This step should then be followed or accompanied by a comprehensive evaluation by a drug-counseling professional; if necessary, contact a well-respected drug and alcohol abuse treatment program near you by calling 1–800–729–6686.

Talk to Your Kids

I cannot stress enough the need to engage in a candid discussion with your child about your concerns and your intentions; again, approach your child out of love and with a sincere desire to help him or her. Unfortunately, in a recent study, teenagers graded parents C- in preventing kids from doing drugs. Many kids claim that their parents do not talk to them about drugs, even though said parents claim that they in fact do. Be sure to make it clear to your child that drugs are not OK; even if it feels like you're stating the obvious, take that risk and spell it all out for your child. Setting the family culture regarding drugs will help your child navigate peer pressure and other temptations (like Internet solicitations) to use drugs. Fifteen-year-old Eileen told me, with tears in her eyes, that "the thing that would have helped me stay away from drugs the most is if my parents had given me clear boundaries in the early years." These teens are all but begging parents like you and me to not just learn but to master the prominent technologies of your child's generation.

Here are some sample rules, explanations, and consequences to use as conversation starters:

Rule #1: You may not use alcohol, tobacco, drugs, or any other illegal substances.

The Conversation: I've been thinking lately that I may not have ever specifically told you this, but I do not want you taking drugs or drinking alcohol, ever. I'm always going to stand by you and always love you and guide you, but I don't want you making the wrong choice and then having bad things happen in your life. My job as a parent is to help you become the wonderful, competent adult that I know you'll be. I know you can't do that if you use drugs or alcohol.

The Consequence: Because you broke our rule about drug and alcohol use, I am disallowing Internet and phone usage. You will also be reading extensive information about the harmful effects of drugs, tobacco, and alcohol. I may even have you write a research paper for me (perhaps have him write out his hopes and dreams and how each one could be squashed by a drug addiction).

Rule #2: If you're at a party and you see that drugs or alcohol are being used, the rule is to leave that party. Call me, and I'll come get you.

The Conversation: Honey, I love you, but you've got to know I'm your parent, not one of your friends. As your parent, I will not put up with your being in a place where drugs are being used. Therefore, do not hesitate to call me at any time to retrieve you from such a situation.

The Consequence: Because you stayed at a party where there was no adult supervision and where people were using drugs, you're not going anywhere—no mall, no movies, nowhere—for one week (up to three). It doesn't matter if you were not participating; the rule states clearly that you cannot be at a party where others are doing drugs or drinking alcohol. Therefore, you have violated our rule. (Or, temporarily restrict friends from coming over to the house and don't allow visits to friends' homes. This includes any text messaging and/or social networking at home.)

Rule #3: You are not allowed to ride in a car with a driver who's been using drugs or who's been drinking.

The Conversation: I care enough about you to let you know that I don't want to see anything bad happen to you. It would be horrible not having you in my life. Therefore, I cannot condone your putting yourself in that kind of danger.

The Consequence: Because you were riding with a friend who had been drinking (or was high), I will give you the consequence that the police would have given you had you been caught. I am taking your driver's license (or learner's permit) from you for two weeks (up to three).

Tips for Parents: How to Know What Your Child Is Up To

(Courtesy of www.theantidrug.com)

1. Have your child check in with you regularly.
2. Make a list of her activities for the coming day and put it on the fridge, on a calendar, or in your wallet.

3. Walk through your neighborhood and note where kids your child's age hang out.

4. Know your child's friends. Have a small party at your house and invite the parents of his friends. Have his friends stay for dinner. Ask them about their parents.

5. Make a point of meeting your child's friends' parents—find them at a PTA meeting, back-to-school night, soccer practice, dance rehearsal, or wherever the kids hang out.

6. Work with other parents to get a list of everyone's addresses, e-mails, and phone numbers so you can keep in touch with your child.

7. Show up a little early to pick up your child so you can observe her behavior.

8. Lots of kids get in trouble with drugs right after school—from 3 PM to 6 PM Try to be with your kids then, but if you can't, make sure your child is involved in a positive activity that is supervised by an adult.

Teens *Will* Try to Hide It

A fact of life when dealing with teenagers is that most of them will not hesitate to operate in secrecy. Of course, they usually term it "privacy." And therein lies the difference in perspectives: it's normal for a parent to want to know everything his child is doing, and it's normal for a teenager to seek distance from his parent. Teens aren't inherently dishonest; they are simply growing up. And an important developmental step in maturation is breaking away from one's parents and attaching more to one's friends. Unfortunately, teens today feel like this separation necessitates a hidden life. The issue is not to get your teen to tell you everything, but to minimize the amount of secrets he keeps—or at least the types of secrets. When it comes to dangerous behaviors like sex and drugs, obviously the fewer secrets the better. Fifteen-year-old Danny told me, "Technology has definitely helped me hide my drug habit from my parents, especially the wireless Internet since it's always available and I don't have to ask permission to go online. Plus, my laptop is invaluable. I can sit in my room for hours and surf MySpace for any new drug combos out there."

A young man I interviewed whom I'll call Ernie confirms that he took advantage of his parents' trusting nature. He explains that "while on MySpace, I found all sorts of good links to sites where I could order drugs. I would just take money or blank checks or a credit card out of my mom's purse that she left lying around. I was always receiving packages from eBay for my bottle rocket hobby anyway, so when another package arrived (filled with ampheta-mines or hallucinogens), she never thought twice about it." As par-ents, it is our job to "think twice" about what our kids are doing, especially in this era of drugs on demand for preteens and teens. Just read sixteen-year-old Cindy's perspective on her parents: "I'm good at wearing masks. I schemed out my parents by telling them little bits of information about mistakes I'd made in order to build up trust. You know, they thought I was so honest with them. That way, they felt good and I could get away with more partying." Drugs are addictive, and teens who fall into that trap will do and say anything to anyone to continue to procure a fix. Even "scheme out" their parents.

Friends of mine often laugh about how much more their child knows about computers or cell phones than they do; I've made some jokes myself. But simply accepting your role as "in the dark" is exactly what drug promoters expect and want you to do, because it makes reaching your kids without your knowledge that much easier. We *must* educate ourselves *now* in the ways of teens and new technologies. The mother of a recovering teen drug addict told me, "I was ignorant to what she could do with her phone. I thought it was a good tool to teach her responsibility." She also expressed her frustration in not understanding the intricacies of the Internet. The father of a teenage rehabilitation patient laments that he "had no reason to believe there was a problem with [his son]. He was good at keeping his developing habit a secret: he was a good student and never missed curfew. We had no indication that he was as deep into drugs as he was."

My advice is to refrain from relying on the checklists of the past—what I mean is that the old indicators of your child's well-being are no longer necessarily valid. Just because Johnny earns straight As in school, just because Sally dresses conservatively and never wears excessive makeup, just because Jimmy is a star athlete, it doesn't follow that he or she is steering clear of drugs and alcohol. The only surefire way to stay on top of this growing problem is to regularly check in with your kids, no matter how trustworthy or together they seem to be. Remember, you may have total trust in your teen, but you cannot control the influences that constantly bombard her. According to psychotherapist Jonathan Nadlman, the most important thing we can communicate as parents is that our children matter to us, that they are important; then, and only then, can we expect them to make decisions that reflect a healthy self-image, decisions that demonstrate a feeling of self-worth.

So how do we let our teens know that we value them? By simply talking with them, asking them specific questions about their daily experiences, and never allowing their moodiness to discourage us. If they see that we really want to be involved in the minutiae of their world, they will begin to believe that they really matter—and if they believe they matter, they will act accordingly.

Cheyenne says, "If I had anything to share with parents, especially if they are divorced or separated, it would be this: be on the same page about your kid, even if you hate each other. I used my parents against each other all the time, making it easier for me to get in trouble. Check in with your kid often, and sneak around if you suspect something."

Advice to Parents from Teens Who Are in Drug Recovery Programs

- Don't assume your kid is innocent just because she gets good grades
- Check the web history on your kid's computer to see what sites he's been visiting
- Check your kid's cell phone bill religiously and make note of any numbers you don't recognize or that keep popping up, especially on weekends
- When your child is not around, feel free to answer his cell phone
- In the evening or around bedtime, take the cell phone away from your child; she should *never* go to bed with her cell phone
- Do the same with the laptop (or remove the desktop's keyboard at night)
- Take preventive measures like strengthening the bond with your child during the preschool years, before he's old enough to be influenced to take drugs; establish a significant presence in his life by engaging in regular activities together (attending ball games, building engines, bird watching), attending an annual parent-child summer camp for a week together each year, or even just showing up at the majority of his school or athletic events. Bonds are created and fortified simply by being together, so plan your days with your toddler wisely.

Monitoring Your Child's Internet Activity

"Learn how to check a computer history log. If my mom knew how to do that, she would have discovered my problem a lot earlier. Fact is, I never erased it. And think to yourself, 'something is up' if you keep seeing blank screens every time you walk by your kid's computer or get a lot of 'nothing' type responses when you ask 'what are you up to?'" —Cheyenne

If you decide to access your child's MySpace page (more on this in chapter 9), pay attention to how he is portraying himself. Sometimes it's as simple as your profile name and headline. For instance, if your child's MySpace name is "Burn One Down," I recommend you inquire into why she chose it. Is she referring to a joint? Also, if your child's picture includes drug paraphernalia, you obviously have grounds for an important discussion and most likely a drug test. Profile wallpaper is a common method of communicating interest in making drug connections; many drug users display the typical green marijuana leaf. Sometimes all it takes is a few links to drug sites like Erowid.org or legalizemjnow.org prominently displayed. Remember my student, Cherie, who advertised that she would "like to meet" people who wanted to get high—being direct works, too.

Don't overlook blogs—believe it or not, many teens write regular entries about their drug use. Although, like diaries, they often contain a person's innermost feelings, blogs are *public* writings, and you have the right to read them, especially if you are concerned about your child's well-being. The following entry, from "SaraNwrapper," reveals a young lady who is in dire need of an intervention:

I wish I could stop hurting so much. I wish I could stop taking pills to—try—to take the pain away. The sad truth is . . . I'm going back on my words. I told myself I wouldn't get caught up in drugs . . . that I would never let them become a part of my life . . . not like a hobby . . . but, heh, let's face it, it's all there is now . . . it's like I can't function if I haven't had some sort of mind-altering substance . . . I've moved from just NyQuil to pot and pills and I'm testing the waters of alcohol again. I don't know if I'm going to go swimming again or not . . . we'll see. I'm just trying to keep everything under control . . .

The desperation in this girl's blog is apparent, and I would argue that her publishing these thoughts classifies as a call for help. If you feel uncomfortable reading your child's blog, ask your child what he or she writes about. Or, try to establish a dialogue with some of your child's friends and occasionally inquire into what types of topics he or she blogs about. Although they may not tell you explicitly about drug use, chances are they would indicate if something were wrong. I am sure that one of SaraNwrapper's friends would be concerned enough, if not to outright alert a parent if asked, at least to hint that she was not doing well. Most teens with whom I spoke are more concerned about their friends than themselves, and they unanimously agreed that they would do whatever they could to get their friends help before they would consider helping themselves.

The above blog entry includes the verb *swimming*, a popular term among teens that means drinking alcohol to excess. Perhaps you did not know that term. Although SaraNwrapper's blog posting makes no secret of her drug habit, many postings allude to drug usage with coded phrases. One of the reasons it is easy for teens to communicate with each other about drugs and parties is the ever-changing slang terms they use. (Sometimes I'm convinced there is an underground publishing company devoted solely to changing teen lingo and keeping adults out of the loop.) Here follow the latest drug terms that every parent of a teen should know:

Popular Street and MySpace Terms for Drug Usage

- 420:   marijuana use/national marijuana use day

- A-BOOT: Under the influence of drugs

- A-BOMB: anything rolled with heroin or opium

- AGONIES: Withdrawal symptoms

- AMPED/SPUN/ CRANKED/LIT/ POLLUTED/ TWEEKED: to be high

- AMPHEAD: LSD user

- ARE YOU ANYWHERE?:   Do you use marijuana?

- AUTHOR: Doctor who writes illegal prescriptions

- BABYSITTER: The person who takes care of you when you're high

- BAGGING: Sniffing or inhaling fumes from substances sprayed

- BANG: When you inject a drug

- BLUE BOOGERS: Snorting Adderall or Ritalin

- BLUNT: Marijuana

- CARPET PATROL: Crack smokers searching the floor for crack

- CHALKED UP: Under the influence of cocaine

- CLOSET BASER: User of cocaine that prefers anonymity

- COKE, CRACK, BLOW, SNOW, 151:   Cocaine

 201

- CRISTY, GLASS,
  ICE, AMP, CRANK,
  LA GLASS, WHITE
  CROSS, ALBINO
  POO, 222, TINA: Crystal methamphetamine

- DIME: 10 dollars' worth of marijuana/
                           coke/crystal meth

- DUB: 20 dollars' worth of marijuana/
                           coke/crystal meth

- E, XTC, ROLLS, ADAM: MDMA (or Ecstasy)

- HEAVEN AND HELL: PCP

- HIGHBEAMS: Wide eyes associated with
                           taking crack

- HONEYMOON: Early stages of drug use
                           before addiction

- HYPE STICK: Hypodermic needle

- LEAN: Drinking prescription cough
                           syrup with painkillers and soda

- MISS: To inject a drug

- O, OC, OXYCOTTON,
  OXY80, KILLERS: OxyContin (Popular among
                           teens, this drug is a combina-
                           tion of the active ingredients
                           in prescription painkillers
                           percoset and percodan.)

- OZONE: Inhalants

- PAPER BAG: Container for drugs

- PHARM PARTIES: Parties centered around teens
                           taking large doses of prescrip-
                           tion drugs (pharmaceuticals)

- PHARMING: Raiding medical cabinets to
                           trade and consume prescrip-
                           tion drugs

- PIGGYBACKING: Simultaneous injecting of two different drugs

- QUAD: 40 dollars' worth of marijuana/coke/crystal meth

- ROBOTRIPPING: Drinking cough medicine to get high (originates from Robitussin brand)

- SACRAMENT: LSD

- SAM: Federal narcotics agent

- SERIAL SPEEDBALLING: Sequencing cocaine, cough syrup, and heroin over a one- to two-day period

- SLANG: To sell drugs

- STARDUST: Cocaine

- TEX-MEX: Marijuana

- TRAIL MIX: Baggies filled with random prescription pills

- TRIPLE C: Coricidin HBP Cough & Cold tablets

- TWEAK MISSION: On a mission to find crack

- TWEAKER: A person who uses methamphetamine

- TWEAKING: High on amphetamines

- WAKE UPS: Amphetamines

As we have seen, more and more kids are quickly forming virtual coalitions against their parents; as caring parents we need to do the same thing. We need to mobilize our communities and form parent groups devoted to keeping these online drug businesses accountable for what they allow to happen. We need to be proactive in busting sites like Erowid.org and badgering sites like MySpace that do not effectively monitor age or content. No one else is going to take control; no one else is going to take the painstaking measures needed to shelter our kids from this insidious world of drugs.

I also recommend contacting a reputable drug-recovery center in your area with the purpose of arranging for your as-of-yet drug-free child to meet one-on-one with a recovering teen addict. Why? Well, kids are most honest with other kids, and a strong message of regret from one sixteen-year-old who has spent the last nine months in recovery may impact your child in a huge way. While we as parents should always be emphasizing the negative results of drug use, it is just that much more powerful when it comes from another, more experienced, teen. If tackling this unorthodox method feels overwhelming to you, I recommend your suggesting that your child's school host teen speakers who can share their stories; I have witnessed many of these programs, and they never disappoint.

Remember that you are your child's most important role model. She notices everything you do and say. If you use the Internet or your cell phone excessively, she interprets that as acceptable behavior. If she sees you drinking or doing drugs, she might think it's OK for her, too. If you make jokes about getting drunk or using drugs, or if you allow minors to drink in your home, your child might think that substance abuse is not a serious matter.

Conversely, if she knows you have an interest in getting to know her friends, she'll think the company she keeps is important. If she senses that you sincerely miss her when she shuts herself up in her room each night, she'll no longer use the Internet as her sanctuary. And if she has a wise adult in whom to confide, she'll come to realize her friends do not have all the answers.

Unsolicited Space

A Place for Porn

"Pornography is no longer a sideshow to the mainstream . . . it is the mainstream."

—*Frank Rich,* New York Times Magazine

"We have a good web blocker on our computer, and my son doesn't know the password. I'm not concerned about any pornographic images reaching his eyes."

—*Jill, parent*

"My daughter wanted to have a bikini party for her thirteenth birthday, but I wasn't all that comfortable with the idea. At one point she asked if they could all take their tops off and take pictures of each other . . . Where is she learning this?"

—*Veronica, parent*

"I just read the best book ever! It's the life story of a real porn actress; I couldn't put it down, Mrs. Kelsey. Can't you assign it for summer reading?!"

—*Sophia, 17*

Jenna Jameson is on MySpace. She has 797,288 friends. Tera Patrick has a profile, too—although she boasts a more modest 79,186 friends. Do these names sound familiar to you? Chances are your teenager knows exactly who they are, and could even be one of their "friends." Jenna and Tera are but two of today's many popular—and ubiquitous—porn stars.

You may be surprised at one of my students, as quoted above, openly sharing her excitement about a biography of a porn star with me, her English teacher, but I assure you that her candid approach is not rare these days. In fact, while I hosted an early Saturday morning advanced-placement practice exam session, one of my female students chose to bring a book of erotica to read in case she finished early. Without hesitation, she dove into the pages of this text in front of her peers and me. Strangely enough, I was the only one who took notice; apparently her fellow seventeen-year-olds were unfazed. Several years later, I was substitute teaching a class of seniors, and as is often the case, the absent teacher left barely enough work for his class. While circulating the room, I noticed a copy of *Maxim* magazine beneath a table; assuming it belonged to a boy, I asked the nearest gentleman to dispose of it. I was quickly chagrined to learn that it belonged to the girl sitting next to him. Happy to take any opportunity to talk to teens about real issues, we then engaged in a discussion about pornography, soft-core and hard-core, and what they thought about it.

I was eager to learn how and why this seventeen-year-old girl would not only purchase said magazine, but publicly share her interest in it. In an effort to crystallize what I'm sure you can imagine was a lively discussion, this young lady declared, "What's a girl to do when she's horny?" She was comfortable, proud even, advertising her sexual appetite and had no reservations exposing her urges to look at other women posed provocatively on the glossy pages of a soft-core magazine. It is my observation that teens today are incredibly comfortable with the existence of pornography; there's little shock value for the average teen who sees it on the Internet or in a magazine. Its presence has become as ubiquitous as television commercials for automobiles. And the result is a generation of teens who equate pornography with normal sexual expression. So what has pornography come to mean today?

Billboards advertising the euphemistic "gentlemen's clubs," pamphlets scattered across an urban sidewalk depicting women giving oral sex to men, websites dedicated to the chronicles of women who have sexual relations with animals, online pictorials boasting underage girls in compromising positions with other underage girls, digital photographs of scantily clad men and women posed in sexually provocative positions . . . the list goes on and on. Pornography ranges from soft core, without graphic sexual images or male nudity, to child pornography, the victimization and rape of young children who have been abducted and exploited. All of which find homes, and patrons, on the Internet—Internet porn is a $1 billion industry. It is not uncommon for a young child, for instance, to be searching for information on a science project and be confronted with an unsolicited pornographic image on screen. One evening I was searching for a large easy chair that would fit my toddler and myself while I nursed my new baby; I searched for "mother–daughter chairs" and hoped to find a good IKEA or Crate & Barrel link. Unfortunately, I was given a slew of options for mother–daughter sex videos, photos, and websites. At my age, I felt sick to my stomach. I can only imagine how a nine-year-old girl must feel when she is confronted with some of the images that pop up while she is searching for information on, say, flowers.

The pornography industry is vigorously trying to make porn mainstream, but let's not be fooled—it's still built on the degradation of women by way of "actresses," many of whom have been sexually abused as children. Psychiatric literature reports that at least 60 percent of female sex-industry workers have been molested as children, and, incidentally, suffer from dissociative identity disorder or post-traumatic stress disorder. As Bruce Watson and Shyla Rae Welch conclude in their article "Just Harmless Fun?" pornography is "not about real human sexuality: it's about a dehumanized, synthetic version of sex that eliminates love, honor, dignity, true intimacy, and commitment." Unfortunately, the commonplace presence of pornography in our culture today, especially for teens, results in a harmful ingestion of its damaging messages. The basic message of pornography—that a woman's sole function is to satisfy a man sexually—reinforces the stereotype that women have no value, no worth, no meaning beyond what they're willing to perform sexually on demand.

Exposure to Pornography *Is* Harmful to Children

Dr. Williams, a therapist who writes for *Enough Is Enough* (a magazine dedicated to educating parents about the dangers of online pornography), declares, "When a child experiences reality beyond their readiness, they have no means of processing the material intellectually or emotionally." Of course, not every child who witnesses pornographic images will be traumatized for life, but many certainly will suffer because of it. According to a recent study, one-third of all child molesters admitted to being aroused by pornography prior to committing their acts, and 53 percent of them deliberately sought out pornography in preparation for their crime. Eighty-seven percent of child molesters admitted to using pornographic images as a method of coercing their victims into thinking that because "this person is enjoying this act," their victim might like it, too.

Children also act out what they see; as parents we know that what our children witness, they are quick to imitate. This also goes for deviant sexual acts, unfortunately. In his study of six hundred junior high and older boys and girls, Dr. Jennings Bryant found that 66 percent of the males and 40 percent of the females who had been exposed to hard-core pornography reported having strong desires to try out the behaviors they had witnessed, and 31 percent of the high school males admitted to having acted out these fantasies in real life "within a few days after exposure." Finally, premature exposure to pornography has the strong potential to result in a damaged child, emotionally and psychologically. According to psychologist Dr. Victor Cline, pornography short-circuits and "distorts the normal personality development" of a sexually developing adolescent, leaving him or her "confused, changed, and damaged."

And since I am not ashamed to say that porn—*especially* in the presence of minors—is violent, damaging, and changing the face of society as we know it into a hostile place for healthy relationships, I'm here to usher you through the reality of the porn industry's unofficial relationship with teen hangouts like MySpace.com. As social commentator Rebecca Hagelin says, MySpace is a "pornographer's playground." Yes, most kids are using MySpace simply to hear new bands or keep in touch with friends from camp. However, it's now time for parents to sit up and take notice of the very real and conspicuous underbelly of this "place for friends."

Pornography and MySpace

The University of New Hampshire's Crimes Against Children Research Center recently published a report that revealed the rate at which young Internet users were exposed to unwanted sexual material has increased. In 2000, 25 percent of children saw pornography that seeped through online filters and monitoring software. By 2005, this figure was up to 34 percent—more than one-third of kids. Take, for instance, the nonprivate MySpace profile I recently came across that posts explicit photos of lesbian sex acts. On the profile, there were lists of pornographic movies to check out, recommended sex groups to join, links to porn-star profiles, and even video links for soft-core and hard-core porn movies. Am I shocked that this element exists on the Internet? Of course not. Am I intent on your realizing that at any time your child could land on this profile—or one of the thousands like it? You bet! Seventeen-year-old Aaron said, "I've learned more about what to ask a girl to do while surfing MySpace than looking at any magazine or video."

While it's virtually impossible to quantify the number of porn-actress profiles on MySpace, a rudimentary search using the phrase "porn star" uncovered over five thousand personal profiles. Keep in mind, many of these pages surely belong to amateurs and teenage porn-star wannabes; nevertheless, the point is that a large amount of MySpace profiles revolve around said goal. Let's take a peek at a legitimate porn actress's MySpace profile.

This woman begins by posting a super-glossy full-frontal shot of her body with only her nipples and a tiny strip of her crotch covered, and her blonde hair cascading down her bare, glittering shoulders. Her tagline is nothing worth mentioning, but the background music is Pat Benatar's "Hit Me with Your Best Shot." In her "About Me" paragraph, this porn star assures her fans, "Yes, it's really me! I will continue to shoot the hottest pics and movies you can sink your teeth into! So stay tuned, bitches, there's lots more to come!" Underneath an endless montage of half-naked beach, pool, and bathtub photographs (not without girl-on-girl poses), this star posts the groups to which she belongs, one of which is the "Sexiest Women of MySpace." Because this endeavor is her business, she wastes no time plugging her services, and prominently posts, "If you're interested in booking me for corporate events, celebrity promotions and club appearances, please email. . . !" Above her Friends List, she provides several erotic photos of herself, each with instructions on how to copy and paste the banners into one's own profile, clearly encouraging the sharing of her images around

MySpace. Finally, she has received a variety of messages from her friends, some of which are as follows: "Hi boys! Wanna see me [f**k] her? Wanna see me [f**k] on film? Cumming soon X," and, from a fourteen-year-old girl, "You are so gorgeous!"

Not only do porn stars have their own profiles available to all MySpace members, but porn companies also have a ubiquitous presence. MySpace hosts over 135 online groups catering to professional porn stars and additional groups devoted to amateur porn actors and actresses. Most of these groups are public, which means *anyone* who claims to be eighteen can join—and remember, MySpace is open and marketed to anyone age fourteen and over. A man whose profile calls him "Monstar," the leader of "Monstar's Porn Star Group" on MySpace, explains on www.xbiz.com that "MySpace has been exploding with porn stars. It's a great tool for many performers who just want to have a place on the Net where they can be easily found by friends and fans. The best part is they can literally build a page and be up and running in minutes." According to the same website, as of February, Monstar's profile boasts 3,409 friends and links to "more than 300 erotic performers with MySpace pages."

Use of the "Groups" feature on MySpace is a strategy used by adult entertainment companies to recruit visitors to their websites outside of MySpace. There are thousands of groups devoted to sex and pornography; in fact, one cull revealed the following groups actively operating on MySpace: "Sex in a Hot Tub," "Sex Fantasies," "Sex Addicts," "Casual Sex Wednesdays," "Cam Sex," "Web Cam Sex," "Gang Bang Sex Groupies," and "Sex Stories." Another such group is entitled "Mingle with Masturbators." I know about this one because I received what was I'm sure one of thousands of invitations to join their MySpace group—*even though that specific profile of mine claims I am only fifteen.* When the invitation arrived in my Inbox, I was asked to approve the invitation. As of now, there is no restriction on invitations to groups based on age. A group that is clearly rooted in adult content is free to contact your child with an invitation to join. Now, technically a minor is not allowed to join an adult group, but all our children have to do is alter their age to eighteen or older, and they are in. And once they're in, their profile picture is permanently displayed as a member of the group. I could find no way to delete membership from a group. Incidentally, as you can imagine, the group for masturbators offered all sorts of advice about how, where, when, and why to engage in the act, as well as several links to sites such as "Live Web Cam Performances by Wet Teens!"

Speaking of webcams, in fact, after setting up my own page, in just one weekend I received *over seventy solicitations from webcam girls*. How, I wondered, is this not being filtered out? These ladies prop themselves in front of their camera and either strip or perform sexual acts; often the appeal of webcam sex is the ability to direct or request actions for the person to perform. Thankfully, the dangerous world of webcam sex was made public by a *New York Times* investigative report on the experience of teen victim Justin Berry. From age thirteen through eighteen, this young man got sucked in further and further to the webcam industry, eventually setting up PayPal accounts for his adult customers. Justin first invested in a webcam as an effort to meet new friends; "I didn't really have a lot of friends," he recalled, "and I thought having a webcam might help me make some new ones online, maybe even meet some girls my age." But it quickly went wrong. What began as taking his shirt off on camera for a proposed $50 ended in his having sex with prostitutes live on camera in Mexico for $300 an hour—all for the voyeuristic delight of his customers. Even law-enforcement officials were baffled at the extent Justin's business had reached. "We've been aware of the use of the webcam and its potential use by exploiters," said Ernie Allen, chief executive of the National Center for Missing and Exploited Children, a private group. "But this is a variation on a theme that we haven't seen. It's unbelievable."

Links from a Porn Star's MySpace Profile

And while many MySpace profiles link to pornographic sites, take a look at the reverse. These are some of the results of my searching the Internet using the key words *MySpace* and *porn*:

- "Top MySpace Porn Sites" www.onthetopof.com
- "Looking for MySpace porn?" www.lycos.com
- "MySpace porn in the free online enclyclopedia" www.thefreedictionary.com
- "MySpace Porn" www.redzee.com
- "MySpace Porn on the Best Broadband Site on the Internet" www.heavy.com
- "MySpace Hotties" www.profile.myspace.com/hotties (a profile on MySpace that encourages users to "rate hotties" and "browse 1000s of photos of sexy singles")
- "Suicide Girls" (the first blog site that appears when a user clicks on the "Blogs" tab on the MySpace home page; this blog is nothing short of a soft-core porn site)
- Or take a look at the MySpace group called "We Jerk It to MySpace Pics" at http://groups.myspace.com/jerkofftomyspace, whose name says it all.

MySpace Policy

So what does Rupert Murdoch think of all this? While I was unable to reach him for comment, he has claimed in interviews that his "underlying philosophy is that all media are one." While he may not be directly speaking to the issue of pornography, he makes apparent that, to him, there exists a solidarity among all genres of media and mediated information.

Let it be understood that the official MySpace stance is to forbid any pornographic images on the site; in fact, their Terms of Use forbid any content that "contains nudity, violence, or offensive

 213

subject matter or contains a link to an adult website," and they explicitly threaten to delete any accounts that violate this rule. Did I hear a collective sigh of relief from parents everywhere? Well, I feel more comfortable knowing that the MySpace folks are aware of and officially opposed to the existence of adult content on the site. However, we obviously should not take this at face value. First, let's ask *why* they even need to include this edict in their Terms of Use. Clearly, there is a serious presence of porn on the site. Second, let's assess the reality of their monitoring the space for such material: with only approximately two hundred employees at MySpace (of which only a third are allocated to regulate content) and over 140 million existing profiles, can they really regulate as well as they (and we) would like? I repeatedly contacted MySpace about these issues, but did not receive a response. My first question would be: *Why don't you start by investigating users with names like "hornyslut-girls"?* In fact, I would be interested in knowing exactly how many profiles have been deleted by the MySpace hall monitors. Of all the teens I interviewed for this book, not one knew of a person who had had his profile deleted for offending the Terms of Use, although they knew of many that had violated the terms. Remember, MySpace is a business, and deleting customers is bad for any business.

I think it's safe to say that there is no lack of adult content being generated via MySpace, however they manage to skirt Hemanshu Nigam's radar. My next questions for Mr. Nigam: Why are well-known porn stars like Jenna Jameson allowed to have MySpace profiles without the risk of being deleted? Why are minors permitted to access them? Why are so many sexually explicit MySpace pages falling through the proverbial cracks?

And, what exactly is the relationship between MySpace and livebycam.com?

Advertisers are noticing. What do Weight Watchers, Verizon, and

Starwood Hotels have in common? Well, all three deserve our kudos. Apparently, the proliferation of inappropriate content on MySpace inspired them to pull their advertising from the site. Meanwhile, recently *Playboy* magazine established its own MySpace page; they also purchased ad space. (I'm not sure how this purchase was approved considering the Terms of Use we looked at earlier—are you noticing some contradictions?) The purpose of *Playboy's* arrival on MySpace? They promoted a search for women to pose in an issue devoted to a pictorial spread called "The Girls of MySpace." The magazine's editor, John Thomas, explained, "MySpace is a very hot piece of pop culture," and they didn't want to miss out on the buzz. Please make note that MySpace did not "participate" in the pictorial, but according to Thomas, "They are, as I understand it, [OK] with us being embedded in their site." So much for disassociating from "nudity . . . or adult content" as stated in MySpace's Terms of Use. *Where are you, Mr. Nigam?*

Official MySpace
Terms of Use

"You are solely responsible for the Content that you post on or through any of the MySpace Services, and any material or information that you transmit to other Members and for your interactions with other Users. MySpace.com does not endorse and has no control over the Content. Content is not necessarily reviewed by MySpace.com prior to posting and does not necessarily reflect the opinions or policies of MySpace.com. MySpace.com makes no warranties, express or implied, as to the Content or to the accuracy and reliability of the Content or any material or information that you transmit to other Members."

How Is MySpace Any Different?

Some may argue that sexual images are simply a part of our culture; kids see more sexually charged content just walking down a busy street than being on MySpace. And I agree—it's everywhere. During one spring while teaching at a private middle/high school in West Hollywood, I left my classroom around 4:00 PM and began exiting the all but empty building. While fumbling with my oversize leather bag, I noticed a bevy of flyers tacked to the walls, restroom doors, water fountains, and lockers advertising our annual school fund-raiser. Much to my chagrin, however, these flyers used sexualized images of women: for example, one was a close-up shot of a woman's red-lipstick-layered mouth, her tongue seductively licking a string of pearls between her teeth. In my outrage, I tore one down and went straight to our assistant principal. Within minutes the school's director of development, who engineered the campaign, was calling me a prude. He defended these inappropriate flyers with that annoying cliché, "Sex sells." If a school fund-raiser can drive a career educator to feel justified in using sexual images to attract the attention of sixth-grade students, imagine what the men and women of the porn industry are willing to do.

So, yes, sexual imagery is in our faces relentlessly; however, there is a difference when it comes to your teen and MySpace. The physical relationship between a child and a computer or other electronic device is quite personal; it's one-on-one, it's not a group activity. In short, your child is surfing alone. And we all know the pitfalls of being alone when facing a temptation. Also, many times kids are on the site late at night, even into the wee hours of the morning, a time when exhaustion sets in and good judgment seems to doze off. But beyond that scenario, what are the other new ways these images could be reaching your teen?

Murdoch's Marketing Factory

As adults we know that the kids who tend to be leaders are quite influential in their peers' lives, whether for better or worse. But what marketing companies realize is that those so-called leaders are still young and inexperienced and can, therefore, also be easily influenced by advertising. Once called "opinion leaders" or "trendspotters" by marketers, today's teenage leaders are aptly dubbed "influencers." These teens are working feverishly to "net" the eyeballs of their friends and serve them up for a good old fashioned corporate American fish fry.

According to Teenage Research Unlimited (TRU), the much-quoted youth marketing research outfit, "influencers" are that 10 or 12 percent that the majority of kids, or as they put it, "conformers," look to for their advice. MySpace has no lack of influencers operating successfully on the site; in fact, it's the fastest growing trend on MySpace. In a new study by Jupiter Research, 22 million teens are online, and 17 percent of them are potential "teen influencers," a group that is highly active online, style conscious, popular, and *extremely persuasive.* These influencers are usually a little older and wealthier than the average teen, spend more hours a week on the Net, and are 53 percent female. Most Americans are familiar with the blurring of commercials and entertainment, just look at the excitement surrounding the Super Bowl advertisements, but the idea of blurring commercials with socializing is novel at best and degrading at worst. Teen influencers mark a new low in corporate marketing strategy.

Jacquie, a fifteen-year-old private high school student in Los Angeles, received a flyer at an underage teen club in Hollywood; the flyer caught her eye because of its glossy, sexy look, and because the tag line claimed to need her help. Jacquie contacted the phone number on the card and quickly became involved in what she thinks is an "exciting, important mission." She is in charge of advertising local strip club events to all her MySpace friends, and she actively sends messages to boys and girls in her "extended network" of acquaintances. She's the perfect influencer because she has a powerful presence on MySpace, interacting with hundreds of other teens. Let me reiterate that she is fifteen. Why would she participate in this exchange? Well, she's not making any money, but she does get to feel important, pretend she's a rebel, and get a lot of attention from her male classmates. Influencers are the Oompa-Loompahs of Murdoch's cyber factory — used, happy, and manipulated into feeling important.

The Mini-Porn Industry

Explicit and suggestive images are also making their way into other forms of technology. Recently my husband decided to trade in his antiquated cell phone for a modest upgrade; apparently the sand-encrusted, faded number pad finally got to him. When he brought the new phone home, I decided to help him out by setting up all his exciting new options. After deleting all the random numbers our three-year-old had entered over the years, I decided to find him a fun screen saver. I was quite surprised when, amid images of balloons, cats, and city skylines, I was faced with an option entitled "Hot Girls." So now it's a standard feature on any cell phone to download pictures of half-naked women in sexual poses? Considering every teenager I know has a cell phone (and usually they demand the latest, most expensive models), it is more than likely that they would have access to the "Hot Girls" feature. And the fact that it is even an option, a standard option, sends a message— both to girls and to boys. Adolescent girls are reminded daily that their objectification is integral to their value, and that they had better start sexualizing their image in order to have any chance at all to get a boy's attention. Our culture has embraced the adult entertainment mantra of sex now, sex everywhere, and sex without relationship. The major risk with boys' exposure to mainstreamed soft-core porn is tenfold; we have an entire generation of boys who are at risk of not being able to see women as human beings worthy of respect and who may not be able to have fulfilling monogamous relationships. As parents, we need to be aware of these subtle ways our children's innocence is compromised.

Pornography is no longer a desktop plague; it is spreading to all the small-screen, pocket-sized electronic devices that our kids so cherish. According to Jason Lee Miller, WebProNews.com staff writer, one-fifth of all mobile Internet Google searches in 2005 were for adult content. (Don't forget . . . MySpace just teamed up with Google!) In fact, according to CNET News.com, mobile phone users spent roughly $400 million on pornographic pictures in 2005. The prediction for 2006? $791 million.

And what do Spiepod.com and OnTheGox.com have in common? Both are popular websites that offer adult films specially made for iPods. That's right, for as little as $4.99 anyone with iPod access can download a pornographic video, known as "podporn" in the business. Just like MySpace, the iPod is no longer just for music! When Apple's Steve Jobs announced the video feature on the new iPod, the adult entertainment industry organized faster than ants at a Fourth of July picnic.

Handheld pornography, or, as an industry veteran labeled it, "flesh-colored crack," is a global business. In Japan, for example, adult film companies released pornographic videos compatible for download onto the Sony PlayStation Portable in 2005, as reported in the *Washington Post*. Clearly, any concern for the age of users is erased by the need to be the most edgy and most image-heavy device on the market. The appeal of porn on such small screens is the anonymity and privacy afforded to the user, as well as the inability of parents (or spouses) to monitor or filter the content. And the porn is always at your side for private viewing; there's no need to be in your home, to stay up late, to surreptitiously switch to a screen of solitaire cards when someone walks in—just slip the cell phone or the MP3 player into your pocket or backpack. These products are in such demand that peddlers are getting very rich.

Porn Is Knocking on Your Child's Door

Harvey Kaplan is an Internet porn veteran who pioneered his company, Xobile, to exclusively sell porn for cell phone and hand-held devices, and his business is booming. With over a thousand manufacturers, he offers in excess of 100,000 movies on his site currently. His goal? To provide those people who "are searching for adult content right now on the web" the ability to "download this stuff to their handheld cell phone, PDA, iPod, and carry it around with them." Kaplan expects wireless adult content to become a multimillion-dollar business by 2008; he explains, "Most people won't buy a 3G cell phone so they can access a Disney trailer, but they will for adult content." The way it works is fascinating. Guys like Kaplan do not have to cajole any mainstream carriers like Verizon Wireless and Sprint Nextel to associate themselves with his company, because the pornographic videos can be downloaded straight to the consumer via the Internet. Any mini electronic device that boasts of Internet capability has total access to the Xobile photo collection. The hottest new cell phone on the market, the Helio "don't call it a phone" gadget, is being marketed heavily to teens for its ability to offer MySpace access in the palm of your hand. And in December 2006, Cingular inked a deal with MySpace to offer the site on its phones as well.

On MySpace, however, few users have even heard of Xobile; there, the photo archive of choice is Photobucket.com, a free site founded in 2003 that lets users store photos and videos with the intent to be displayed elsewhere (usually MySpace). The company is arguably the heart of the image obsession thriving on the site. In an article from the *Pittsburgh Post Gazette*, Photobucket founder and CEO Alex Welch says, "MySpace would be very dark without

Photobucket content." Unfortunately, many of the images stored and accessed via Photobucket are pornographic and making their way onto MySpace pages. As far as the MySpace Terms of Use are concerned, please note that MySpace in no way has condoned any ads for pornography. However, there is really no way to stop adult website companies from sending users messages "directly through their profiles," according to the same article. And they do.

Take a look at this sample e-mail sent to a teenage girl's MySpace account:

> Hey! i know this is really random but i found your myspace under "cool new people" and im looking to get the word out about that bitch Katie Holmes. i found her sex tape for free online @ CelebrityPornCam.com. can you believe it? this site is crazy, with sex tapes of Angelina Jolie, Jennifer Lopez, and Britney Spears all for free. anyway go check it out, and hit me back with a message if you liked the site as much as me!

The method to their madness is this: first, these adult companies sign up multiple MySpace accounts and upload alluring photos to pepper the profiles and attract interested users. Then, these companies send out endless friend requests in the hopes that their profile will be viewed. Of course, on each profile are links to adult porn sites that aggressively solicit users to sign up. While one way to fight this insidious method is for teens to report the profiles using the "Flag as Spam/Abuse" safety tab provided by MySpace, the reality is that not many fifteen-year-old boys are likely to scroll down to the option after being barraged by these kinds of images. Plus, once a teenager clicks on such a MySpace profile, his page is likely to be flagged as one to flood with solicitations. Keep in mind that most porn companies have automated programming devices that send mass spam messages to any and all profiles with no deference to age or gender. The sad reality is that parents (and children) are somewhat helpless against such obvious attacks that take place on MySpace.

The Cool Girl

Unfortunately for our adolescent girls, they fall prey to the pressure to compete with such images. One of my female students shared her frustration with the climate of high school parties today. She lamented that it has become as commonplace for a high school party to have some alcohol and occupied bedrooms as a wide-screen television displaying a continual stream of pornographic movies. "You have no idea how bad it is to be a teenage girl today, Mrs. Kelsey," she told me. When I asked if anyone thought of turning the TV off and explaining it was offensive, she laughed. "Why would I get myself blacklisted from the good party scene?" she asked, apparently shocked by my naïveté.

The truth is, teenage girls don't stand up alone against this porn culture for a variety of reasons. First of all, there is an inordinate amount of pressure on girls to prove that they are the "cool" girl-friend who can "hang with" the guys. The most coveted label for a girl is "she's cool," meaning she doesn't challenge any of the guys. If my student had acted outraged by the porn and demanded that somebody turn it off, what would have happened? She would have been laughed out of the party not only by the guys, but particularly by the other girls who are more concerned with earning the label "cool girl" than preserving any semblance of sisterhood. Plus, an opportunity to out a fellow female at a party is rare and cannot be overlooked; chances are, in this girl–against–girl social hierarchy, the other girls would turn have turned on my student, ostracizing her rather than supporting her. After all, the goal for most teen girls in these scenarios is to impress a guy or to get attention from a group of guys, and what better way to do that than to scoff at the prude who questioned the sex flick? And how much more of a prude must she feel like if these images are "normal" each time she signs on to her "place for friends," a place that is so integral to her social life?

While some girls are merely gritting their teeth and tolerating it, others are joining in. I found the following blog on MySpace written by a sixteen-year-old girl. She brags,

> You may think I'm quiet and shy, but once you get to know me for real, you'd be surprised. What I do in private is CRAZY! I'm on [MySpace] to meet YOU because I'm bored....LMAO... Help me do some modeling if you can... I'm OBSESSED with being a porn star!

While she obviously has very real self-esteem issues and clearly is striving to receive validation from boys, what she may also receive is an invitation to actually *be* in porn. Look at the following "Who I'd Like to Meet" statement from an actual porn company executive's MySpace profile:

> I make smut. [I'd like to meet] Cool people not kids but young adults or people who fell like young adults that are open minded and like porn and want to be apart of my movement to make it better... If you want to be a porn star... I'm the guy that can make that happen for real... but I'll look you in the eye first to make sure you can hang... any Emo, punk, or goth kids... your all my friends... be stylish and cute as hell.

Why are young girls clamoring to be porn stars? As I mentioned in chapter 1, many girls are happily acting out fantasies of celebrity via their profiles. The opportunity to post photos from their weekend jaunts, blogs describing the amazing things that happened to them that day, and a collection of fans in the form of a Friends List all provide the grist for the celebrity mill these girls crave. Unfortunately, it doesn't stop there. In a culture that allows porn-star autobiographies on the top sellers list and broadcasts the annual Adult Video News Awards, while mainstream television shows like *Flavor of Love* glorify female prostitution, it is no mystery that sexually blossoming tweens and teens feel drawn to experimenting with exhibitionism.

"If I don't make out with my friends at parties, some other whore will, and then where will I be? Nowhere!" says Leah, sixteen. When I was in high school, it was commonplace for girls to have nose jobs, but today I can name several former female students of mine who negotiated breast augmentations as high school graduation gifts from their parents. Taking it a step further, is it any wonder that the hottest new plastic surgery procedure is vaginoplasty, a restructuring of the vaginal labia to resemble those of porn stars/models? Our girls are feeling like they have to degrade themselves to the level of porn actress in order to get noticed.

Teens At Risk

"One day I was hanging out with a friend when I was twelve. My friend showed me some pictures. I looked up websites and things would pop up and lead to other sites. It led me to having sexual intercourse at age thirteen, trying to do what I saw on the Internet."

—*Bill*

"When I was ten, my sister's boyfriend and I opened up a website on pornography. It caused me to be curious. I wanted to see more.

My mom wanted to take me to Wet & Wild Water Park. I got on the Internet and typed in 'Wet & Wild' to find out how much it cost. When I clicked on the site, it was lesbian pornography; more pop-ups came and hours of this went on. I saved more than 1,000 pictures on floppy disk and printed them out. It's amazing how the words 'Wet & Wild' can lead you to something entirely different that will get you into bondage. It corrupted my mind. When I would see a girl all I could picture was seeing them naked. I judged girls on their body, and not their personality."

—*Hosea*

—*Courtesy of Donna Hughes Rice, www.protectkids.com*

Former attorney general John Ashcroft predicted that nine in ten teens have been exposed to pornographic images. That's an awfully large percentage of teens, especially since many of these teens are susceptible to developing addictions or compulsions to view these images. Remember our discussion in chapter 1 about the seven key vulnerabilities of teens: *Separation, independence, peer influence, role model influence, need for control, experimentation,* and *sex appeal.* Also, recall the teen brain research that substantiates why teens are particularly susceptible to addictions of all kinds. The term *addict* may not sit well with some parents. Most parents will initially minimize the problem, hoping their son or daughter is simply "experimenting." Today, however, Internet pornography is a potential path to sex addiction. Remember that children's minds are still in the process of developing to maturity, and addiction can happen quicker than we would like to think.

While there is no recognized Internet pornography addiction as a mental illness, the American Psychiatric Association does acknowledge sexual addiction as a legitimate disorder. According to the *Diagnostic and Statistical Manual of Mental Disorders,* sexual addicts "are those who engage in persistent and escalating patterns of sexual behavior acted out despite increasingly negative consequences to self and to others." According to psychologist Patrick Carnes, a researcher who was instrumental in the initial identification and treatment of the condition, over fifteen million people in the late 1970s suffered from this disorder; the figures are much higher today. The following is a list of addictive disorder criteria, from TeenPaths.org:

"Some experts suggest that if three or more of any of the following are concluded about your teen and this continues for more than thirty days, that they may be considered an addict.

- Frequent engaging in a behavior to a greater extent or over a longer period than intended
- Persistent desire for the behavior or one or more unsuccessful efforts to reduce or control the behavior
- Much time spent in activities necessary for the behavior, engaging in the behavior or recovering from its effects
- Frequent preoccupation with the behavior or preparatory activities
- Frequent engaging in the behavior when expected to fulfill occupational, academic, domestic, or social obligations
- Giving up or limiting important social, occupational, or recreational activities because of the behavior
- Continuation of the behavior despite knowledge of having a persistent or recurrent social, financial, psychological, or physical problem that is caused or exacerbated by the behavior
- Need to increase the intensity or frequency of the behavior to achieve the desired effect, or diminished effect with continued behavior of the same intensity
- Restlessness or irritability if unable to engage in the behavior"

Reread the above checklist with the idea of your child's relationship with the Internet, specifically Internet porn or sex, at the forefront of your mind. Should you be concerned?

In an article titled "The Cyber Porn Generation" published in *People* magazine in April 2004, "thirteen-year-old Ryan Cleary . . . admits to looking at Internet porn occasionally as a kind of research tool, so he'll know more about what he's supposed to do with girlfriends." Adolescents, boys especially, are particularly hormonally charged, but the typical male fascination with seeing women undressed is not at issue here. Healthy curiosity and experimentation with things sexual are integral to the coming-of-age of both boys and girls. However, an unhealthy amount of exposure to unhealthy images is a concern. In the same *People* article, young Troy Busher says cyberporn skewed his view of women. "'A guy starts treating a girl like a ho,' he says. 'They're just a piece of meat. Not a person with a name, history, feelings.'" After all, according to Eric Griffin Shelley, author of *Sex & Love: Addiction, Treatment & Recovery*, "The beginnings of sexual addiction are usually rooted up in adolescence."

During this time of extreme emotions and frequent feelings of boredom and anxiety coupled with increasing hormonal developments, adolescents often look to sexual experimentation as a replacement act. Many addicts, especially teens, do not publicly seek stimulation; instead they find fulfillment surfing the Internet for hours. The *DSM* criteria note that such teens spend extensive time "surfing the Net, downloading and reading information on sex bulletins, and exchanging sexual information with others in sexual chat rooms or directing their own live sex shows on interactive sites." And it makes sense, since the Internet provides the isolation, secrecy, fantasy, and total availability that sex addicts crave.

What You Can Do

I trust my daughter; she would never click on any of these pornographic sites. My son is a good kid; he knows better. We have blocking software, so I'm not concerned. I've told my son to report any sexual stuff that shows up on his MySpace page. Sound familiar? While it's important to trust our children and terrific that so many parents are doing so, and have had conversations about the adult content on MySpace, the reality is that some teenagers in the throes of puberty are unable to effectively process even the most tame solicitations or images. Our kids are trustworthy, but it's the adult entertainment industry that is not ... and that is aggressively searching for girls like your daughter. This industry wants to hook as many young people as possible.

Dr. Harris Faigel, a Boston-based pediatrician specializing in adolescent medicine, explains, "Children start having sexual feelings around the age of four. Those feelings don't go away and suddenly reappear at puberty. It's important for parents to treat ongoing questions about sex as they would any other part of their child's education." Remember not to discourage your child's curiosity, especially when he or she comes to you with the questions; once our children learn that we are not willing to talk about sex, they won't stop searching, they'll just search elsewhere. Debra Haffner, former president and CEO of Sex Information and Education Council of the United States (SIECUS), advises: "Don't wait for your teens to ask you about sex—they may not. We don't wait to talk to our kids about other important matters of health and safety. Why should the subject of sex be any different?" In fact, it should be one of the most important topics we broach with our children. The healthy sexual development of our kids determines so much of who they become and how they find fulfillment in the world.

Fifteen-year-old Miles kept the top drawer of his bedroom desk locked; the key was hidden in a tin of mints at the back corner of his school locker. His parents had no reason to suspect anything inappropriate taking place in Miles's social life. He did fine in school, played soccer, talked to girls on the phone occasionally, and, like most teens, complained of being tired each morning. The locked drawer seemed harmless to his mother, who was adamant about allowing her son his privacy; in her mind, he had pictures of a girl he liked in there, or maybe some love notes he wanted to protect.

However, when Miles's mother received a call from the computer teacher at school, she became puzzled. Why would Miles pilfer stacks of computer disks? Little did she know, Miles was stockpiling hundreds of disks to house his thousands of pornographic downloads. But it wasn't until Miles's mom became suspicious of repeated charges for a strange website on her credit card statements that she decided to confront her son. Late one night, Miles's mother entered his room to find his bed covered in disks and her son feverishly typing away at his computer, sending pornographic images to his cyber-friends.

If you are concerned that your son or daughter has developed an unhealthy relationship with pornography via exposure either on MySpace or the Internet in general, what should you do? The first bit of advice is to accept that as devastating as this realization may be, the fact that you have made the realization puts you ahead of the game. Also, I implore you to look at your choices regarding the intake of sexual images into your home. In the words of the nineteenth-century humorist Josh Billings, "To bring up a child in the way he should go, travel that way yourself once in a while." In other words, if you've got a stack of *Playboy* magazines in the master bathroom, you may have a difficult time communicating to your teen about his or her relationship with pornography. Barring such a situation, once you have accepted the impact these images have had on your child, pat yourself on the back, have a good cry, and take steps to help your child.

Five Steps to a Porn-Free Teen

1. Take Responsibility

Don't start pointing fingers; chances are that everyone in the child's life bears some level of ownership. As a parent, ask yourself how proactive you have been in providing an open and healthy means of discussion regarding sex. Have you emphasized and reinforced how special sex is, how sacred it is, or have you reinforced the view of sex as casual? What messages about sexual relations have you exposed your child to over the formative years? Reevaluate the types and frequency of media you have allowed into your home. Do you or your spouse subscribe to or house any pornographic materials for your own consumption? Are the television programs, video games, and lyrics you take in promoting respectful messages about sexuality or are they slowly eroding such principles of human dignity in your child's mind? Finally, please don't overlook the possibility of sexual abuse in your child's past; more times than not, a traumatic sexual experience like incest, rape, or inappropriate touching can lead an adolescent into the world of pornography. Acknowledgment and treatment of the abuse is paramount if healing is to occur.

2. Don't Minimize the Problem

It is easy to want to sweep this problem under the proverbial rug. But you want your own teen to face up to a frightening, and embarrassing, problem, so you have to model the courage to deal with unpleasant things, too. That's not to say that the climate of the home may become one of awkward silences, explosive reactions, and unexplained tears, but please realize that your child is most likely feeling quite ashamed. Encouragement, compassion, and love are the three most productive tools at this time. Don't feel discouraged if your child resists all of the above; your job is to persist. Also, many teens will promise never to look at porn again—if this occurs, please do not consider the problem solved! If your child struggles with pornography or is acting out sexually, chances are the behavior did not occur overnight, and neither will the solution. Remember, just because your child got caught does not mean he is suddenly able to control his behavior.

3. Establish Family Principles of Integrity

The main difficulty in holding your child accountable in this manner is the personal nature of the addiction; it touches the very core of one's secret desires, intimacy, and private life. The best way to remove the personal aspect of the problem is to make it about the family's principles of integrity. Sit down as a family and discuss your core values at length; create an agreed-upon list of what behaviors are acceptable in your family and what behaviors are a breach. Then, when your child is tempted to look at porn, he or she will be at risk of violating a well-defined, published set of core family principles. While the addiction is still highly personal, it is now public within the family, and accountability is at work rather than shame.

4. Set Firm Boundaries

While boundaries may not instantly change a child's behavior, they do communicate that you are serious about an issue and that you love them enough to enforce difficult parameters. In this situation, you must regulate the media input your child receives: Internet usage only with adult supervision, filtering and monitoring software, television set removed from bedroom, cell phone package restricted without any image or picture options, iPod downloads blocked, etc. While these restrictions may feel too strict or even Draconian, remember to institute them out of love—communicate on a regular basis with your child; don't just cut them off from all their gadgets. Conversation must take place *every day*.

In addition to the now standard video camera feature on most laptop computers, cell phones also come equipped with camera capabilities. For the sex or porn addict, the temptation is too great to avoid recording inappropriate pictures. Also, most cell phones offer some database of images of bikini-clad or scantily clothed females for the downloading. Most recently, of course, is the technology of downloading actual pornography, stills, and movies onto phones, iPods, PDAs, and even video-game consoles. Be wary before you buy your child the latest electronic device; do your research and find out what the darn thing is actually capable of and then ask yourself if you want your child to face that temptation.

5. Seek Professional Help

It is up to you to make that difficult phone call; I realize it is one thing to call a counselor and explain your child has depression and quite another to explain that your child has a problem with pornography. But the way I see it, that is all the more reason to be aggressive in getting your child help—it's a big deal, it's scary, and it's not going away. There are many therapists who specialize in teen porn addiction, and they will equip you to approach your child. Don't feel defeated if it reaches this point—teenagers are incredibly resilient, especially when they feel loved and nurtured by their parents.

How to Report Pornographic Images on MySpace

Some pornographic images are displayed on the main profile page of a user; however, other photos are only accessible by selecting the "View My Pics" link beneath the member's name and picture. Once you've clicked on this link, a full gallery of photos will be opened (assuming you are a member yourself—you cannot view pictures without a MySpace account, which is less a safety measure and more an incentive to lure new users). If you feel one of these photographs is pornographic and would like to report it to MySpace, follow these simple steps:

1. Click the "Report This Image" link beneath the specific picture you wish to report.
2. A pop-up window will ask you: "Are you sure you want to report this image as inappropriate?"
3. Click "OK" to proceed with your report.
4. Next, you will see a page detailing MySpace's policies on inappropriate images; you will be asked: "Do you want to report this image for us to review?"
5. Click "Report This Image."
6. Wait patiently for a response.

These steps apply for the overwhelmingly inappropriate classified ads posted on MySpace as well. Since there are no restrictions on fourteen-year-olds accessing these frequently sexually explicit ads ("*horny college student seeks orgy partners*"), the most we as parents can do is to report the ones that violate MySpace policy.

Protecting Your Child

Most of my research regarding pornography on the Internet and its access by teenagers revealed a prevailing attitude that "there's nothing you can do about it." The majority of advice to parents of teens consists of platitudes such as, "Teach your child to look the other way" or, "Avoid that site." Ideally, yes, but you know that a sexually curious preteen or teen will have difficulty looking the other way, and you know that exposure to deviant sexual images is harmful to the sexual identity formation of a child. So how do you go about monitoring your child's Internet usage and protecting your child? Here are some techniques.

Install the most up-to-date remote filtering software on all computers (home, desktop, laptop, etc.) and demand that your school's computer lab do the same.

Contact the parents of your child's friends and share with them your excitement about the newest content-blocking software you have discovered; you can't tell them what to do, but you sure can provide a positive example for them.

Don't shelter your child from the presence and importance of sex.

The worst thing you could do is try to keep your preteen or teen in the dark about sex; you must accept that he or she *is* a sexual being, has real desires, and will pursue knowledge about sexuality in one way or another. It is up to you to hold the reins and ensure that this exploration is healthy and productive, not damaging and destructive. Let your child know that sexual urges are normal, but that acting on them prior to being in a committed relationship can cause very real emotional pain, especially for girls. I recommend reading Lauren F. Winner's book *Real Sex* either on your own or with your teenager. Winner provides a down-to-earth tone that most teens will appreciate, and she explains the not-so-emphasized but vital risks involved in acting on our every sexual craving. Advocating abstinence with teens is terribly ineffective without candid discussion. Taking the approach that all things sexual are bad or prurient is just as damaging as being exposed to pornography, I would argue. If sex is so ugly, a teen may reason, then why is everyone so obsessed with it? *As parents we must emphasize the beauty of sex.* It is only then that a teenager will be able to see how ugly the perversions are.

Educate your child on the "business" of sex.

Take opportune moments to point out the marketing value of sexy images in an effort to elucidate your child as to his or her status as a pawn, a consumer. Walk your child through the logic behind *why adult entertainment companies exist.* Help them to see the ploy to make money at any cost. Some of my students struggle with this discussion, arguing that "if it makes money, how can you blame them?" To which I respond, "Then what's wrong with men who kidnap toddlers and force them into child pornography or drug dealers that prey on elementary school students? They are just making money!" That usually works, but it really takes a series of discussions to affect any shift in this generation's reverence for corporate moneymakers. I also recommend exposing them to the ugly facts surrounding the behaviors that exposure to pornography encourages—incest, child molestation, drug use, addiction, inability to have meaningful relationships (especially marriages), suicide, and, of course, STDs and AIDS. Contact a local teen crisis center or pregnancy center to find out about programs dealing with these issues, either for you and your child to attend or to request your school to book for an assembly.

Begin a petitioning or letter-writing campaign demanding that cell phone companies, PDA companies, MP3 player brands, etc., research, invent, and offer filtering options.

As you know, the home computer is now only one of many ways your child can be exposed to pornography via the Internet. There has to be real pressure on handheld electronic device companies to take responsibility for their Internet features, especially since they market so heavily to teens.

All of the above.

Yes, it takes quite a bit of work to usher your teen into this new terrain of being a sexual being in a sex-saturated culture, but such is the work of good parenting.

Your Assignment

This assignment might not be that easy. We've discussed the prevalence of sexual images barraging our teens on a daily basis and from every angle; we've looked at how a website like MySpace.com, geared toward teens as young as fourteen, is unable to effectively regulate the presence of adult content; we've learned that teens are particularly vulnerable to sex image addiction and looked at the emotional and sexual well-being of our teens. Now I challenge you to go a step further.

For five to seven days, take an intensive inventory of the image intake in your family's life. This means keeping a log or a journal to record each sexual image you encounter. I caution you that, at first, you may not see many because your eyes are so accustomed to them. However, really work to heighten your awareness of the billboards, the sides of buses, the television commercials, the pop-ups on your e-mail account, the magazine covers on your coffee table, etc. Jot down a daily list including each image, describing it, and then, at the end of the day, write a few paragraphs in response to the images you saw—*what do they communicate, how do they make you feel, and how might they shape your teen?* At the end of the week, reread the entire journal. Record your thoughts and reflections. Don't take any actions immediately; chances are that this exercise has been a bit overwhelming, and you need to let your reflections and observations settle. But after about a week or ten days, I recommend the final step: sharing your realizations and epiphanies with your teenager. Talk about the images that flooded your week; discuss the power such exposure has over both you and your teen. While this conversation may be awkward at first, I promise that it will afford a newfound level of intimacy, trust, and sincerity between you and your child. And isn't that what we want more than anything?

Taking the Tour

Getting to Know Your Cyber-Child

"When you're a mother, it's not called invading privacy, it's called 'cleaning.'"

—*Roseanne Arnold in* Roseanne

"If my mom ever looked at my MySpace page, I would flip out. I mean, it's none of her business; it's for me and my friends only. It's my private space. Like my underwear drawer."

—*Marta, 15*

"My dad's seen my page, and he's cool with it. My mom, on the other hand, would lose it if she knew how I talked on there. She couldn't handle the language."

—*Calvin, 14*

"I would never take a peek at my son's MySpace. It's his special place, and it clearly means a lot to him. Why would I pry into it? I trust his judgment anyway."

—*J. P., parent*

"I regularly check my daughter's MySpace page—and her friends' pages, too. I don't care what anyone thinks; she's a child and I'm in charge of her, and I take that pretty seriously. When she's eighteen, I'll stop checking up on her . . . I think."

—*Carla, parent*

"My daughter has accused me of stalking her; however, as I explained to her, I have a very real challenge: how can I allow her privacy and autonomy when she continually breaks our family's Internet usage rules? I told her, 'Until you are able to make better choices, I will continue to monitor your Internet activity.'"

—*Jenique, parent*

Does My Child Have a Profile?

How can you tell if your teen participates in MySpace? If she's not already mentioning it, one way to know is simply to ask her neutrally: *Do you have a MySpace? Have you ever had one?* Most teens I know would answer honestly; after all, they don't see anything wrong with the site. The only reason some secrecy may enter into the picture is if they feel condemned for having a MySpace profile, which of course is not the approach you will be taking. So, assuming your child shares with you that yes, he or she does have a MySpace page, the next issue is whether or not to view your child's page.

I recommend wholeheartedly that you make every effort to establish proper trust and credibility with your child in order to make him feel comfortable enough to show you his page. Quite frankly, your goal is to be privy to your child's cyber-world and cyber-personality. As the parent, this information is vital. However, being ushered in is a delicate procedure, one that requires patience, timing, self-reflection, and courage. And believe me, your child will be scrutinizing your every move once you bring up the concept of his MySpace page, so be ready to handle this strategic step.

First, patience is key. If you've ever owned a cat, you know that they operate on their own schedule. But there are those moments when they crawl onto your lap and purr for an hour. The secret is waiting, respecting their space, and knowing that eventually they will approach you because, really, they want your attention. Your teen is just an overgrown cat (who makes a lot more of a mess). Plant the seed that you are interested in the whole MySpace scene, but then do nothing else about it. The idea that you are interested will percolate long enough for them to either ask you about it or to obsess about it with their friends.

Second, timing is everything. Approaching your teen with the idea of viewing her MySpace page while she is in the midst of a fight with a friend, working on a stressful paper for school, agonizing over which boy to ask to the holiday dance, or stewing about how many chores she has to do on the weekend is counterproductive. (I realize it's an odd moment when she's *not* stressed out—but try to find one!) It's also unwise to broach the subject when she has an easy out—the cell phone is on, *Project Runway* is about to come on the television, or she is anywhere near an iPod. The best environment in which to bring up the seemingly preposterous idea of your seeing her MySpace page is while you have her captive. Set out for a long drive, perhaps during rush hour traffic, so she has nowhere to hide. Or, begin the conversation while waiting at the doctor's office or for a table at a busy restaurant. The point is, you want to have an extended amount of uninterrupted time to work through this important conversation.

The third requirement on your part is a hefty amount of obvious self-reflection. This is where you put on a show for your child. You want them to see how deeply you've investigated this issue of MySpace and how thoroughly you've contemplated its worth. Share with your child what you've been reading, how you've created your own faux site, when you've surfed random profiles, and how it has affected you. Talk about what you have found, what has impressed you, what has frightened you, and what you want to learn more about. While this may freak your child out to some extent, it will undoubtedly strike them as a sincere attempt on your part to learn more about their world. And there is not a teenager alive who doesn't want to feel like her world is intriguing and worthy of study.

Finally, you're ready to view your child's page when you've truly prepared yourself for what you might find. This is where the courage comes in play. Diving into your own child's MySpace page is not for the faint of heart; as you've read in the previous chapters, sometimes the discovery you make will rock your world. Or, perhaps you've come this far in the book and realize that your child's cyber-persona or -personae are not information you need or want to have. Such a decision, if based on a rational, well-informed, and loving foundation, is not a "wrong" one. However, for those of you who feel compelled to at least witness who your cyber-child is, this chapter will guide you through the steps to help make that process go as smoothly as possible. In addition, you will find helpful tips regarding age-appropriate guidelines for online social-networking membership. At what age should you allow your child to be on MySpace? Have total access to Facebook without any parental involvement? Until what age should you insist on knowing your child's password? Read on.

Should I Look at My Child's Page?

At this point in the book, you are ready to make a choice—to look at your child's (and her friends') MySpace profile or to let it lie peacefully swaddled in its digital crib. Is ignorance bliss? Should you look at all? *Wait a minute*, you might be saying. *I'm not ready to do this. I don't really want to know what my child is doing on MySpace.*

I might learn something I don't want to know. And I completely under-stand—the fact that your teen may be in the midst of healthy experimentation with identity, expression, and even sexuality on the cyber-screen can be daunting. I mean, how much *should* Mom or Dad be privy to during these coming-of-age years? Should you know that your daughter is in a bitter argument with two of her closest friends? Should you know which girls your son finds attractive? Do you really need to read about your child's friend who feels hopeless about French class? Many psychologists feel teens need to have their own space, their own private domain in which to play with their desires, curiosities, and dramas. It's not always necessary for parents to be intimately involved in such matters. After all, allowing teens to experience and resolve their own conflicts is simply part of the maturation process that is so integral to becoming a healthy adult.

But It's Not Private

Of course, a MySpace page or a LiveJournal blog is not a private diary or person-to-person e-mail; these are public, and accessing your child's page is *not* akin to steaming open a sealed letter or unlocking a personal diary. So now the waters get a little murky. Why should you ignore your child's private profile when hundreds of so-called friends are viewing it freely anytime and anywhere? The other issue at hand is the interactive element of a MySpace profile. While it may take some restraint for a concerned parent to refrain from opening that mysterious letter or diary, there does exist some sense of comfort in knowing that these items are truly private. Although our children seem to believe we are aliens from one of Saturn's rings, we have all received special letters, sent private e-mails, and kept personal journals. We can understand that landscape, so allowing our kids that level of privacy is really not that scary—it's culturally familiar.

241

However, a MySpace presence is culturally *un*familiar to most parents. And as columnist Ellen Goodman puts it, "The central struggle of parenthood is to let our hopes for our children outweigh our fears." Even with the help of the previous chapters, including your week of MySpace adventures, you're still only an immigrant (on a temporary visa), and therefore not completely at home with it all. It's not that easy to refrain from snooping. And most importantly, the fact is that one single MySpace profile can (and does) attract thousands of random add requests, unedited advertisements, endless messages, unsolicited images, and total access to terribly inappropriate content. In short, your child can surf or link to any number of adult content groups, forums, blogs, or profiles. A MySpace profile is not a letter, an e-mail, or a diary; it is a public, social, *adult* site that poses many risks for teenagers. This is one reason why I believe you are fully justified in making an appointment to meet your cyber-child.

Should you spy?

On the one hand, you are the adult, the parent, the protector who is responsible for the adolescents in your care; on the other hand, taking a peek without permission and then calling the content into question may seriously damage the trust that you've been building with your child—trust you must have in order to successfully communicate.

Under most circumstances I don't recommend snooping. Nothing builds responsibility and autonomy in your child more than the knowledge that he or she is being trusted to figure things out independently, and that it is OK if he or she makes a mistake or two. In regard to MySpace, much of what I've witnessed from my own students is pretty innocent behavior, negotiating the wobbly steps on the path of adolescence. For many kids, MySpace and other online social networks are not dirty little secrets kept hidden under the mattress, so there should be no reason to snoop. Most teen experts agree that spying on or performing surveillance on your child is not a wise approach.

The exception is if you suspect your child is involved in dangerous behaviors or relationships and you are having difficulty asserting parental control. Of course, in this instance, your child's involvement on MySpace is a secondary concern. If you suspect your child is involved in an abusive relationship, self-mutilation, drugs, or pornography, and you are getting nowhere talking with them, *please* by all means search your teen's room, backpack, cell phone records, and Internet profiles in an effort to help them. And then seek professional help or counseling for your child. But barring this extreme, you may feel torn about how to approach the issue of meeting your cyber-child.

Enlist your child's help

I believe you absolutely *must* enlist your child to escort you on a tour of their page. Teenagers like to feel that they are in control, and soliciting their assistance will feed that desire. Also, because MySpace is so personal and so teen-centered, proceeding without their guidance would only provoke indignance and irritation from your child. Still, asking your child to escort you through his profile may not be well received. If you're worried, just remember what Bette Davis once said: "If you have never been hated by your child, you have never been a parent." But the reality is that most kids won't feel so averse to showing you their page; most teens I've spoken to are quite proud of their page and eager to show it off. Your child may surprise you.

After conducting an impressive study about the role MySpace plays in teens' lives, in which he interviewed over 1,200 MySpace teens and their parents, psychologist Larry D. Rosen, PhD, declared, "You absolutely need to ask your child to show you his/her MySpace page." After extensive interviews with L.A. parents, he reports that "38 percent said they had never looked at their child's profile (nor had they talked to their child about their MySpace usage), another 14 percent said they had almost never checked it, and 16 percent stated they only glanced at it every few months." In fact, he found that only one-third of the parents actually checked their teen's MySpace page on a regular basis, and more than 40 percent of parents had never seen the photographs that their teenager posted on MySpace. Interestingly, he adds that "70 percent of the adolescents said they would feel comfortable having their parents look at their MySpace page." Fifteen-year-old Angelo told me, "I would love to show my parents my page, especially since I tricked it out last week; they'd be pretty proud of it."

In my experience, before a teen will open up to you, she first needs to trust you—trust that your intentions are sincere, rational, and coming from a position of love. We all know that the more we condemn something, the more our children will want to do it— basic psychology, right? A report in *Curriculum Review*, a monthly report for educators, recommends this more open approach, to "discuss positive uses of these sites (most MySpace members aren't making mischief) and then explain some of the pitfalls (using real-life examples) before showing children ways to stay safe." Essentially, the desired effect is your child's having an "Aha!" moment, realizing that you're on their side and that you actually *do* want them to have some fun in their life.

Why You Should Look—The Right Intent

I have to tell you, however, that I am not advocating your crossing the threshold of your child's profile in order to find out sensitive or potentially embarrassing personal information. Your purpose is not to learn the inside scoop about your teen's social, emotional, or sexual life. There's a healthier way to do that—spending time together on a regular basis engaged in open and real conversation. No, your purpose here is not to see who they are; it's to see *who they are purporting to be, to whom they are advertising themselves, and for what reason.* You may need to shift your approach a little and be sure that you're committed to digesting your child's created MySpace identity in all its potential horror. If you can come to the tour bus with an attitude devoid of rash judgment and rich with the sincere desire to understand, then you will be successful in the first step toward getting to know your cyber-child.

Remember, your cyber-child is only one aspect of your real child—*a MySpace profile is an experiment in identity.* It is a revolving door of fantasy. Even so, mind you, as a parent you must be aware of how and why your child is playing it up on MySpace.

Taking the right approach with your teen is crucial. Don't panic or raise your voice. You must be calm and prepared, which you now are after reading the past eight chapters on what to expect. So approach your child with a desire to learn about this new phenomenon and an appreciation for the creative and unique things you may see. Praise the profiles that you find to be clever or artistic, and express concern over profiles that appear troubled or insecure. Rather than criticizing or mocking the names, photos, or other personae on MySpace, successful parents will realize that their cyber-children will have multiple names and various ways of representing who they are throughout adolescence.

Your goal is to create healthier possibilities regarding how your child chooses to represent herself. I recommend, for example, suggesting positive-sounding screen name such as Smartgirl, Ambitious1, theRealDeal, LadyBaller, Sideoutchamp, happy2bme, brainynbeautiful, etc. Ask her how she thinks these will influence *how* others talk to her, or *who* chooses to talk to her.

How to Talk to Your Child about MySpace

Before you approach your child with the dreaded request to see his (and his friends') MySpace profiles, it is vital that you've discussed MySpace as an entity in and of itself. Perhaps let your teen know you're reading a book about it. Start a dialogue, but in the beginning, don't let your discussion focus *only* on the negative media hype. By all means reference the recent news stories, as they are important and relevant, but do not come across like you believe MySpace to be solely a pedophile's playground—nothing will alienate your cyber-child quicker. Your goal is twofold: to establish your child's trust that you are sincerely interested and open-minded, and to show off a little to your child that you are somewhat well versed in the world of online social networks. Once your teen realizes you are not approaching his cyber-world with claws extended, he will be more willing to invite you in. Here's a sample conversation:

Parent: I know MySpace.com is a fun place for you and your friends. What do you like about it?

Teenager: (*With suspicion*) Uh, yeah, it's cool. It's fun to make and remake the page and talk to my friends.

Parent: That makes sense. I remember putting up posters of different bands in my room and talking on the phone as much as I could when I was your age. That was the fun part of being a teenager! What bands do you have on your profile?

Teenager: Oh, Mom, you have no idea who they are. Plus, you'd hate their music.

Parent: Well, that may be true, but you're still my child and I'm interested in knowing you better. Don't worry, I don't plan to attend the Warped Tour with you next summer!

Teenager: (*Hopefully laughing at this point*) OK, Mom.

Parent: Listen, why don't you just show me?

Teenager: Show you? Huh?

Parent: Yeah, whenever you're ready, show me how you've designed your MySpace profile. I'd love to see what you've put together. You always were so creative.

Teenager: I'll think about it (*not knowing what hit him*).

Here's a sample conversation that doesn't go quite so smoothly:

Teenager: Why are you reading that stupid book about MySpace? Do you always have to get all up in my business or what?

Parent: I'm reading a book about MySpace because I am interested in what it's like for you to grow up in today's world. I'm happy to share the book with you; in fact, I'd love to get your opinion on what the author is saying. I'm sure you have some interesting thoughts. Would you like to look at it with me?

Teenager: (*with dramatic effect*) *No*, I'm sure you're just going to try to kick me off MySpace now, and I won't be able to have any social life.

Parent: Why are you so convinced that I will feel negatively about MySpace? Isn't there anything redeeming about it that might convince me to let you use it?

Teenager: (*More engaged*) OK, Mom. Yes, there is. But are you really going to listen?

Parent: I have a better idea, why don't you just show me?

Teenager: Show you? What?

Parent: Yeah, whenever you're ready, show me how you've designed your MySpace profile. I'd love to see what you've put together. You always were so creative.

Teenager: Maybe.

These sample conversations hopefully provide you with some ideas of how to approach your teenager. Engaging in a conversation

 247

about MySpace by framing it in a positive light sets a foundation for the rest of the discussion. If, say, the parent *began* by citing facts and figures about sexual predators on MySpace, the teen would have immediately tuned out. Also, the strategy of identifying with her son and his teenage experiences by mentioning her own youth reminds her son that she is aware of what it's like to be a teen. An important moment in this conversation is the "whenever you're ready" phrase; it eases any anxiety the teenager may be having and it also gives him time to think about cleaning up his profile (if need be). The final stroke is her casual and seemingly off-the-cuff request to see his page coupled with the compliment to her son's creativity. While the teenager is still not sure if he will share his profile with his mom, he is considering it.

If your child is over the age of sixteen and is already participating in online social networking, I do think it's preferable to engage in conversation about her online activities rather than ban them outright, "site unseen." As seventeen-year-old Ariel explained to me, "The trouble with parents just reacting and grounding their kids—or cutting them off from MySpace completely—as opposed to dealing with the issue on an adult level is that we learn pretty quickly not to tell our parents about any of our online activities. If I'm being cyber-bullied or harassed by a pervert, I'm not able to talk to my parents about it now." Incidentally, most teens already well entrenched in the cyberworld will find their way around a parent ban. You want to be able to *discuss* how your child is representing herself, and that discussion is predicated on her being open to it. Ask your child about the content her friends post to their sites and how she feels about it. Is that how she wants to be represented? Focusing on a friend's site takes a little pressure off your child. This type of dialogue is valuable merely because it shows your child that you are aware and that you care.

Tips for Parents: Opening the Lines of Communication

1. Listen. Don't say "in just a minute" or "not right now." Devote your attention to what your son or daughter is saying because kids know when you're pretending.
2. Ask open-ended questions that encourage conversation. Avoid questions that kids can answer with a simple yes or no.
3. Make it clear that you are listening and trying to understand your child's point of view. When your child describes events, repeat what you think your child has just told you.
4. To show that you're listening, try the following phrases:
   a. "Sounds like you're saying . . ."
   b. "Do you mean that . . ."
   c. "When that happens to me, I feel like . . . Is it like that for you, too?"
   d. "I'm having a hard time understanding what you're saying. What do you mean?"
5. Establish regular weekly "together time" in which you and your child do something alone with each other that allows your child to talk and allows an organic conversation to unfold. Go for a walk, a drive, or an ice cream.

Teachable Moments

Viewing your child's or your child's friends' MySpace profiles is an excellent time for you to start an ongoing discussion. In fact, research shows that teenagers whose parents are aware of their child's media influences (television shows, music, etc.) are less likely to smoke, drink, or use drugs. This MySpace interaction with your child is an excellent teachable moment. I actually recommend linking to your child's friends' pages *before* scrutinizing your child's page. Of course, begin on your child's page, but scroll down to her Friends List, her Top 8, and click away. This strategy eases the nerves

 249

of both you and your teen, as it takes the spotlight off her page and puts it on another's. Plus, you'll get a better, more honest look into how your child conducts herself by seeing the messages she sends her friends, and these messages only show up on her friends' pages. And, by discussing your child's friends' methods of self-representation, you can plant the seeds of thought in your own child.

If a friend's profile has a photograph of her drinking alcohol, you could start a conversation with any of these opening lines:

- "I wonder what her family thinks about her drinking at parties?"
- "How would her mom or dad feel if they saw these pictures?"
- "Where do you think this person will end up in life?"
- "What do you think her teachers would think? Her neighbors? Her pastor?"
- "Why would she want other people to know about her drinking?"
- "How do you think she'd feel about my looking at her profile?"

If a friend's profile has a photograph of her dressed provocatively or posed inappropriately, you could start a conversation with any of these opening lines:

- "I wonder what her father/mother thinks about her sharing her body so freely?"
- "How would she feel if these pictures were seen by everyone she knows?"
- "What type of attention do you think she is trying to get with these pictures?"

- "What kind of attention do you think she will get with these pictures, and why?"
- "How could she get the positive attention she really wants?"

If a friend's profile has explicit or inappropriate language on their page, you could start a conversation with any of these opening lines:

- "What is he trying to say with these words?"
- "What would be a more creative way to express that sentiment?"
- "How might his mother or father react if they saw him using this type of language?"
- "Who's he trying to impress with this language? Why?"

Viewing Your Child's Profile

Now that you've spent some time looking at and discussing your child's friends' MySpace profiles, it is time to transition to the hallowed ground of your child's space. Gulp. If you like, you could look at three different aspects of her page on three separate days, so as not to overwhelm. The first day might focus solely on your child's profile picture, screen name, tagline, and song. If these are harmless and don't concern you, your first day is through, and you can go about your business of the day with a sigh of relief. However, if these three elements cause you some concern, well, then you have plenty of grist for the mill of discussion. The second day (and these days do not have to be consecutive) might tackle the blogs, surveys/quizzes, and videos/pictures. On the third day, you might look at the Friends List, the messages from friends, and the messages sent to friends.

Sit with your child in a quiet place, both at the computer with equal access to the screen, keyboard, and mouse. Be sure all cell phones are turned off and that no one else who could possibly distract you is nearby. Not only will you communicate to your child that his cyber-life is important to you, but you will also ensure that you both don't feel rushed and get enough time to explore, discuss, and possibly argue about what you find.

While you both sit at the computer, it is important to let your child hold the reins. Let her control the pace initially, signing in and navigating to her page. If she moves too fast, don't react. She's probably nervous and unsure of what to expect from you. Once she begins to calm down and is more at ease, then ask her to go back to certain elements. The goal is to keep your child as calm and willing as possible; you don't want a combative environment when asking your child to share personal information with you. Besides, the only things to focus your attention on initially are the following: *your child's profile name, photo, tagline, and song.*

I've included a worksheet in three stages, which you can look at or fill out either with your child present or alone.

Assessing Your Child's Profile: Worksheet, Part I

My child's profile picture communicates _____

_____

My child's profile picture makes me feel _____

_____

My child's tagline/personal quotation communicates _____

_____

My child's tagline/personal quotation makes me feel _____

_____

The song that plays on my child's profile is _____ by _____

This song communicates _____ _____

This song makes me feel _____ _____

Now that it is Day 2 of your MySpace Tour, your goal is to look at the blogs, surveys/quizzes, and videos/pictures.

Assessing Your Child's Profile: Worksheet, Part II

My child has the following pictures posted _____ _____

These pictures communicate _____ _____

These pictures make me feel _____ _____

My child has the following video/s downloaded _____ _____

These videos communicate _____ _____

These videos make me feel _____ _____

My child seems to write blogs mostly about _____
_____

If I didn't know my child, I would think that he/she is _____
_____

Finally, Day 3 allows you to look at the Friends List, the messages from friends, and the messages sent to friends.

Assessing Your Child's Profile: Worksheet, Part III

I know _____ of the Top 8 friends on my child's page. My child offers the following personal information _____
_____

The most disturbing information my child shares is _____
_____

Reading this information makes me feel _____
_____

Three adjectives that describe the overall layout of my child's page are_____

I really like that my child's profile includes _____
_____

I am impressed by my child's profile because _____
_____

I am disappointed in my child's profile because _____
_____

Some elements that may be difficult to discuss with my child are

_____

because_____

_____

Beware of "Shadow" Profiles

I do caution you about one risk: some teens use a "shadow" profile to dupe their parents. A shadow profile is a faux display intended to assuage a nosy parent's concerns, and, sadly, it usually works. Unfortunately, many a parent has been shown a shadow page and, after a hefty sigh, slept better at night. How do you know if you're being shown a dummy MySpace profile?

It's actually easier than you might think. Few teenagers throw together their MySpace page with a flick of the wrist. Most teenagers spend hours, days, even weeks perfecting or "tricking out" their page; remember, designing one's profile is the sole purpose of being a member. Their profile is a magnum opus. Ask yourself—does it look detailed? Check out the level of work that has gone into the page; if it feels insincere in any way, you may raise an eyebrow. If your child spends hours and hours on MySpace each night, but the page you're being shown seems a bit light on social interactions, meaning the last friend comment was one week earlier or the last photo posted was from a party six months ago, be suspicious.

Make note of the dates of the latest messages sent from friends and the latest blogs or bulletins. How recent are they? Are they clustered within a few days or over the span of months? Does your daughter love her digital camera, but few photos have been posted? Check out the bio—do the interests listed match your child's? For example, if you know your teen is a huge music fan, but he hasn't bothered to upload a song or provide a full listing of bands he likes, that may be a clue. If you do find out that you've been shown a shadow page, I recommend being more assertive with your child—if not investigative—about finding the real page; the use of a shadow profile is a good indication that the actual profile is being hidden for a reason. Also, at this point the trust has been broken, and you need to know why.

If Your Child Is Resistant

Your child may be quite resistant to your viewing her page, and understandably so. Remember, she sees it as *her* space. In a way, it is a good problem to have. I say that nothing is a more obvious red flag that your child is involved in some questionable behavior than if she is adamant about your not knowing who she purports to be online. So in some ways, you are ahead of the game if your child forbids you to see her MySpace or Facebook page. Ah, but what do you do about it? Here's what takes courage—the courage to be the parent . . . no matter the reaction from your child. You know what is best and healthiest for your child, and quite frankly you are obligated to provide that for him or her. Your child has no one in the world to look out for her well-being, no one to protect her from negative influences, no one to tell her that her choices are poorly made—no one, that is, except *you*.

I see it in the classroom and I see it with my students' parents. The one consistent desire teenagers have is to know their boundaries. Honestly, they care less about what those boundaries are and more about if they will be consistently reinforced. Teens just want the security of knowing where they stand and what's expected of them—the song-and-dance tantrums in response to strict rules is just that—a performance. It's just something they've seen on a bad TV movie or read in some "How to Be an Annoying Teenager" pamphlet. The fact is, teenagers crave rules, boundaries, and consistency. All that being said, if your teen refuses to let you see her

MySpace page, it is time for you to establish your authority and let her know that your request is no longer a request, but now a requirement. However, do give your child a period of time to digest your change in approach . . . and to clean up her profile, if need be. Even in the throes of asserting your authority, remain fair and loving and respectful.

They Don't Need a "Cool Parent"

Please don't make the mistake of trying to be the "cool" parent. Working with parents almost as much as I work with students affords me a unique perspective on the different methods of parenting. Unfortunately, I've seen all too often the parent who can't say no to his teenager. Nine times out of ten it is born out of a fear of their child's not "liking" them, not thinking they're a "cool" parent. And nine times out of ten it damages the child. The following is an extreme example; nevertheless, it illustrates my point well.

Several years ago, I became close to a female student of mine whom I will call Stefanie. Her stepfather was occasionally physically abusive, and her mother clearly felt guilty about the situation. Her mom worked harder than most of Stefanie's peers to earn her daughter's friendship—her approval, really. Her mom would indulge Stefanie's every whim for a party, including supplying the alcohol and letting kids hang out in the bedrooms. She would listen to the same music as her daughter and even dressed as youthfully as her body would allow. This warped inversion of the mother–daughter relationship really took its toll on Stefanie. This young lady became confused about her sexuality, angry toward her peers, and depressed on a daily basis. She had what most teenagers would covet—control over her mom—but she was miserable. As Rosalind Wiseman writes in *Queen Bees and Wannabes*, "You don't need to be your daughter's best friend. Even if she says she hates your interference and accuses you of violating her privacy, rest assured her hatred is temporary." Obviously this is an extreme example of a parent refusing to be a parent, but as parents we shouldn't give our kids what they want, but what they truly need.

What Teens Really Want from Parents

Compiled from hundreds of interviews with teen MySpacers:

- To be asked about what I'm studying in each of my classes
- To be required to introduce my friends to my parents, and to be expected to include them in my family's activities
- To be encouraged to open up and talk more freely with my parents
- To be left alone when I really need to be
- To be praised for what I do well
- To spend more time having fun and laughing together
- To see them show up at one of my school functions
- To be kept safe

The Importance of Self-Reflection

For many years I taught at a high school that, like many others, required its teachers to chaperone the students for a week on an outdoor education trip, usually camping in tents to places like Joshua Tree National Park, Catalina Island, or Yosemite National Park. The L.A.-born-and-raised students, of course, bemoaned having to "rough it" in tents or cabins, but the most outrage came from their not being allowed to bring any electronic devices—no cell phones, video games, iPods, or headsets of any kind. The idea of having to ride on a bus for several hours without any electronic distractions was, at first, simply too much for them to compute. But after a week of nature hikes, rock climbing, and kayaking sans volume knobs and colored pixels, my students seemed to evolve by a couple million years: they were relating to each other, being physically active, and caring less about their appearance (most of them, that is).

Without fail, I noticed the same reaction on the bus ride home: as we reentered civilization, we faced an onslaught of billboards, man-made structures, and lots and lots of garish sights, especially when we exited the freeway and made our way down Sunset Boulevard. The kids' reaction? "It's so ugly!" "Ewww, I'm not ready for this." "I miss the quiet!" "Let's go back!" "I hate this place." These materialistic and media-saturated kids had been detoxed of the total assault of media distractions for a significant period of time, and they grew to appreciate it. Much like my TV-Turnoff experiments, I realized that teens are inherently self-reflective, they just cocoon themselves in endless layers of technological distractions that keep them from seeing beauty, listening to others, and getting to know their true selves.

How and Why to Encourage Self-Reflection in Your Cyber-Teen

The best way for your child to make good decisions about what he is posting online is to be able to self-reflect. To be able to take stock of yourself is to walk in a realm of exceptional awareness, a realm that eludes most adults, let alone most teenagers. One of the most effective teaching tools I use is requiring students to reflect after a major paper or project, spending time analyzing the choices they made or the approaches they took while looking to the future to anticipate how they may perform differently. Without fail, once my students are comfortable with the steps of self-reflection, the results are fruitful, both academically and personally.

I recommend training your cyber-child in the art of self-reflection. For, when faced with questions of "why" and "how" and "if," your child will be operating at a much deeper level of self-awareness and will be forced to acknowledge that he has a self that

is valuable and worthy of being true to. It's easy to represent ourselves poorly or to mishandle our own reputations when we are
disconnected from who we are. It's much more difficult to abuse
ourselves when we know what we like, who we want to be, and
why we want to pursue specific goals. And your specific goal is to
guide your child into that difficult but rewarding endeavor that I
liken to ice fishing—cutting a hole in a frigid surface, waiting for
hours in discomfort, and eventually (and joyfully) pulling out a fish
for the fire. Such is the work of self-reflection.

Now that you have discussed your child's cyber-ways as
encouraged in the previous worksheet, it is time for you to help
your child to engage in their own self-analysis on a regular basis.
Whether it's a journal or a file on the computer, present this set of
questions as a starting point. (However, do not let your child blog
these thoughts and feelings . . . they are private.) Once your child
is in a quiet place, have them consider the following:

1. How do I feel right now?
2. What do I think about the world around me?
3. List three values or personal standards that you would
    never compromise, and explain why.
4. What adjectives would I use to describe myself to
    myself? To my friends? To my parents? To my teachers?
5. How do I see myself in the future?
6. What kind of work do I like?
7. What kind of relaxation do I enjoy?
8. How have I changed since I entered puberty?
9. What kinds of people do I respect, and why?
10. How am I similar to and different from my
    mother/father?
11. What mark do I want to make on society?
12. What makes me really angry?

13. Why should the college of my choice accept me?
14. Why should the college of my choice *not* accept me?
15. What would I be proud to share with my future son or daughter?

Now that you've walked through the fire—and by the way, congratulations!—it's time to clean up some of the debris. First of all, the conversations *must* continue; they are futile if they happen once in a while rather than on a regular basis. After all, nothing creates a bond better than meaningful discourse. I implore you to engage your child in ongoing, organic discussions not only about MySpace, but about how he or she represents him- or herself both to peers and to strangers in everyday life.

In the next chapter, we'll look at the conversations every parent must have with their teen about Internet privacy, as well as what level of intervention is required of you as the parent. Will you install monitoring software? Will you forbid MySpace altogether? Will you take the computer out of your child's bedroom? Will you require access to your child's password? Hopefully at this point you have a good idea of where your child stands in terms of his or her involvement with MySpace. Please look to the next and final chapter for more help in protecting your child online.

10 MySafe Child

Practical Advice for Protecting Your Online Adolescent

"We do not raise our children alone . . . Our children are also raised by every peer, institution, and family with which they come in contact."

—*Richard Louv*

"My husband and I keep a wicker basket on our dresser; each evening at 9:00, we collect our three teenagers' cell phones, turn them off, and drop them in the basket. It's not that we don't trust them, it's that we love them. We want them to get their homework completed and to fall asleep at a healthy hour. If they're talking or texting all night, their quality of life will diminish. It's our job to protect them."

—*Barb, parent*

"Until my son turns eighteen, his keyboard is mine each night from 10 PM on. I take the temptation away from him as an act of parental love."

—*Lynne, parent*

"Yeah, it kinda sucks that my parents are so in tune with what a lot of teenagers do online. I've never done anything stupid, but that's probably because my parents are always a step ahead of me. I tell my friends how lame they are, and they all feel so bad for me. I mean, I can't even have a TV in my room, let alone a laptop. But I guess it's pretty cool that I don't have to worry about the peer pressure to stay up late gossiping."

—*Gigi, 15*

———

In February 2006, Detective Frank Dannahey of the Rocky Hill, Connecticut, Police Department went undercover as a teen male named "Matt" on MySpace.com in an experiment to circumnavigate the MySpace safety features and see what kind of personal information he could glean from teenage users. Here's what he discovered:

"Once 'Matt' was allowed on the teenagers' MySpace pages, a feat he accomplished easily via simple friend requests, it became immediately obvious that personal information was readily available and easily volunteered. I was able to find out information such as where a teen lived, worked, their full name and date of birth, where they went to school, as well as home and cellular phone numbers. Photos posted on teens' sites were usually photos of themselves that could assist in locating them. Some of the photos posted are highly inappropriate, if not provocative. As 'Matt' became friends with teens online, he had access to messages known as 'bulletins.' Through these bulletins, I was able to gain much personal information about my online friends. Teens readily discuss their social activities and provide phone numbers to contact them.

"In one case, I saw a real-time message from a teen telling the exact location that she and her friends were about to walk to. If I had a devious intent, I could easily stalk or intercept her and her friends. Many of the teens use the bulletins to post surveys that reveal very personal information about them. Surveys that can be viewed by the general public are also a common sight on a teen's page. In one case, I found a 377-question survey on the site of one of my online 'friends,' who was a fifteen-year-old female. This survey included the teen's personal information as well as her likes and dislikes. These surveys assist predators in establishing a dialogue with a teen as they attempt to infiltrate that teen's online world.

"One of the most concerning incidents of the 'Matt' online experiment occurred when one of my online friends suggested that we meet in person. The in-person meet is the most dangerous scenario online. Teenagers meeting an online stranger sometimes become the victim of a sexual assault, or worse. The sixteen-year-old female that made the suggestion to meet in person communicated with 'Matt' on a daily basis. This teen later said that she allowed 'Matt' to be one of her online friends because she saw that other teens she knew were also friends of Matt's. I found that teens are very trusting of people they meet online and are very willing to share their personal thoughts and information with virtual strangers."

Officer Dannahey's experience is a lesson for all parents and teens in the MySpace generation. Keep in mind, however, that online predators are rare, and most teens are savvy to the typical suspicious friend request. In fact, 95 percent of the teens I interviewed knew exactly how and what to post and not post on

MySpace; now, whether they stayed true to what they know or not, I couldn't tell you. That being said, many teens still make poor decisions in the interest of social pressure or curiosity or even ego, and that's where parenting enters the picture. It is important for you to be aware of how much personal information your child is presenting online.

- For instance, one Connecticut man is arrested repeatedly for sexual assault charges in direct relation to his use of MySpace—he's on his tenth arrest. Clearly, some teenage girls are not being discerning enough.
- Another reason to sharpen your safety radars is the discovery that at least thirty Texas death row inmates have their own profiles on MySpace. "I think I'm a pretty funny guy. I have a wacked sense of humor," blogs one inmate, who was convicted in a 2000 shooting death of a police officer.
- A twenty-two-year-old man was recently charged with having sex with a fourteen-year-old girl whom he met and established a relationship with via MySpace. A forty-six-year-old man was recently charged with attempted sexual assault after police caught him in a parked car with a fifteen-year-old girl he met on MySpace.
- On a September school day, a crazed gunman took six girls hostage at a Bailey, Colorado, high school. Apparently he had composed a list of exactly which girls he wanted thanks to countless hours of research on MySpace.com. Unfortunately, this unstable man was able to obtain extremely personal information about a number of teenage girls, so much so that he was able to find where they went to school, and which class they would be in at what time of day.

Again, the stories are few and far between compared to the volume of online participants . . . but they keep happening. And until we are able to go a day without hearing about another case of falsified age or sexual assault of a minor, we—and our cyber-children—need to be hypervigilant.

Predators have always lurked at the fringes of our society, but now they've simply moved onto the Internet to prey—and to mobilize. Says one California police offcer, "In the days before the Internet, criminals preyed upon kids in playgrounds, schools, and in public gatherings. Today, with the advent of MySpace and the like, these criminals prey upon kids by coming into the house via the phone or cable lines. Parents believe that their kids are safe because they have burglar bars and good locks, but these criminals, posing as teens, lure kids into counterproductive and often illegal activities. Law enforcement can only react to incidents after the fact."

Years ago, in the nascent stages of the Internet, pedophiles simply swapped images; today they infiltrate chat rooms, teen web hangouts, and child gaming sites pretending to be other teens in an effort to connect with kids. Online social networks, for example, provide a ripe environment for these creeps to do just that—"network" with each other by way of sharing tips for getting near children at camps, through foster care, at community events, and online. In their minds, pedophiles truly believe that the child is "consenting" to sexual contact. Perhaps even more frightening, according to a recent *New York Times* article, they even make use of technology to "help take their arguments to others, like sharing online a printable booklet to be distributed to children that extols the benefits of sex with adults." Did you know that these pedophiles have their own community, their own subculture, their own radio stations, charities, jewelry, coffee shops, and vacation spots?

No, these menaces to society are not just trolling the profiles of teenage MySpacers, they are mobilizing for an all-out legalization of their perverted way of life. It is essential for you as a parent to know the dangers of your teen's cyber-world in an effort to protect your kids from it. In an experiment that garners my respect, the *New York Times* monitored conversations among pedophiles in virtual exchanges via message boards and instant messages. Findings reveal that these men "view themselves as the vanguard of a nascent movement seeking legalization of child pornography and the loosening of age-of-consent laws." In fact, they found cause for celebration when in May a group of pedophiles in the Netherlands earned court approval to exist as a viable political party. So what's the problem with these sick men finding a place to unite via the Internet? The Netherlands debacle should be the first indication that wired pedophiles find solace, encouragement, and even justification for their behaviors on the Internet. "It is rationalization that allows them to avoid admitting that their desires are harmful and illegal," said Bill Walsh, a former commander of the Crimes Against Children Unit for the Dallas Police Department, adding, "That can allow them to take that final step and cross over from fantasy into real-world offenses."

Where might you find this new breed of "social-activist" pedophiles? Some post deceptive Internet classified advertisements looking for babysitting positions; some search postings for weekend estate sales since "plenty of bored minors show up accompanying inattentive parents"; some create seemingly mainstream websites that may be devoted to helping children. My point: technology not only enables predators to reach your kids, it also encourages a sense of solidarity among even the most warped of individuals. And solidarity is power.

There are over 550,000 registered sex offenders in the United States alone. To the credit of MySpace's chief security officer, Hemanshu Nigam, the site is taking new action against registered sex offenders who sport MySpace profiles—accessing those databases and deleting the profiles of any registered sex offenders. Mr. Nigam states, "We are committed to keeping sex offenders off MySpace." Unfortunately, *how* he plans to locate many of these profiles is still a bit of a mystery; after all, I assume most of these predators do not use their real names or details. As explained earlier in this book, it is quite simple to register for a profile on MySpace without using any genuine personal information (age, zip code, name, photo, etc.).

Basics of Internet Safety

Now I recognize that this ultra-disturbing information will make you want to ban the Internet altogether! At the very least, I hope I have grabbed your attention enough to motivate a renewed interest in your child's Internet activities. But, there are very simple methods of keeping your kids safe from these monsters. It's *vital* to remind our kids that you never can truly know whom you're talking to online—or who is looking at your personal information. But sometimes, when we keep hearing the same warnings over and over again without feeling any consequences, we fail to really get it. For instance, take a look at the following text from a MySpace profile that offers unnecessary personal information.

A Word from the Wise

"The particular focus is the public nature of [online social networks]. That seems to be what surprises students most. They think of it as part of their own little world, not a bigger electronic world."

—*Tracy Tyree,*
Susquehanna University's Dean of student Life

 269

In "LalaBurger's" profile, she writes the following "About Me" paragraph: "Hey, my name is lara and I AM 15 YEARS OLD. Gymnastics is my LIFE. I train and compete at PACIFIC COAST GYM in Newport Harbor. I go to high school at NEWPORT HARBOR ACADEMY with the coolest girls on earth—we love to party and meet new people! Well I'm silly and goofy and I love to hang with other partiers. I'm always up for a fun time when my folks are out of town (every weekend!), so IM me!" LalaBurger's profile is also replete with photographs of her in her leotard either doing gymnastics or posed provocatively with her fellow gymnast girlfriends.

Unfortunately, too many kids don't realize that the inclusion of the above kind of information is dangerous. If I were a predator with the intent of meeting this girl, I would not have a difficult time of it. First of all, I know what she looks like from her pictures, and I know which girls she hangs out with at her gym. I would be able to find her gym simply by using the Yellow Pages, and I would be able to wait outside her high school, especially on a Friday, when I know she is going home to an empty house! How I wish these girls would be more careful. But, according to danah boyd, "Teens today grow up in a state of constant surveillance where there is no privacy, so they can't really have an idea of its being lost. The risk of [someone uninvited] coming in and looking at their MySpace site is beyond their consideration." Teach your child to be careful.

The #1 Thing You Can Do to Protect Your Kids Online

Fifty percent of parents say their child has a computer in their bedroom. *Move the computer out of the bedroom and into a centralized area like the living room instead.* If there's protesting, Trent Lewis of HighSchoolRevolution.com offers a reminder. Let your kids know it could be a lot worse:

"Something to remember is that the computer is not required; it's a privilege, not a right. Today that sounds silly, but I heard about a parent whose child insisted that they *had* to have a computer. After breaking the rules of content and staying online too long, the parent removed the child's computer. All papers that year were typed on a typewriter (remember those?). All research was done with a weekly trip to the library, where they used books. When the parent was asked about the hassle it was for them, she replied, 'It was a pain for everyone, sure, but this is my child. It's more than worth it.' The easy thing to do is to not look into this. I admire the parent who refuses to take the path of least resistance."

Set Profiles to "Private"—
But Know They May Not Always Be Private

I'll just have my child set her MySpace profile to "private," then she'll be safe from all these sickos. If only it were that simple. Setting a profile to private is a feature that blocks random users from viewing a profile in full. Although it does provide an initial wall of protection, it's a wall with as many holes as a pound of baby Swiss. Of course, I advocate using the private option. But I caution you not to place an unquestioning trust in this much-advertised feature—it is not a catchall safety measure.

Even if a profile is set to private, the person's photograph and user name (including some personal information) still appear, it's only that to the right of this private information is an ironic banner announcing, "THIS PROFILE HAS BEEN SET TO PRIVATE." Unfortunately, the private setting doesn't stop someone from forwarding the page to anyone else with whom they may want to

 271

share it. And, of course, it does not stop them from contacting your child. And all unbeknownst to your child, there is no alert that one's profile has been forwarded, a feature that MySpace should consider offering. If an undesirable user is forwarding your child's profile, picture and all, to other undesirables, shouldn't you know about it?

Also, once your child has joined a forum or a group, her picture will accompany any of her comments, and again, anyone can view it. Also, even though the profile is set to private, her membership in a MySpace group diminishes her privacy slightly: a stranger can now, more readily, view her profile. Be aware—your child isn't likely to think of this as a big deal. As sixteen-year-old Kristopher told me, "We're willing to give up some of our privacy to connect with people easier. The realization that people can find you online isn't that threatening to this generation." Again, teens are aware of predators and myriad Internet risks; however, they are not careful and tend to operate as though they are impervious to any harm.

"Block" Unsolicited Users—
But Know It Doesn't Completely Block Them

Blocking a user prevents you from receiving messages from that person. However, if your child blocks another user from accessing her profile, say for bullying or using inappropriate language, the effects are not as powerful as you might think. While this person will be excluded from your child's Friends List and therefore be denied full access to his or her profile (assuming it is set to private, of course), a blocked user can still view your child as a "favorite" on his profile. Being designated a "favorite" means that the blocked user may still see your child's:

- Photograph
- Sexual orientation

- Motive for being on MySpace (dating, serious relation-ship, networking, etc.)
- Age
- Location
- Date the profile was last updated
- Date he or she was last online
- Status concerning whether your child is online now

Another aspect of the blocked-user scenario to consider is that said user may still compose and send MySpace e-mail messages to your child; the blocked user has no idea that they are not being received. In other words, the user is not notified of his being blocked, and therefore may assume he is being ignored . . . and if he's not the most rational person, that may inflict a feeling of rejection and resulting anger. The only way a user is informed of being blocked is if said user attempts to subscribe to your child's blog. He will receive the following message: "You are blocked by this user." The benefit of blocking a user is denying him key access to your infor-mation, but it doesn't totally protect you from the person.

Don't Open Unsolicited Messages—
But Know They Will Still Be Received

Even a private profile is not immune to friend requests from strangers. *Anyone* can send your child a message requesting to be added to their extended network of friends. This request may be denied or granted: once it is granted, of course, the person is afforded total access to your child's profile and is bestowed all rights and privileges that go along with friend status (access to blogs, pic-tures, etc.). In the best-case scenario, your child will deny or block any and all friend requests from unknown users; however, there is always the chance that your child may be tempted to add an unknown "friend" who perhaps shares the same musical tastes, claims to know of a swanky after-hours party, or seems particularly intriguing for whatever reason. Remember, the whole purpose of online social networking is to meet new people. In fact it is strongly encouraged by the MySpace administrators.

When I signed up for my profile, I was bombarded with messages from MySpace to circulate my profile and invite as many friends as possible. I'm still disturbed by the emphatic order posted on my profile that states: "You haven't added your school yet! Click here—add your school now!" I think we all know how dangerous it would be for a teen MySpacer to provide her school name and location—a basic safety no-no. I also find it disquieting that while a profile is set to private, the little red blinking icon below the profile picture actively indicates whether the person is "online now" or not. Isn't that information *private*?

You Are the Webmaster

Now that you've broached the subject of MySpace and had that difficult but fruitful conversation with your child, you're ready for the next step. The most effective way to ensure that your child is as safe as can be on MySpace, or the Internet, is to assert your authority over the cyber-life of your family. Be aware, however, that asserting your authority does not mean becoming an unbearable tyrant or mounting a guerrilla-style coup over your children. Remember that as the parent, you're in charge, but with that comes responsible leadership and loving discipline. So, whether you are proficient in C++ computer programming or still can't figure out how to cut and paste, you need to appoint yourself the webmaster of your household. No one loves your child like you do, right? So who better to act as the safety net as your child surfs the Net than you?

Recommended Technology Guidelines

It's difficult to know when your child is ready to venture into a new technology. I know the sight of my daughter with white iPod cords trailing from her preschool uniform is a little unsettling, even though she's only rocking out to Mary Poppins's "A Spoonful of Sugar" and gets bored after about two minutes of not being able to ask me a question. Clearly she's too young to have a headset blasting in her ears (someone please let my husband know that), but when the age limits aren't so obvious, what should parents do?

After many years of working with preteens, teens, their parents, and school psychologists, I have compiled the following scale of general readiness regarding our children and technology. Of course, you know your child's maturity level best.

Age 11 and under

These preteens are far from being mature enough to understand the risks and responsibilities inherent in any personal electronic device beyond an extremely modified cell phone or PlayStation. There is no reason for an eight- or nine-year-old to acquire a personal laptop, desktop, iPod, or PDA, all of which afford Internet access. Any homework that needs to be done via computer should be completed in the presence of an adult. Without question, this age group should be shielded from any online social networking in the realm of MySpace, Facebook, or Xanga.

Age 12 to 13

These tweens are ready for watered-down versions of most electronic devices, especially the thirteen-year-old crew. And the fact is that most of them are now actively using these devices either at school or at friends' homes. Because computer use is necessary for most school assignments, your tween will surely be clamoring to use the family computer. But at this age, I cannot stress enough that word-processing capabilities are all that is necessary for school— and socializing. As a teacher, I can tell you that nightly Internet access does more harm than good for the majority of students. If electronic sources are required for research, which is not as often as some kids would like you to believe, I recommend utilizing the local public library. Most public libraries provide cutting-edge technology, helpful staff, and flexible hours, not to mention a sense of community.

Even though they will accuse you of sabotaging their social lives, I don't believe a twelve- or thirteen-year-old is ready to be networking online. As for cell phones, this is the perfect age for a child to make his first commitment to a phone and a calling package. However, I encourage you to select one of the phones listed at the end of this chapter, with an extremely limited calling plan and keypad.

Age 14 to 15

Flying in full swing of teenage antics, this group of young adults is ready to experience more freedom on the technological plane. Cell phones with more calling and contact capabilities, including text messaging, are appropriate for this age group, although I would be less quick to grant it to the fourteen-year-olds, as their concept of social-izing is still terribly unformed. I still do not recommend a cell phone, however, that provides Internet access, as these youngsters do not yet have the self-control to resist the many temptations associated with that. I also don't recommend a personal laptop or a personal desktop computer in the bedroom, for the same reason. However, relatively unrestricted access to the Internet on the family computer located in a public space (for IM or perhaps blogging or research for school) is acceptable for this age group. I do not advocate any fourteen- or fifteen-year-old having her own MySpace or Facebook profile.

Age 16 to 17+

These soon-to-be adults are ready for unrestricted access to the family computer located in a public place, but may still not be mature enough to handle the dangers of a personal computer in a private space. Unrestricted use of cell phones, iPods, and PDAs is acceptable at this age, barring any trust issues. That being said, I urge parents to still follow the safety guidelines laid out in this chapter, including ongoing conversations about online choices and activities. As for online social networks like MySpace, I firmly believe that this age is the youngest acceptable limit allowable, and profiles should be set to private. My argument is the previous nine chapters. Perhaps a mature sixteen-year-old is ready for MySpace, but for the majority of the sixteen-and-younger crowd, the free-doms and influences inherent on sites like MySpace are not age appropriate.

According to the guidelines in "Protecting Our Kids," provided online by the Los Angeles District Attorney's Office, you, as the family webmaster, are responsible for the following initial tasks:

- Informing your children that you have the right to mon-itor their computer use and that *if you suspect there is a problem, you will randomly monitor their Internet activities*
- Not allowing your child to have multiple e-mail accounts or screen/IM names
- Prohibiting your child from using private chat rooms as well as adult-oriented sites
- Educating your child about how to be safe and smart on the Internet
- Becoming familiar with the web browser your children use and restricting the type of content (violence, sex, and language) that can be viewed

The first order of business as the family webmaster is to famil-iarize yourself with advice from the experts. And as much as I wish

MySpace were doing even more to protect kids, the MySpace safety guidelines are an excellent place to start. Take a close look at what Hemanshu Nigam, the safety czar at MySpace.com, has published, and go over these points one by one with your kids:

MySpace makes it easy to express yourself, connect with friends and make new ones, but please remember that what you post publicly could embarrass you or expose you to danger. Here are some common sense guidelines that you should follow when using MySpace:

- **Don't forget that your profile and MySpace forums are public spaces.** Don't post anything you wouldn't want the world to know (e.g., your phone number, address, IM screen name, or specific whereabouts). Avoid posting anything that would make it easy for a stranger to find you, such as where you hang out every day after school.
- **People aren't always who they say they are. Be careful about adding strangers to your Friends List.** It's fun to connect with new MySpace friends from all over the world, but avoid meeting people in person whom you do not fully know. If you must meet someone, do it in a public place and bring a friend or trusted adult.
- **Harassment, hate speech and inappropriate content should be reported.** If you feel someone's behavior is inappropriate, react. Talk with a trusted adult, or report it to MySpace or the authorities.
- **Don't post anything that would embarrass you later.** Think twice before posting a photo or info you wouldn't want your parents or boss to see!

- **Don't mislead people into thinking that you're older or younger.** If you lie about your age, MySpace will delete your profile.

The second order of business in your new leadership role is to sit down with your child and verify his or her MySpace settings. Please see the following checklist:

Parents' Checklist for Securing Your Child's MySpace Profile Settings

Use this helpful but ponderous checklist to verify that your child has, in fact, made his or her profile as safe as possible. I recommend walking through this process with your child, so he or she will be aware of both how serious you are about safety and how wise you have become. First, get on your child's MySpace page. Once there, click on the "Edit Profile" tab. Next, check off the following statements once you are certain they are completed:

- My child is not using a picture of him- or herself; a suitable image, clip art, or cartoon figure is used instead.
- My child's "Name" is not their real name and is an appropriate nickname.
- My child's "Interests & Personality" answers are appropriately vague and tasteful.
- My child's birth date is false, and the year selected makes my child one hundred years old and therefore out of the range of a profile search.
- My child has left blank or used the "No Answer" option for the "Body Type" and "Marital Status" questions.
- My child has indicated "No Answer" to the "Background & Lifestyle" questions that include hometown, education, school, and children.

- The music that plays on my child's profile is acceptable and represents her in a positive manner. (As for the music used on your child's profile, use your own values and judgment to determine whether you feel it is appropriate or not.)
- I have clicked on "Account Settings" and verified that my child's profile is set to "Private." (Be sure that every privacy option is selected except "Who Can View My Profile: Anyone under 18.")
- I have taken a look at the e-mail address my child has used to register with MySpace. (Make sure you recognize it, and that it is an appropriate moniker.)
- I know my child's password. (In regards to the "Change Password" option, if you do not know your child's password, you need to change it now and memorize it. As discussed earlier, *I recommend your knowing the password and your child's not knowing it.* You must be in control; you are the new webmaster of your household, remember?)
- My child has indicated that he or she does *not* want to receive "Notifications" or "Newsletters" from MySpace.
- For the "IM Settings," my child has checked that either "No one can IM me" or "Only Friends can IM me." (This distinction is entirely up to you and predicated on whether you want your child instant messaging on MySpace or not.)
- My child has unselected *all* mobile settings.
- My child has unselected *all* group settings.
- My child has unselected "Display Groups I belong to."
- I have clicked on "Upload/Change Photos" and approved or deleted any pictures posted.
- I have clicked on "Manage Blog" and selected "Customize Blog." Under the section called "Side Module" I

have double-checked that all the settings (gender, status, age, sign, city, etc.) are set to "No."

- I have read and continue to read the blogs my child has and is posting. *I recommend forbidding any blogging altogether; journaling should always be kept private, especially when written by a minor.*

The third order of business is to solidify your rules in writing. It's about now that your child is realizing how serious you are . . . and you are beginning to like being a webmaster, right?

Teen Talk

"To me MySpace is like NyQuil; it's only as dangerous as you make it. If you overdose or abuse it, it can hurt you."

—*Shanta, 15*

Put It All in Writing

I implore you to compose and use a contract specifying rules and expectations for your child as long as he or she is a denizen of MySpace. Part of the problem of MySpace is the nebulous nature of the site, including what role you should play in monitoring your child, but a solid contract that outlines your own Terms of Use is well within your rights (in fact it is your responsibility) as a parent of one of today's e-teens. Plus, when your child violates an agreed-upon tenet, there can be no arguing. Below I have included a sample contract modeled after one found on the helpful site www.theparentsedge.com, but I do encourage you to involve your child in the composition of the contract—let him or her have some input, so there exists some sense of ownership.

 281

You will notice a few lines provided at the end of the contract for the specification of consequences; be sure you think these through before committing to them. I do recommend consequences that relate directly to the type of violation—in this case, the Internet; therefore, try stripping away computer privileges one by one. For example, if your child downloads a video without your permission, forbid him or her to use the computer for one week. *But be prepared to back it up should the contract be violated; without consistent consequences, the contract is pointless.* And if your child is breaking the contracted rules, chances are he or she is putting him- or herself in potential danger of attracting predators, scam artists, or phishers. Please see this sample contract, courtesy of www.the-parentsedge.com:

Family Internet Safety Rules and Usage Contract

Have your child read these three statements out loud to you and then initial them:

1. Nothing on the Internet is private. _____
2. People online are not always who they say they are._____
3. People are not always truthful online._____

I _____ agree on this date ___/___/___ to:

• Never give out our last name, address, phone number, or any personal information without parental consent. This includes the name of my school, where I play sports, the names of my family members and anything else included below:

- Additional "Never give out rules":_____
  _____

- Never give out my password to anyone other than my parents.
- Always let my parents review existing and new screen names, e-mail addresses, user logins, and all passwords.
- When asked where we live, we all agree to say this online: _____ Examples: ("can't give out this info," "the moon," "state," "OZ," "N/A.")
- Never upload or download pictures without parental consent.
- Never download games, music or videos without parental consent. (Many viruses infect your computer this way.)
- Get my parents' permission before I sign up for anything on the Internet.
- Never order anything online, even if it says "free," without parental consent. (Remember, nothing is free, some places just want your e-mail address so they can bombard you with spam, i.e., garbage e-mail.)
- Stop what I am doing and immediately get my parents or an adult I trust if someone asks to meet me in person. (A very serious matter not to be taken lightly.)
- Stop communicating with someone if the conversation gets uncomfortable, or if crude or inappropriate language is used.
- Never give out my age or any of my family or friends' ages online.
- Never use inappropriate language online.

- Never click on a pop-up banner or sign. (Just click on the X to close them.)
- Report a bully immediately to my parents and never bully someone else.
- Never enter a site that states, "You must be 18 to enter"
- Limit my time on the Internet to: _____ a day; homework is excluded here.

The Adults Agree:
- If my child comes and tells me that they saw something online that was inappropriate, I will discuss this openly with them.
- If my child reports a violation, I will discuss the matter with them first before calling the contract broken.
- If this contract is broken, the consequences will be:

_____

_____

_____

_____

I agree to abide by this contract.
Parent's signature:

_____

Kid's signature:

_____

Signed on ___/___/___

Now be sure to display this contract in a prominent spot near the computer as a constant reference and reminder!

Safety Recap

Caution! Remind your child to never disclose the following pieces of information in any form online: last name, address, school name, school address, regular hangouts, phone number, social security number, password, financial information, personal calendar of upcoming events or schedule, and personal data about family or friends.

Ask the Tough Questions

The fourth order of business is open and honest discussion. As you know, a signed piece of paper has its weight, but it is never a foolproof method. I know this firsthand as a teacher who has seen signature after signature on my class syllabi agreeing to the late-homework policy; without fail, I have students and parents argue my policy even after having signed it. Where is the disconnect? Frankly, I think a piece of paper is easily forgotten, and I don't believe people today value the gravity of a signature the way we once did. Nevertheless, the contract is a necessary and perhaps powerful step in the cyber-safety process. More important, however, is how we as parents follow up with it. I mentioned previously that proposed consequences must be applied consistently. And now, I propose that you engage in a regular, biweekly dialogue with your e-teen that consists of five tough questions, courtesy of Internet safety expert Donna Rice Hughes author of *Kids Online: Protecting Your Children in Cyberspace.*

- Have you seen any pornographic pictures?
- Has anyone online talked dirty to you?
- Have you met anyone online whom you don't know?

- Has anyone asked you for personal information?
- Has anyone asked to meet you in person?

As uncomfortable as it may be to address these questions with your teenager, trust me when I tell you that *you have to*! In an ideal world, your teen would still be playing blindman's bluff or Malibu Barbie, but the culture has evolved (or digressed, actually) and suppresses any sense of innocence as quickly as possible. And the Internet is leading the charge. So deal with the blushing and the stammering and begin discussing these issues immediately.

Cell Phone Safety

As a parent, we want our tweens and teens to have access to a cell phone for safety reasons and basic communication needs, but it's frustrating to know all the potential dangers that come with it. After consulting many parents, developmental experts, and educators, I have composed a checklist of good reasons to get your child a cell phone:

- My child is often home alone after school
- My child walks to and from school, as well as work
- My child is frequently on the road for sports, theater, or other activities
- My child goes out with friends on weekend nights
- My child has a driver's license, or his friends are driving
- My child is involved in extracurricular activities

If your child is a good candidate for a cell phone, you may wish to be selective in the type of phone and service plan you purchase. I have a few viable options: try the *LG Migo VX1000* from Verizon Wireless ($49.99 with a two-year contract); it is a child-friendly, simple phone with no text messaging, no games, and no camera.

The feature I really dig is that it has only four numbered buttons, which can dial four preprogrammed phone numbers (and they can't be changed without a password). For an extra $9.99 per month the phone offers a "chaperone service" with GPS capabilities to track your kid—if you're that neurotic. Try *Enfora's $99 TicTalk*; this walkie-talkie-like cell phone lets parents authorize certain numbers to call in and dial out, and the lack of a keypad forbids any text messaging or elaborate contact lists. A similar phone is the *Firefly Mobile*.

Recommended Monitoring and/or Filtering Software

Finally, to consummate your role as the family webmaster, you've got to implement monitoring and filtering software. However, please keep in mind that most mobile, handheld, or pocket devices offer access to the Internet, and therefore offer access to unmonitored and unfiltered adult content! Please do not buy into the myth of monitoring and filtering software as a cure-all. But, by all means, it should be one line of defense. *Any techie parents out there want to create a program for cell phones and iPods?*

If you decide to allow your child to participate in online social networks, please consider installing a filtering software program. More than half of parents do not have filtering software on their computers, according to facts provided by www.protectkids.com, even thought such programs block inappropriate content from your child's computer. No matter how much you trust your child, filtering or content-controlling software is a must. In terms of monitoring software, however, I recommend your considering it if you have been unsuccessful in reining in your child's Internet behavior. Monitoring software is like a built-in surveillance camera, and while I definitely don't advocate spying on your teen *unless* he or she has given you adequate reason to do so, using monitoring software gives you the ability to track your child's whereabouts online, viewing most activities and identifying online contacts.

These programs give you a better understanding of what your child is doing online. Information garnered from such programs should be used to finely tune your family's Internet contract. Hopefully, you see the benefits in both. However, please remember that these programs are merely a Band-Aid; while they are somewhat worthwhile, it is imperative for parents to realize that tech-savvy kids can usually get around them (and, in fact, pride themselves on doing so), as can the many less than honorable websites that prey on teens. As the intellectual Thomas G. Halliburton once said, "The suspicious parent makes an artful child." In short: nothing beats ongoing conversations, so do not rely solely on monitoring or filtering devices. Below please find a pretty good survey of the existing programs:

WebWatcher, $99.95 (www.awarenesstech.com)

With WebWatcher's web-based monitor you can check your recorded data from any computer in the world. This software lets you see what your children are doing as they are doing it. While some applications allow you to monitor your child, and some allow you to block the Internet, WebWatcher does both.

CyberPatrol, $39.95 (www.cyberpatrol.com)

This software will filter or block websites, newsgroups, and search engine image results based on all CyberLIST database categories, which can be fine-tuned by adding your own blocked or allowed sites or list of sites. CyberPatrol uses a combination of powerful layered filtering technologies comprising the CyberLIST database, as well as dynamic filtering technologies that capture new sites not yet in the database.

Net Nanny, $39.95 (www.netnanny.com)

Among other assets, Net Nanny stops illicit material from invading your child's computer by filtering and blocking web content while they surf.

CSWEB with PredatorGuard, $39.95 (www.securitysoft.com)

This software allows parents to *remotely* monitor and change filter settings on their home computer. Learn what your children are doing online and whom they are communicating with. Get screen captures of violations e-mailed to you instantly, or configure your own reports on all PC activity.

IamBigBrother, $29.95 (www.software4parents.com)

This software really is like Orwell's "Big Brother." It provides a complete list of all websites visited with the web page URL, title, and time visited. Another useful feature is to let IamBigBrother capture the screen when certain keywords are typed. If any of the words you set up are typed, IamBigBrother will capture the whole screen and save it for later viewing by the parent.

More Remote Monitoring Software

SafeEyes, $49.95

This software reports instant messaging chat, Web use, and file sharing with alerts via phone or e-mail.

eBlaster, $99.95

eBlaster e-mails copies of chats and reports Web use with e-mail alerts.

IM Einstein, $40

This product records IMs and chats and alerts via e-mail, phone, or PDA.

Finally, I recommend Trakzor 2.0, a tracking device designed specifically for MySpace.com. This software allows you to track any guests that click on your child's profile; it even displays these visitors on an interactive map. Go to www.trakzor.com for more information, including price.

You love your child. You're well aware of the many influences circulating the Internet that threaten to damage your child in some way. You want to honor your teen's coming-of-age process even though that means allowing him or her new freedoms. And it's overwhelming and ever evolving. Exactly! That's why your child is blessed to have you as his or her parent. Because you acknowledge their social reality and don't ignore it, because you trust them, because you realize that all is not bleak and that your child is a normal, healthy child trying to make sense of a sometimes abnormal, sometimes dysfunctional cyber-world. Simply put— your child is ahead of the game because you are in the picture.

If there's one thing I have come to realize in my many years of teaching middle and high school students, it is that *they are resilient.* Preteens and teens can weather a great deal of negative influences, harmful experiences, and discouraging words. I've seen countless seventh-grade girls dance on the fringes of dangerous behavior only to land safely in the center of normalcy. The process is no less jarring; to witness someone you love dabbling in potentially perilous activities, especially for a parent, is almost too much to take. However, I urge you to maintain the perspective that all will be well if you continue to love your child, talk to your child, and be the parent. My hope is that this book has reached the heart of your inner parent, and that I have been able to help you to more fully understand the new adolescence in this age of MySpace.com.

Resources

Introduction

Abe, Debby. "The Siren Call of MySpace.com." *The News Tribune*, January 8, 2006.

Anonymous. Adolescent Brain Development "The Brain Shapes 'What's the Matter with Kids Today.'" *Harvard Mental Health Letter*. Boston, MA, Harvard Health Publications: Boston, 2005.

Anderson, Nikki. "Local Teens Find Themselves Addicted to Social Networking Web Site." *The Ledger-Dispatch*, April 14, 2006.

Angwin, Julia. "Parental Guidance: How Safe Aare Top Networking Sites for Teens?" *The Wall Street Journal*, July 24, 2006.

Arnold, Thomas K. "The MySpace Invaders." *USA Today*, July 31, 2006.

Associated Press. "MySpace.com Links Politicians, Friends." www.newsmax.com, August 17, 2006.

Carlisle, Wendy. "Background Briefing." ABC Radio National, December 18, 2005.

Colker, David. "On the Cell, MySpace Is Crammed but Livable." *Los Angeles Times*, May 11, 2006.

Coxx Communications Press Release. "New Study Rreveals 14% of Teens Have Had Face-to-Face Meetings with People They've Met on the Internet." May 11, 2006.

Demos, Telis. "Making Friends — And Money — On MySpace." *CNNMoney.com.* May 8, 2006.

Dumenco, Simon. "Screwing Up MySpace: A News Corp. How-To Guide." *Advertising Age,* June 26, 2006.

Easterbrook, Gregg. "The Heart of a New Machine." In: J. Zerzan and A. Carnes, *Questioning Technology.* Philadelphia: New Society Publishers, Philadelphia.1991.

Eggerton, J. "Hundt Hits Television Violence." *Broadcasting and Cable,* January 31, 1994.

Fearing, James. "The Symptoms of Computer Addiction." www.warningsigns.com.

Harris, Dan. "MySpace.com's Extreme Makeover." ABCNews.com, April 11, 2006.

Hempel, Jessi, and Paula Lehman. "The MySpace Generation." *BusinessWeek Online,* December 12, 2005.

Irvine, Martha. "Not So Fast: Slower E-Mail Can't Keep Up with Young." *The Washington Times Insider,* July 20, 2006.

i-Safe America Survey. www.isafe.org, 2003–2005.

Lenhart, Amanda, Mary Madden, and Paul Hitlin. "Teens and Technology: Youth Are Leading the Transition to a Fully Wired and Mobile Nation." Pew Internet and American Life Project, July 27, 2006.

Mander, Jerry. Interview via telephone, August 29, 2006.

McCarthy, Caroline. "'My Name is Earl' Promotion Launched on MySpace." CNET Networks: Www.News.com, August 11, 2006.

McCluhan, Marshall. *Understanding Media: The Extensions of Man.* M.I.T.Press: Cambridge, MA. MIT Press, 1964.

Miller, Jason Lee. "Deeper iInto the Shadows of MySpace." www.webpronenews.com, April 4, 2006.

Mueller, Ken. "Dear Diary, Dear World." The Center for Parent/Youth Understanding. www.cpyu.org, 2005.

Nolan, Clancy. "Venture Firms Help Ffund Social Sites." *The Wall Street Journal,* September 21, 2006.

Norris, Michelle, and Spencer Reiss. "The Ascendance of MySpace." NPR: *All Things Considered*, July 12, 2006.

Olsen, Stephanie. "Google Pledges $900 Million for MySpace Honors." CNET Newstworks: Www.News.com, August 8, 2006.

Pace, Natalie. "Q&A: MySpace Founders Chris DeWolfe and Tom Anderson." Forbes.com, January 4, 2006.

Pew Internet & American Life Project. "Protecting Teens Online." March 17, 2005.

Potkewitz, Hilary. "Major Media Paying Big Bucks to Reach Youths." *San Diego Business Journal*, August 8, 2006.

Rainie, Lee. "Life Online: Teens and Technology and the World to Come." Speech to Annual Conference of Public Library Association, Boston. Pew Internet & American Life Project, March 23, 2006.

Reardon, Marguerite. "Helio to Open Retail Stores." CNET Networks: www.News.com, August 14, 2006.

Reeves, Byron, and Clifford Nass. *The Media Equation*. Stanford University: CSLI Publications, 1996.

Resnikoff, Paul. "Bebo Battles MySpace Music, Attracts Early Following." www.digitalmusicnews.com, August 19, 2006.

Resnikoff, Paul. "MySpace Officially Launches in Australia." www.digitalmusicnews.com, August 19, 2006.

Reuters. "MySpace Heat Raises News Corp. Profit." CNET Networks: www.news.com, August 9, 2006.

Reuters. "MySpace May Be Worth $15 Billion." CNET News.com, September 28, 2006.

Rideout, V. G., U. G. Foehr, D. F. Roberts, and M. Brodie. *Kids and Media*, Executive Summary. Menlo Park, CA: Kaiser Family Foundation, 1999.

Rimm, Sylvia, Ph.D. *Growing Up Too Fast: The Rimm Report on the Secret World of America's Middle Schoolers*. New York: Rodale, Inc. New York, 2005.

Romano, Lois. "Teens Are Right — Mom and Dad Really Are Clueless." *The Day*, August 18, 2006.

Smith, Andrea. "A Parent Learns About MySpace." ABCNews.com, February 21, 2006.

Spinks, Sarah. "Inside the Teenage Brain." *Frontline*. PBS Transcript, January 31, 2002.

Taylor, Lewis. "30 Million Find a Place on MySpace." *The Register Guard*, October 8, 2005.

van Krieken, Mark. "Parents Need to Know the Risks of Weekend Teenage Parties." Berkeley High School Newsletter, January 2006.

Wikipedia. "MySpace." www.wikipedia.org.

www.43things.com. "Worth Doing!"

www.bewebaware.com. "Internet Addiction."

Yamamato, Mike. "How Cyworld Could Trump MySpace." CNET News.com: August 11, 2006.

Zimmerman, Stephanie. "Scams Begin to Target Users of MySpace." *Chicago Sun-Times*, May 22, 2006.

Chapter 1

Abe, Debby. "MySpace.com Becomes a Social Necessity." *Tacoma News Tribune*, January 24, 2006.

Acuff, Daniel S., and Robert H. Reiher. *Kidnapped: How Irresponsible Marketers Are Stealing the Minds of Your Children*. Dearborn Trade Publishing: Chicago, 2005.

Alderman, Rob. "My Addiction to MySpace." *Relevant Magazine*. www.relevant-magazine.com, 2005.

Anonymous. "43 Things." www.43things.com. 2005.

Anonymous. "Adolescent Brain Development." *Harvard Mental Health Letter*. Boston, MA: Harvard Health Publications. July 2006.

Boyd, danah. Interview, August 19, 2006. www.sephoria.org/thoughts.

Lewis, Trent. . . "MySpace . . . . What Parents Need to Know." www.high-schoolrevolution.com. The Church at Rocky Peak: Student Ministries, 2006.

Nadlman, Jonathan. Interview. August 14, 2006.

Chapter 2

"Online Safety Tips." Connecticut Internet Crimes Against Children Task Force. Connecticut Department of Public Safety. www.ct.gov/dps/lib/public/public_information/files/brochures/online_safety.pdf.

"Protecting Our Kids." See www.lacountyda.org/pok.htm.

Anonymous. "Finding Teenagers Online: A Step-by-Step Approach to Navigating Their Online World." The Center for Parent/Youth Understanding. www.cpyu.org.

Boyd, danah. "Identity Production in a Networked Culture: Why Youth Heart MySpace." American Association for the Advancement of Science. www.danah.org/papers. February 19, 2006.

Boyd, danah. Interview on August 19, 2006. www.sephoria.org/thoughts.

Dale, Laney. *A Parent's Guide to MySpace*. Redondo Beach, CA: DayDream Publishing: Redondo Beach, CA. 2006.

Erskine, Chris. "Maybe Rename Iit DadSpace?" *Los Angeles Times*, June 15, 2006.

Farnham, Dale and Kevin. *MySpace Safety: 51 Tips for Teens and Parents.* Pomfret, CT: How-To-Primers, Pomfret, CT. 2006

Garrett, Grant. "Parenting and Technology: Social Networking Web Sites and More." www.modernmom.com.

Healy, Jane, Ph.D. *Failure to Connect: How Computers Can Affect Our Our Children's Minds—and What We Can Do about It*. New York: Simon and Schuster: New York, 1998.

Hunt, Caroline. "Holden's MySpace: Assessment of Characterization and Voice." Summit View School, spring 2006.

Lenhart, Amanda. "Testimony to the House Committee on Energy and Commerce Subcommittee on Telecommunications and the Internet Hearing on H.R. 5319, the Deleting Online Predators Act of 2006." July 11, 2006.

Lewis, Trent. "MySpace . . . What Parents Need to Know." www.highschoolrevolution.com. The Church at Rocky Peak: Student Ministries, 2006.

Rebello, Justin. "MySpace: Facebook's Gay Cousin." www.pointsincase.com,. June 12, 2006.

Rosen, Larry D. "Adolescents in MySpace; Identity Formation, Friendship, and Sexual Predators." Academic study. California State University, Dominguez Hills. June 2006.

See www. missingchildren.com/cyber_safety.htm. Adapted from *Teen Safety on the Information Highway* by Lawrence J. Magid. Copyright(c) respectively 1994 and 1998 National Center for Missing & Exploited Children (NCMEC), 1994, 1998.

Weinstein, A. "Unlocking Your Teen's Profile." *Red Herring*. August 7, 2006.

Chapter 3

Anonymous. "Comprehensive IM Shorthand List,." in "Protecting Our Kids." Web pamphlet. Los Angeles County District Attorney, www.lacountyda.org/ pok.

Anonymous. "Keeping Your Kids Safe Online: Slang Every Parent Should Know." Internet Slang Dictionary & Translator, www.noslang.com.

Carroll, Lewis. "Jabberwocky." Please see www.jabberwocky.com.

Huffaker, David A., and Sandra L. Calvert. "Gender, Identity, and Language Use in Teenage Blogs." Children's Digital Media Center, Georgetown University, 2004.

Chapter 4

Associated Press. "MySpace Blog Disrupts School, Sparks Probe." *Chattanooga News-Free Press*, October 2, 2006.

Bansal, Rashmi. "Networking = Net Worth." *Business World*, September 2004.

Barrie-Anthony, Steven. "Take a Number, Pal." *Los Angeles Times*, May 10, 2006.

Boyd, danah. Interview, August 19, 2006. www.sephoria.org/thoughts.

Bryant, J. Alison, and Ashley Sanders-Jackson, and Amber M. K. Smallwood. "IMing, Text Messaging, and Adolescent Social Networks." *Journal of Computer-Mediated Communication*. Department of Telecommunications, Indiana University, 2006.

Downes, Stephen. "The Semantic Social Network." Posted www.downes.ca. February 14, 2004.

Duffy, Jonathan. "The MySpace Age." *BBC News Magazine*, September 2006.

Healy, Jane. *Failure to Connect: How Computers Affect Our Children's Minds—And What We Can Do about It*. New York: Simon and Schuster: New York, 1998.

Kornblum, Janet. "Campuses Connect Students Online." *USA Today*, August 16, 2006.

Kornblum, Janet. "Many Love 'Friending,' but Some Question Its Value." *USA Today*, September 20, 2006.

Lewis, Trent. High. "MySpace . . . What Parents Need to Know." www.high-schoolrevolution.com. The Church at Rocky Peak: Student Ministries, 2006.

Peters, Amanda. "'I have 208 Friends' — Real Friends vs. MySpace Friends." *New America Media*, July 26, 2006.

Srinagesh, Soumya. "Teen's Tips for Avoiding MySpace Dorkiness." CNET News.com, August 2, 2006.

Turkle, Sherry. "Living Online: I'll Have to Ask My Friends." *New Scientist*, September 20, 2006.

www.netfamilynews.org. "Social Influence Techniques Used Online."

www.zephoria.org. "Attention Networks vs. Social Networks." *Apophenia*. November 29, 2005.

Chapter 5

Associated Press. "College Students Warned about Internet Postings." CNN.com, August 2, 2006.

Head, Will. "Teachers Urged to Tackle Cyber-Bullying." www.vnunet.com, August 16, 2006.

Lau, Calvin. "Whose Space Is MySpace?" www.theeyeopener.com, April 4, 2006.

Olsen, Stephanie. "Youth Centers Grapple with MySpace." CNET News.com. June 23, 2006.

Rapoport, Ian R. "The MySpace Dilemma." *The Clarion-Ledger*, August 6, 2006.

Sullivan, Bob. "Cyberbullying: the Newest Threat to Kids." Blog. www.redtape. msnbc.com, August 9, 2006

Tseng, Nin-Hai. "Districts Grapple with Web Bullying." *Orlando Sentinel*, August 9, 2006.

Zhou, Kevin. "MySpace.com Invites Bullying, Possibly Danger." *Danville Weekly*, online edition, March 10, 2006.

Chapter 6
Barrie-Anthony, Steven. "Take a Number, Pal." *Los Angeles Times*. May 10, 2006.

Huffaker, D. A., and S. L. Calvert, S. L. "Gender, Identity, and Language Use in Teenage Blogs." *Journal of Computer-Mediated Communication*, 10(2), article 1, 2005.

Levy, Ariel. *Female Chauvinist Pigs: Women and the Rise of Raunch Culture.* Free Press: New York, 2005.

Mazzarella, S. R. *Girl Wide Web: Girls, the Internet, and the Negotiation of Identity.* Peter Lang: New York, 2005.

Subrahmanyam, K., P. M. Greenfield, PM, and B.& Tynes, B. "Constructing Sexuality and Identity in an Online Teen Chat Room." *Applied Developmental Psychology*: 25, 2004.

Chapter 7
Angwin, Julia. "MySpace Draws Ads by Offering Safe Content." *The Wall Street Journal*, June 21, 2006.

Anonymous. "Teens & Technology Fact Sheet." National Youth Anti-Drug Media Campaign. www.mediacampaign.org. July 21, 2006.

Anonymous. "What Are Teens Hiding on MySpace?" ABC News. www.abc-news.com,. May 18, 2006.

Berton, Justin. "Generation Gap: Parents, Exhibitionist Young People Differ on NSA Spying." *San Francisco Chronicle*, May 20, 2006.

Davis, Wendy. "Teens' Online Postings Are New Tool for Police." *The Boston Globe*, May 15, 2006.

Payne, January W. "MySpace, MySickness: The Dark Side of the Popular Website." *The Miami Herald*, July 18, 2006.

Sand, Paul. "MySpace: Meet People, Talk Music, Fight Crime." The News Tribune.com, March 12, 2006.

Selingo, Jeffrey. "Back to School, with Cellphone and Laptop." *The New York Times*, August 17, 2006.

Stone, Jessica. "World 'Weed' Web and 'Sell' Phones: Teens Use Technology to Score Drugs, Get High." Newsletter, Pathway Family Center. July 13, 2006

Sweeney, Annie. "Internet Was Way into Drug Life: Teens." *Chicago Sun-Times*, July 19, 2006.

Chapter 8

Anonymous. "MySpace Comedy! How About MySpace Porn?" www.myflakes.com, 2006.

Anonymous. "MySpace Promotes Lesbian Lust to Fourteen-14 Year-Olds." www.myflakes.com, 2006.

Anonymous. "MySpace Youth—Fun Outlet for Aggression, Hate, Misery, Despair, Racism, Crime, Rape, Mayhem." www.myflakes.com, 2006.

Bissonnette, Emily. "Youth Choose Abstinence oOver Sex." *The Cincinnati Enquirer*, September 30, 2006.

Gupta, Shankar. "*Playboy* to Publish Women of MySpace." www.mediapostpublications.com, 2006.

Hagelin, Rebecca. "Porn, Pedophiles, Our Kids, and MySpace." WorldNetDaily, May 30, 2006.

Heredia, Christopher. "How Mom Can Affect a Teen's Sex Life." *The San Francisco Chronicle*, September 5, 2002.

Hoffman, Claire. "'Baby, Give Me a Kiss': The Man bBehind the 'Girls Gone Wild' Soft-Porn Empire." *The Los Angeles Times*, August 6, 2006.

Horning, Rob. "Meet Joe Francis." Permalink. www.popmatters.com, August 8, 2006.

Hosley, Ryan, and Steve Waters. "Dangers and Disappointments of Pornography." www.pureintimacy.org. Focus on the Family. March 9, 2006.

Hughes, Donna Rice. "Teen Testimonials on Internet Porn and Recovery." Courtesy of House of Hope, Orlando, Florida. www.protectkids.com.

Jackson, Rob, M.S., LPC, LMHC, NCC. "Advice for Parents of Teenage Porn Addicts." *Pure Intimacy*. www.pureintimacy.org.

Jacobs, Rodger. "MySpace Now a Porn Fav." www.xbiz.com. February 17, 2006.

Lewis, Trent. "MySpace . . . What Parents Need to Know." www.highschoolrevolution.com. The Church at Rocky Peak: Student Ministries, 2006.

Makow, Henry, Ph.D. "Why All Porn Is Gay." www.savethemales.ca, February 11, 2006.

Miller, Jason Lee. "Cell Phone Better Choice for Porn." www.webpronews.com, February 24, 2006.

Musgrove, Mike. "Mini-Porn Could Be Mega Business." *The Washington Post*, November 15, 2005.

National Center for Missing and Exploited Children. "Online Victimization of Youth: Five Years Later." www.missingkids.com, 2005

O'Malley, Gavin. "'*Seventeen*' Gets Its Own MySpace Page." *Advertising Age*, June 29, 2006.

Richard, Jerome, Joanne Fowler, Devan Stewart, Joanna Blonska, Pam Grout, and Jason Bane. "The Cyberporn Generation." *People*, April 26, 2004.

Saillant, Catherine. "Testing the Bounds of MySpace." *Los Angeles Times*, April 8, 2006.

Samson, Jeri, and Beth Keen. "Pornography on the Internet." www.notmykid.org, 2006.

Tuttle, Allison. "MySpace: Kiddie Porn for Millions?" www.associatedcontent.com, 2006.

Woods, Ann. "Teenagers and Risk-Taking at Camp: An Interview with Lynn Ponton." *Camping Magazine*, January/February 2002.

Chapter 9
Anonymous. Special Report. "How to Cope with MySpace Invaders." *Curriculum Review*, April 1, 2006.

Erskine, Chris. "Maybe Rename It DadSpace?" *The Los Angeles Times*, June 15, 2006.

Lamb, Sharon, and Lyn Mikel Brown. *Packaging Girlhood: Rescuing Our Daughters from Marketers' Schemes.* St. Martin's Press: New York, 2006.

Chapter 10

Anonymous. "Rules "N Tools for Social Networking Sites," www.protectkids.com.

Anonymous. "How to Cope with MySpace Invaders." *Curriculum Review,* April 1, 2006.

Anonymous. "Kids Are Easy Victims." Protecting Our Kids. Online Pamphlet. Los Angeles County District Attorney. www.lacountyda.org/pok.

Anonymous. "MySpace Contract." www.theparentsedge.com, 2006.

Conklin, Andrea. "MySpace Banned from Many School Computers." KGBT4 News: Harlingen, Texas, March 1, 2006.

Dannahey, Frank. "Making the Internet Safe for Kids: The Role of ISPs and Social Networking Sites." Written testimony given before the Committee on Energy and Commerce Subcommittee on Oversight and Investigations, United States House of Representatives. June 28, 2006.

Eichenwald, Kurt. "On the Web, Pedophiles Extend Their Reach." *The New York Times,* August 21, 2006.

Erskine, Chris. "Maybe Rename It DadSpace?" *The Los Angeles Times,* June 15, 2006.

Finder, Alan. "For Some, Online Persona Undermines a Résumé." *The New York Times,* June 11, 2006.

Garrett, Grant. "Parenting & and Technology: Social Networking Web Sites and More." www.modernmom.com, August 14, 2006.

Hughes, Donna Rice. *Kids Online: Protecting Your Children in Cyberspace.* Fleming H. Revell Company: Grand Rapids, MI, 1998.

Jackson, Rob. "Advice for Parents of Teenage Porn Addicts." Pure Intimacy. www.pureintimacy.com. Focus on the Family, 2004.

Jesdaunun, Anick. "UNH Study Finds Decrease in Online Sexual Solicitations." www.boston.com, August 9, 2006.

Keeker, Kory. "MySpace, Horse Porn—Apparently It's All Evil." www.juneauempire.com, July 27, 2006.

Anonymous. "Deleting Online Predators." The Norman Transcript. www.acsblog.org, 2006.

Kuhlenschmidt, Richard. "Remote Monitoring Software." www.blog.famundo.com, June 1, 2006.

Lewis, Trent. "MySpace . . . What Parents Need to Know." www.highschoolrevolution. com. The Church at Rocky Peak: Student Ministries, 2006.

Lewis, Trent. "The Internet . . . Simple Steps to Guard Your Students." www.highschoolrevolution.com. The Church at Rocky Peak: Student Ministries, 2006.

Lewis, Trent. "The Internet . . . Simple Steps to Guard Your Students,." www.highschoolrevolution.com. The Church at Rocky Peak: Student Ministries, 2006.

Lewis, Trent. "The Internet . . . Simple Steps to Guard Your Students." www.highschoolrevolution.com. The Church at Rocky Peak: Student Ministries, 2006.

Lukianoff, Greg. "I Am All for Free Speech—but I Draw the Line at People Making Fun of Me!" Fire's "The Torch." www.thefire.org, May 30, 2006.

Magid, Larry. "Protect Kids on MySpace." CBSNews.com, February 3, 2006.

Mann, Denise. "Challenges of MySpace-Era Parenting." CBSNews.com, August 11, 2006.

Palank, Jacqueline. "Face It: 'Book' No Secret to Employees." The Washington Times, July 17, 2006.

Poulsen, Kevin. "MySpace Backlash." www.wired.com, February 27, 2006.

Puzzanghera, Jim. "Bill Seeks to Block Access to MySpace in Schools." The Los Angeles Times, May 12, 2006.

Thierer, Adam. "The MySpace Middleman Isn't the Problem." www.heartland.org. The Heartland Institute, August 1, 2006.

Wallace, Stephen G. "Their Space. . . . or Yours?" Summit Communications Management, 2006.

WikiHow. "How to Defeat a MySpace Addiction." www.WikiHow.com, July 29, 2005.

Wright, Sarah H. "Experts Discuss MySpace Issues." Academic Forum. Massachusetts Institute of Technology, May 24, 2006.

Zeller, Tom Jr. "A Lesson for Parents on 'MySpace Madness.'" *The New York Times*, June 26, 2006.

Recommended Reading, Surfing, and Viewing

Chapter 1

Recommended Reading

Currie, Elliott. *The Road to Whatever: Middle Class Culture and the Crisis of Adolescence.*

Mindell, Jodi, and Judith Owens. *Take Charge of Your Child's Sleep: The All-in-One reesource for Solving Sleep Problems in Kids and Teens.*

Perlstein, Linda. *Not Much Just Chillin': The Hidden Lives of Middle Schoolers.*

Rawlings, Gregory J. E. *Moths to the Flame: The Seduction of Computer Technology.*

Walsh, David, and Nat Bennett. *WHY Do They Act That Way: A Survival Guide to the Adolescent Brain for You and Your Teen.*

Young, Kimberly. *Caught in the Net: How to Recognize the Signs of Internet Addiction.*

Helpful Websites

www.notmykid.org
www.bewebaware.com
www.webmd.com
www.helpyourteens.com
www.warningsigns.com

Chapter 2

Recommended Reading

Dale, Laney. *A Parent's Guide to MySpace.*

Farnham, Dale and Kevin. *MySpace Safety: 51 Tips for Teens and Parents.*

Harris, Marc. *MySpace 4 Parents: Learn How to Protect Your Child in MySpace.*

Hupfer, Ryan, and Mitch Maxson. *MySpace for Dummies.*

Magid, Larry, and Anne Collier. *MySpace Unraveled: What Is It, How to Use It, and How to Stay Safe.*

Chapter 3

Recommended Reading

Burke, David. *Street Talk 2: Slang Used by Teens, Rappers, Surfers, & Popular American Television Shows.*

Crystal, David. *Language and the Internet.*

Danet, Brenda, and Susan C. Herring. *The Multilingual Internet: Language, Culture, and Communication Online.*

Holt, Richard. *Dialogue on the Internet: Language, Civic Identity, and Computer-Mediated Communication.*

Horwitz, Sil. "The Language of the Internet." An article from PSA *Journal.*

Myracle, Lauren. *TTYL (Talk To You Later).* This novel is cleverly written entirely in IM language; it's a great read on many levels, if not for you then definitely for your teen.

Young, Kenn W. *Naz's Dictionary of Teen Slang.*

For Fun

Evslin, Tom. *hackoff.com: An Historic Murder Mystery Set in the Internet Bubble and Rubble.*

Chapter 4

Recommended Reading

Self and Society: Is Social Life Being Transformed?

Beane, Allan L. The Bully Free Classroom: Over 100 Tips and Strategies for Teachers K-8.

Ben-Ze'ev, Aaron. Love Online: Emotions on the Internet.

Haythornthwaite, Caroline, and Barry Wellman. The Internet in Everyday Life.

Joinson, Adam N. Understanding the Psychology of Internet Behaviour: Virtual Worlds, Real Lives.

Packer, Alex J. The How Rude! Handbook of Friendship & Dating Manners for Teens: Surviving the Social Scene.

Romain, Trevor. Cliques, Phonies, and Other Baloney.

Simmons, Rachel. Odd Girl Out: The Hidden Culture of Girls' Aggression.

Valentine, Gill, and Sarah Holloway. Cyberkids: Youth Identities and Communties in an On-line World.

Wiseman, Rosalind. Queen Bees and Wannabes: Helping Your Daughter Survive Cliques, Gossip, Boyfriends, and Other Realities of Adolescence.

Recommended Films

A Better Place. Eion Bailey.

Suburbia. Penelope Spheeris.

Chapter 5

Recommended Reading

Beane, Allan L. *The Bully Free Classroom: Over 100 Tips and Strategies for Teachers K-8.*

Borba, Michele. *Nobody Likes Me, Everybody Hates Me: The Top 25 Friendship Problems and How to Solve Them.*

Romain, Trevor. *Bullies Are a Pain in the Brain.*

Simmons, Rachel. *Odd Girl Out: The Hidden Culture of Girls' Aggression.*

Stofel, Robert. *Survival Notes for Teens: Inspiration for the Emotional Journey.*

Verdick, Elizabeth, and Marjorie Lisovskis. *How to Take the Grrr Out of Anger.*

Wiseman, Rosalind. *Queen Bees and Wannabes: Helping Your Daughter Survive Cliques, Gossip, Boyfriends, and Other Realities of Adolescence.*

Recommended Websites

www.bullypolice.org

www.kidpower.org

www.stopbullyingnow.com

www.bridgew.edu/marc

www.safeyouth.org

www.pacerkidsagainstbullying.org

www.isafe.org

Chapter 6

Recommended Reading

Anderson, Kristen. *The Truth about Sex by High School Senior Girls.*

Barker, Teresa, and JoAnn Deak. *Girls Will Be Girls: Raising Confident and Courageous Daughters.*

Brashich, Audrey. *All Made Up: A Girl's Guide to Seeing through Celebrity Hype . . . and Celebrating Real Beauty.*

Brown, Lyn Mikel, and Sharon Lamb. *Packaging Girlhood: Rescuing Our Daughters from Marketers' Schemes.*

Courtney, Vicki. *Teenvirtue: Real Issues, Real Live . . . A Teen Girls' Survival Guide.*

Fass, Paula. *The Damned and the Beautiful: American Youth in the 1920s.*

Gurion, Michael. *The Wonder of Girls: Understanding the Hidden Nature of Our Daughters.*

Gruver, Nancy. *How to Say It to Girls: Communicating with Your Growing Daughter.*

Hummel, Patti M. *This Is Now: Girl to Girl Devotional for Teens.*

Klar, Barry. *Citizen Sex: The Girl Next Door on the Adult Internet.*

Levin, Diane. "So Sexy So Soon," a chapter in *Childhood Lost.*

Levy, Ariel. *Female Chauvinist Pigs: Women and the Rise of Raunch Culture.*

Machoian, Lisa. *The Disappearing Girl: Learning the Language of Teenage Depression.*

Peiss, Kathy. *Hope in a Jar: The Making of America's Beauty Culture.*

Pipher, Mary. *Reviving Ophelia: Saving the Selves of Adolescent Girls.*

Ponton, Lynn. *The Sex Lives of Teenagers: Revealing the Secret World of Adolescents.*

Schrum, Kelly. *Some Wore Bobby Sox: The Emergence of Teenage Girls' Culture, 1920–1945.*

Shalit, Wendy. *A Return to Modesty: Discovering the Lost Virtue.*

Snyderman, Nancy L., and Peg Streep. *Girl in the Mirror: Mothers and Daughters in the Years of Adolescence.*

Spears, Aubrey, and Chandra Peele. *Great Love for Girls: Truth for Teens in Today's Sexy Culture.*

Tarbox, Katherine. *A Girl's Life Online.*

Tolman, Deborah. *Dilemmas of Desire: Teenage Girls Talk about Sexuality.*

Weil, Sabrina. *The Real Truth about Teens & Sex: From Hooking Up to Friends with Benefits—What Teens Are Thinking, Doing, Talking about, and How to Help Them Make Smart Choices.*

Recommended Websites

www.girlscoalition.org

www.girlsinc.org

www.newmoon.org

www.smartgirl.com

www.sistagirls.org

www.withitgirl.com

Recommended Organizations

Coalition for Positive Sexuality, www.cps@positive.org

Dads & Daughters, www.dadsanddaughters.org

Third Wave Foundation, www.thirdwavefoundation.org

Advocates for Youth, www.advocatesforyouth.org

Recommended Newsletter

Daughters (the newsletter for parents of girls), www.daughters.com

Recommended Films

Thirteen. Catherine Hardwicke.

Mean Girls. Mark Waters.

Ghost World. Terry Zwigoff.

Recommended Reading for parents of boys

Brinly, Maryann Bucknum. *Oh Boy! Mothers Tell the Truth about Raising Teen Sons.*

Currie, Elliott. *The Road to Whatever: Middle Class Culture and the Crisis of Adolescence.*

Gurian, Michael. *The Good Son: Shaping the Moral Development of Our Boys and Young Men.*

Kendall, Lori. *Hanging Out in the Virtual Pub: Masculinities and Relationships Online.*

Kindlon, Dan, and Michael Thompson. Raising Cain: *Protecting the Emotional Life of Boys.*

Kipnis, Aaron. *Angry Young Men: How Parents, Teachers, and Counselors Can Help "Bad Boys" Become Good Men.*

Middleman, Amy B., and Kate Gruenwald. *American Medical Association Boy's Guide to Becoming a Teen.*

Nikkah, John. *Our Boys Speak: Adolescent Boys Write about Their Inner Lives.*

Pollack, William S., and Todd Shuster. *Real Boys' Voices.*

Pope, Harrison G. *The Adonis Complex: How to Identify, Treat and Prevent Body Obsession in Men and Boys.*

Quinn, Eithne. *Nuthin' but a 'G' Thang: The Culture and Commerce of Gangsta Rap.*

Shaffer, Susan Morris, and Linda Perlman Gordon. *Why Boys Don't Talk—and Why It Matters.*

Chapter 7
Recommended Reading

DuPont, Robert L. *The Selfish Brain: Learning from Addiction.*

Emmett, David, and Nice Graeme. *Understanding Street Drugs: A Handbook of Substance Misuse for Parents, Teachers, and Other Professionals.*

Ensor, Jim. *Future Net: The Essential Guide to Internet and Technology Megatrends.*

Falkowski, Carol. *Dangerous Drugs: An Easy-to-Use Reference for Parents and Professionals.*

Folkers, Gladys, and Jeanne Engelmann. *Taking Charge of My Mind and Body: A Girls' Guide to Outsmarting Alcohol, Drug, Smoking, and Eating Problems.*

Gordon, Dianna. *Surfing for Drugs: Internet Pharmacies Have Proliferated, Offering Consumers Cheap, Mail-Order Drugs.*

Kuhn, Cynthia. *Just Say Know: Talking with Kids about Drugs and Alcohol.*

Marshall, Michael and Shelly. *Ready, Aim, Inspire: Targeting Your Teen's Drug Crisis, with a Focus on Solutions, Not Blame.*

Monroe, Judy. *Inhalant Drug Dangers.*

Palmiero, Karen. *90 Ways to Keep Your Kids Drug Free.*

Ponton, Lynn. *The Romance of Risk: Why Teenagers Do the Things They Do.*

Rogers, Peter D., and Lea Goldstein. *Drugs and Your Kid: How to Tell If Your Child Has a Drug/Alcohol Problem and What to Do about It.*

Rosengren, John. *Big Book Unplugged: A Young Person's Guide to Alcoholics Anonymous.*

Schwebel, Robert. *Saying No Is Not Enough—Helping Your Kids Make Wise Decisions about Alcohol, Tobacco, and Other Drugs.*

VanVonderen, Jeff. *Good News for the Chemically Dependent and Those Who Love Them.*

Recommended Websites, Pamphlets, and Organizations
For Parents
www.theantidrug.com
www.laanidroga.com (Spanish)

For Teachers and Coaches
For Employers
www.theantidrug.com/ParentsatWork

For Faith Leaders
www.theantidrug.com/Faith

For Journalists and Entertainment Writers
www.drugstory.org

For Everyone
www.mediacampaign.org
www.whitehousedrugpolicy.gov
www.helpyourcommunity.org
www.findtreatment.samhsa.gov
ww.health.org
www.nida.nih.gov

For Youth
www.freevibe.com

Make a Difference: Talk to Your Child about Alcohol (U.S. Department of Health and Human Services). www.niaaa.hig.gov or call 1.800.487.4889

Keeping Youth Drug-Free (U.S. Department of Health and Human Services, Center for Substance Abuse Prevention). www.samhsa.gov or call 1.800.729.6686

For a description of effective school and community drug-abuse-prevention programs and strategies, you can also visit http://modelprograms.samhsa.gov.

Recommended Films
Brick. Rian Johnson.
Traffic. Benicio Del Toro.

Chapter 8
Recommended Reading
Hagelin, Rebecca. *Home Invasion: Protecting Your Family in a Culture That's Gone Stark Raving Mad.*
Levy, Ariel. *Female Chauvinist Pigs: Women and the Rise of Raunch Culture.*
Schuster, Mark, and Justin Richardson. *Everything You Never Wanted Your Kids to Know about Sex (But Were Afraid They'd Ask): The Secrets to Surviving Your Child's Sexual Development.*

Chapter 9

Recommended Reading
Glasser, William. *For Parents and Teenagers: Dissolving the Barrier between You and Your Teen.*
Godfrey, Neale S., and Rhett. *The Teen Code: How to Talk to Them about Sex, Drugs, and Everything Else—Teenagers Reveal What Works Best.*

Grigsby, Connie, and Kent Julian. *How to Get Your Teen to Talk to You.*

Paterson, Kathy. *Every Adult's Guide to Talking to Teens.*

Patnaik, Gayatri, and Michelle T. Shineski. *The Secret Life of Teens: Young People Speak Out about Their Lives.*

Peterson, Jean Sunde. *The Essential Guide to Talking with Teens: Ready-to-Use Discussions for School and Youth Groups.*

Rainey, Barbara, and Bruce Nygren. *Parenting Today's Adolescent: Helping Your Child Avoid the Traps of the Preteen and Teen Years.*

Taffel, Ron, and Melinda Blau. *The Second Family: Dealing with Peer Power, Pop Culture, the Wall of Silence—and Other Challenges of Raising Today's Teens.*

White, Joe, and Nicholas Comninellis. *Nine Things Teens Should Know & Parents Are Afraid to Talk About.*

For Fun

Kaplan, Jeffrey P., and Abby M. Lederman. *Finding the Path: A Novel for Parents of Teenagers.*

Chapter 10
Recommended Reading & Viewing
Books/PDFs:

Phillips, Antoinette. *Families Talk—A Manual for Parents—Discussing Danger and Personal Safety with Children.*

Roddel, Victoria. *Internet Safety Family Guide.*

Sullivan, Detective Mike. *Safety Monitor: How to Protect Your Kids Online.*

Freeh, Louis J. *A Parent's Guide to Internet Safety.* FBI Publications (PDF): www.fbi.gov/publications/pguide/pguidee.htm.

Drake, Elizabeth. *50 Plus One Tips to Preventing Identity Theft.*

Frangos, Amber. *No Child Is Safe: From Internet Crime.*

Roche, Steve. *Protect Your Children from Internet and Mobile Phone Dangers: An Easy-to-Understand Handbook for Worried Mums.*

Silver Lake Editors. *Scams & Swindles: Phishing, Spoofing, ID Theft, Nigerian Advance Schemes Investment Frauds: How to Recognize and Avoid Rip-Offs in the Internet Age.*

DVD/CD-ROM/Video:

Aarniokoski, Douglas. "The Safe Side—Internet Safety." (DVD)

U.S. Government. *2006 Essential Guide to Protection from Identity Theft—Federal Information on Financial and Cyber Security, Online Safety, Internet Scams, Web and Email Phishing.* (CD-ROM)

"Internet and Street Smarts: Safety Tips for Kids." (VHS)

Recommended Websites
MySpace-specific:

www.myspacesafetytips.com

www.mycrimespace.com
www.commonsensemedia.org

MySpace.com
1223 Wilshire Blvd., Suite 402
Santa Monica, CA 904043

Parent Guides to the Internet:
www.ed.gov/pubs/parents/internet
www.learnthenet.com
www.ctw.org/parents/techtips
www.webopedia.com
www.safekids.com/parent_guidelines.htm
www.bewebaware.com
www.blogsafety.com
www.socialshield.com
www.isafe.org
www.benetsafe.com
www.missingkids.com
www.netfamilynews.org
www.netsmartz.org

Online Safety for Kids:
www.livewires.com
www.netsmartz.org
www.safekids.com
www.webwisekids.com
www.wiredkids.org
www.tcs.cybertipline.com
www.teencentral.net
www.teenlineonline.org

Government and Law Enforcement Agencies:
www.cybercrime.gov   U.S. Department of Justice
www.fbi.gov   Federal Bureau of Investigation
www.missingkids.com   National Center for Missing and Exploited Children

National Sex Offender Registries:
www.prevent-abuse-now.com/register.htm (U.S.)
www.rcmp-grc.gc.ca/techops/nsor/index_e.htm (Canada)

Acknowledgments

Thanks and praise to my Savior and King, Jesus Christ, without Whose grace and truth I would be nothing.

For that exciting call on a sunny June morning, and for being my agent in the truest sense of the word, a thousand thanks to Sharlene Martin—it doesn't get any better!

For her expertise, diligence, and guidance, an ancient Greek ship full of thank-yous (and literary references and extended metaphors) to my editor, Katie McHugh. I never truly understood the impact of *my* red pen until I met *hers*. . . . Much respect and admiration to my students and their parents for their willingness to share their experiences, thoughts, and feelings, without which this book would not be. And a special nod to Cameron and Chelsea for all their help. . .

I'm overwhelmed with gratitude to my husband, Kevin, for his faith in this book; he "got it" from the beginning and refused to let me back out of it. His wisdom has been a consistent beacon in my life. And his patience with the irrationality of a pregnant first-time author did not go unnoticed. His unconditional love continues to carry me.

To the best sport in the history of three-year-olds, my sweet daughter, Georgia Rae, who put up with a lot for a project she didn't quite understand. And humble appreciation for Mike who was, quite literally, with me every step of the way and unknowingly tolerated being referred to as the "other" due date. To my brother and writing mentor, Chris Balish, who lit the fire under my novice feet, encouraged me daily, and worked tirelessly to see me make this book happen. To my parents, Tom and Jean Balish, for encouraging my writing since I was a child; many thanks also for the proofreading, researching, and all-around über-grandparenting done to bring this book to completion.

To Dale and Marlene "MILOMDs" Bradshaw for seeing the importance in my project and providing countless hours of prayer and grandparenting so I could write.

I am indebted to Dave and Barb Kelsey for their unconditional love, support, and generosity.

Big hugs to my precious nieces and nephews, Hadley, Brynne, Elise, Mikailie, Augustine, and Anton, whose beautiful faces reminded me why I was writing this book, and who provided much needed fun during a stressful sixty day deadline, whether by reading Dr. Seuss, jumping on the couch to classical music, playing charades, shooting air guns in the back yard, or jumping off the side of the house boat.

To the best aunty and unc-y my daughter could ever want, Tom and Jana Balish, whose hospitality and babysitting stamina still amaze me. And thanks to my friend, colleague, and cheerleader extraordinaire, Caroline Hunt, for the endless conversations. Special thanks to my Westside Christian Fellowship and Pacifica Christian High community for their prayers, support, and love, especially Kent and Joan Crawford, Laurie Vander Veen, Liz Hammer, and Scott Comer.

A ton of gratitude to Jonny Nadlman for making his wisdom available to me time and again.

And to the various and sundry coffee shops that allowed me to sit and sit and sit without buying much of anything: The Cow's End in Venice, Bartleby's in Mystic, Dado's Tea in Cambridge, and Sweet Sue's in Arlington.

Index

Generation MySpace

communication
  and images, 59. *see also* photo sharing
comScore Media Metrix, 5
Concerned Women for America, 144
Connectiut Internet Crimes Against Children Taskforce, 41
Conrad, Joseph, 26
consumerism, 98–100, xxv
contract, for MySpace use, 281–284
creating profile, 40–48
creativity, on MySpace, 54
CSWEB with PredatorGuard software, 289
cutting (self-mutilation), 86, 119
cyber-bullying. *see* bullying, cyber-
CyberPatrol software, 288
cyberspeak. *see* language, on MySpace

D

DaCav5, "The MySpace Song", 54–55
dadsanddaughters.org, 165
Dateline (TV show), 69
deleting MySpace profile, 19–20, 52–53
denigration, 109
Depp, Johnny, 100
depression, 11–12, 18
detoxing, from MySpace, 21
DeWolfe, Chris, 84, xiii
Diagnostic and Statistical Manual of Mental Disorders (DSM), 225
Diagnostic and Statistical Manual of Mental Disorders (DSM), 225
Diary Project, xiii
Disney Corporation, 99–100
Drug Enforcement Administration (DEA), 172
drug test, beating, 174, 176
drug use, 169–204
  access through MySpace, 175–176, 181–186
  alcohol, 204
  and blogs, 199–200
  cell phone access, 187–189
  girls and, 179–180
  and instant messaging, 176
  intervention, 193–198
  MySpace postings, 174, 199–200
  and online access, 172, 173, 174, 176–178, 178–179
  prescription, 170, 171–173, 176–177
  prevalence of, 171, 183
  prevention, 191–193, 198, 204
  pro-drug websites, 184, 199, 204
  recovery, 176, 188–189, 198–199
  role modeling, 204
  and sexuality, 180
  signs of, 190–191
  slang terms, 200–203
  trash drugs, 186–187
drug use, signs of, 170
Drugstore Cowboy (film), 7

E

e-mail, definition, 73–74
e-mailing, x
eBlaster software, 289
Edelson, Michael, 51
electronic bullying. see bullying, cyber-
electronic mail (e-mail), 73
empowerment, false, 160, 161
Enough is Enough magazine, 208
entertainment, endless, xxiii–xxiv
entitlement bullies, 115
Erowid.org, 177, 204
Erskine, Chris, 53
exclusion, 109
exhibitionism, 156–157, 185, 223–224, xxviii
  discouraging, 167
extended network, 96–97

F

Facebook, x, xii, xiv–xv
Faigel, Harris, 228
fathers and daughters, 165–166
FBI Publications, *A Parent's Guide to Internet Safety*, 75
Felling, Matthew, 77
female chauvinist pigs (levy), 157
feminist consciousness-raising, 162–165, 208
flaming, 109
Florida Public Schools, 135, 157
friend space, 40
friending, 44–45, 80–89
  advertising and, 221
  bands, 97–99
  brands, commercial, 99–100
  and popularity, 82–83, 85–87, 98–99, 100
  and safety, 273–274
  and status, 82–83
  Top 8, 87–89
friends with benefits, 143
friendship, real, 101–102, 103, 104
Friendster, 142

G

gaming, x
Gilman, Charlotte Perkins, *Herland,* 162
girls, 141–168

319